INSANE CL●WN PRESIDENT

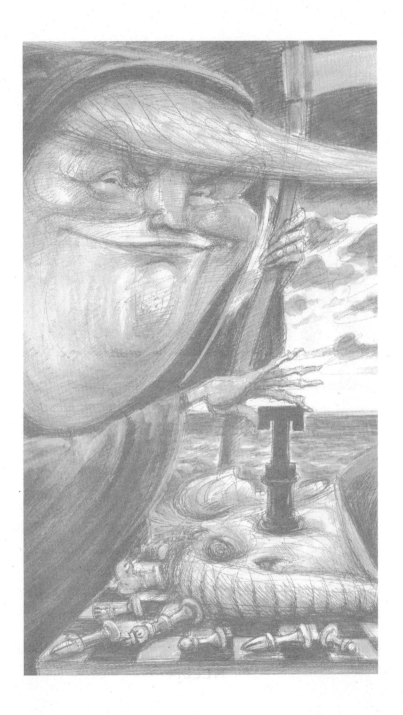

INSANE CLOWN PRESIDENT

Dispatches from the American Circus

Matt Taibbi

1 3 5 7 9 10 8 6 4 2

WH Allen, an imprint of Ebury Publishing,
20 Vauxhall Bridge Road,
London SW1V 2SA

WH Allen is part of the Penguin Random House group of companies whose
addresses can be found at global.penguinrandomhouse.com

Penguin
Random House
UK

Most of the essays which appear in this work were originally published
in *Rolling Stone*.

Chapter 1, excluding the headnote and footnotes, was originally published in
The Great Derangement by Matt Taibbi (New York: Spiegel & Grau, 2008) and is
reprinted here by permission.

Illustrations by Victor Juhasz were originally published in *Rolling Stone* and are
reprinted here by permission of the artist.

Grateful acknowledgement is made to Houghton Mifflin Harcourt Publishing
Company for permission to reprint an excerpt from "The End of the World"
from *Collected Poems 1917–1982* by Archibald MacLeish, copyright © 1985 by
The Estate of Archibald MacLeish. Reprinted by permission of Houghton
Mifflin Harcourt Publishing Company. All rights reserved.

First published in the United Kingdom by WH Allen in 2017
First published in the United States by Spiegel & Grau in 2017

www.penguin.co.uk

A CIP catalogue record for this book is available from the British Library

ISBN 9780753548400

Printed and bound in Great Britain by Clays Ltd, St Ives PLC

Penguin Random House is committed to a sustainable future for our
business, our readers and our planet. This book is made from
Forest Stewardship Council® certified paper.

To my beautiful son Nate, born during this madness

"I believe that ignorance is the root of all evil. And that no one knows the truth."

—MOLLY IVINS

Contents

Introduction

A LITTLE OVER TEN YEARS AGO, WHILE WRITING A BOOK and working as a correspondent for *Rolling Stone*, I thought I saw a new trend in American politics.

I was spending half my time in Washington watching Congress make some very unsavory sausage and the other half hanging around political extremist movements in various parts of the country. In retrospect, the setup probably predetermined the conclusion. Nonetheless, I ended up returning over and over to the same theme, which had a syllogistic formula:

> The country's leaders are corrupt and have become unresponsive to the needs of the population.

> People all over are beginning to notice.

> This being America, as ordinary people tune out their corrupt leaders, they will replace official propaganda with conspiratorial explanations even more ridiculous than the original lies.

This was the core idea behind a book that ended up being called *The Great Derangement*. Between first-person narratives about fringe political phenomena like the apocalyptic "Rapture" movement and 9/11 Truth, the book tried to warn about a loss of faith in national institutions, most notably in my own business, the political media.

I felt sure a collapse of belief in the efficacy of the news media, if it coincided with widespread (and justified) political discontent, could lead in some pretty weird directions. One possible future was one in which politics "stopped being about ideology and . . . instead turned into a problem of information."

The 2016 presidential campaign, simultaneously the most thrilling and disgusting political event of our generation, proved to be a monstrous affirmation of the Derangement. The stunning rise of Donald Trump marked the apotheosis of the new postfactual movement.

Every mechanism our mighty oligarchy had devised to keep people like Trump out of power failed. This left the path to power wide open for anyone who understood, or sensed, the depth of the crippling weaknesses in our political infrastructure.

I didn't see Donald Trump coming. But as a campaign reporter I'd surely seen trouble on the horizon. The most obvious problem was the total alienation of candidates and their attendant media from the population.

I'd struggled with this issue from the first time I was sent out by *Rolling Stone* to cover a campaign, in 2004. One of the first things that struck me was the way the candidates and the "traveling press" moved around the country in what was essentially a roving prison.

Your route was from a bus, to a charter plane, to another

bus, to an event hall (where you were kept behind rope lines most or all of the time), back to the bus, back to a plane. Then the cycle would repeat until you got to a hotel in the next city, at night. You slept six hours and repeated the pattern, day after day, week after week.

This moving prison was so airtight that if you needed cigarettes, you had to ask campaign volunteers (the Kerry crew called them "Sherpas") to smuggle them in.

This seemed like merely a strange detail when I first wrote about it more than a dozen years ago. But it spoke to a much more enormous problem. It was a perfect metaphor for the distancing of the ruling class from the population. Presidential campaigns were bubbles, and the people inside them became myopic codependents. The establishment pols and their lackeys bullied the press into becoming guardians of their orthodoxy. The press in turn savagely policed the agreed-upon lines of decorum.

To campaign professionals, real people became fodder for stylized visual backgrounds and nothing more. In a less self-deceiving future—perhaps under a leader like Donald Trump who better understands that presidential races are now really just big television shows—they will conduct campaigns from a single soundstage in a place like Burbank and just blue-screen in the different crowds and locations.

Campaigns needed "people" only as props. If a candidate wanted to show that he or she was with it on racial issues, that candidate would visit a predominantly black high school and be photographed clapping to a school band performance. If he wanted a worker-friendly image, he'd visit a robotics factory in Wisconsin and be photographed wearing a hard hat and goggles. And so on.

But neither politicians nor reporters were ever in one

place for long enough to see or hear what was really going on with the public. In place of that one-on-one experience, politicians and the press increasingly relied upon polls, and each other, to gauge the temperature "out there." This resulted in a bizarre mutual-admiration-society situation in which everyone inside the plane gradually became more and more removed from the outside world.

When fellow *Rolling Stone* scribe Tim Crouse wrote *The Boys on the Bus* nearly half a century ago, he was mostly describing how pack journalism led to faulty reporting. But his description of the culture on the Bus also accurately foretold the derangement of the whole campaign mechanism, which included the politicians with whom reporters traveled.

Stuck inside the campaign bubble for too long, politicians and journalists alike started to operate like high school Heathers, using abuse and shaming to enforce the myriad social rules inside the plane. If Candidate A fell outside either behavioral or policy lines, fifty reporters immediately cried foul and that candidate quickly retreated, or else.

A classic example was Howard Dean. Now a dependable party creature, Dean in 2004 initially garnered enthusiasm for his opposition to the Iraq War and his heretical reliance upon small online donations as a way around the Democratic leadership's kingmaking corporate donors.

Dean spent much of his campaign's first summer fending off questions from reporters about whether he was too "liberal" or "pointed," not "nuanced" enough, etc. Many of my colleagues really didn't even know what they meant by these harassing questions. They didn't need to. The constant pestering questions were all code. The complaint about Dean was that he wasn't enough of a company man, that he'd stepped outside the lines of the agreed-upon orthodoxy.

When the Vermont governor finally stumbled with that infamous scream in Iowa, the press piled on with what another reporter I know jokingly describes as the "Seal of Death." This is a maelstrom of negative reports that is expected to inspire a plunge in the polls, followed by a series of humiliating rituals.

First comes the Abashed Public Apology, a scene reporters enjoy to the point of it being unseemly. Next comes the short Dead Man Walking period. Candidates, Dean included, usually try to soldier on after being excommunicated by the media, clutching at single-digit poll numbers and speaking in increasingly desperate or even angry tones to half-empty halls. This tragicomic narrative may last weeks, even months.

Finally there is the Anticlimactic Withdrawal, when the already-dead candidate quietly announces his or her exit and disappears for a while to "spend more time with my family" or go into literal or political rehab. Anthony Weiner's recent exile to Tennessee for a stint of horse-riding therapy to treat his sexting addiction is a typical endgame for a Seal of Death victim.

Before 2016, nobody had ever survived the Seal of Death, with the possible exception of Bill Clinton, who pathetically squirmed free from the Gennifer Flowers episode.

In the case of Dean, TV stations around the country played the "scream" tape a whopping 633 times in the first four days after Iowa, according to the AP. They were like piranhas skeletonizing a waterfowl. It was viral media before YouTube. As Dean's campaign manager, Joe Trippi, later put it, "The establishment wanted to stop us and they did."

Trippi's comment implied that reporters were part of that establishment, which was a pretty damning criticism. But it was true. And people noticed.

It's impossible to overemphasize the toxicity of this dynamic. Politicians and political journalists were volunteering to be trapped in an endless conversation with one another about which candidates, and by extension which ideas, were and were not suitable for consumption by the American people.

It wasn't a substantive conversation, either. The big topic on the Bus was who was winning: the horse race. Policy ideas had no meaning except in terms of their efficacy in helping the candidate win the horse race. Of course, an idea that was too popular, like Dean's anti-war gambit, could run up against that internal policing mechanism again and be dismissed as "populist," which was something very bad in the campaign-trail lexicon.

Ultimately, most all of the talk on the Bus ended up being concerned with the narrow question of which party-approved candidate pushing acceptably non-populist ideas would edge out the other. We pretended this was a fascinating intellectual question. It even became fashionable to become a kind of PhD in these moronic dynamics.

Nobody thought it was odd when a baseball statistics guru, Nate Silver, became a godlike figure in the campaign bubble and America's foremost expert on what was going on in the heartland.

I have nothing personal against Nate Silver—I was a big fan back in his *Baseball Prospectus* days—but elevating a bespectacled sabermetrics geek to the role of Nostradamus of middle American attitudes speaks volumes about where the country's political elite was at, mentally, heading into this campaign season.

Even in baseball there's value in looking beyond the numbers and seeing and talking to a player in person. But trying the Moneyball approach in politics is insanity. Reducing people to stats in politics is both a strategic and moral error of breathtaking proportions. Elections may be about winning and losing, but they are not a game—except, sadly, to the people who leading into this campaign season made electioneering their business.

If you want a graphic picture of the cluelessness of the people inside campaign bubbles, just watch Hillary Clinton's now-infamous "Mannequin Challenge."

Watch as the camera pans over the plane full of photogs, aides and pols, proudly clutching their tablets and pens and pizza boxes, all dressed in blazers and "smart glasses" and crisp gingham shirts and buzzed at being on the same plane as two Clintons and Jon Bon Jovi.

As a metaphor for an overconfident and incompetent ruling class that was ten miles up its own backside when it should have been listening to the anger percolating in the population, the "Mannequin Challenge" is probably unsurpassable. Here was a planeload of effete politicos making a goofball video when they should have been frantically bailing water to stave off maybe the most disastrous loss in the history of American presidential politics.

If those people had known the election was even going to be close, they would have outlawed smiling on that plane, let alone making nutty souvenir videos. But they had no clue what was coming.

Why would they worry? After all, there were fail-safe mechanisms built into the campaign infrastructure to prevent any of this foolishness from ever backing up on them.

Until 2016.

Yes, Donald Trump's campaign was massively fueled by racism and xenophobia. But racism and hatred and fear of foreigners were not irreconcilable with hatred of the arrogant establishment that controlled major-party politics. Many voters out there hated both, and some hated those latter folks with the heat of a thousand suns.

Donald Trump was tuned in to this. Better than any candidate we'd ever seen, he ran against the Bus.

The media was the only group on his long list of cultural villains that was actually in the room for all of Trump's enormous rage rallies. We were part of his act. And his triumph over us was a major factor in convincing ordinary people that he could deliver on his rebellious rhetoric.

A key moment in the race came in the days after July 19, 2015, when Trump made his infamous comments about former prisoner of war John McCain: "He's not a war hero. He's a war hero because he was captured. I like people who weren't captured."

Earlier, Trump had made even more outrageous comments, calling Mexicans "rapists." For some reason, that scandal was not seen as immediately disqualifying across the political spectrum.

But insulting veterans? That was a bridge too far, especially for other Republicans. Republican National Committee spokesman Sean Spicer tweeted: "There is no place in our party or our country for comments that disparage those who have served honorably."

New Jersey's Chris Christie added, "Senator John McCain is an American hero. Period. Stop." Wisconsin's Scott Walker said of Trump, "I unequivocally denounce him." Lindsey Graham said, "At the heart of [Trump's] statement is a lack of respect for those who have served—a disqualifying characteristic to be president."

With universal statements affirming that Trump was now "disqualified" from running, reporters rolled out the Seal of Death script. There were a gazillion stories. The vid went viral. Twitter went nuts. We anticipated Trump assuming the position and commencing the Expected Rituals, beginning with the Abashed Public Apology.

It didn't happen. Trump not only didn't apologize, he even denied that he ever said McCain wasn't a war hero.

"If somebody is a prisoner, I consider them a war hero," he said.

Reporters freaked out. How could he deny he said it? It's right there, on video! He said it!

But it worked. Trump not only didn't sink after the McCain incident, he rose in the polls.

This happened again and again and again in Trump's campaign. First, he would say something crazy, something that would have eliminated any previous candidate. Then reporters would try the WWE takedown maneuver, only to find themselves chair-whacked and tossed out of the ring.

For instance, after Trump's comment about Megyn Kelly having "blood coming out of her wherever" in the first primary debate, journalists and political analysts alike harrumphed: "Nobody can win after making a joke about women's menstrual periods." Women were 51 percent of the country. How could any candidate survive alienating more than half the voting population? It was impossible.

Once again, we tried to apply the Seal of Death. But Trump survived the Kelly episode. He similarly survived episodes in which he mocked disabled reporter Serge Kovaleski, threatened to kill the families of terror suspects, promised to ban all Muslim immigrants, offered to pay the legal fees of anyone who beat up people protesting him, insisted that women who had abortions should suffer some kind of "punishment," and a hundred other things.

By the end of the campaign, even more serious accusations and scandals bounced harmlessly off that maddening false pompadour of his, seemingly having no impact at all.

America's population of Otherwise Smart People was stunned. How could the electorate not care that a billionaire admitted to not paying taxes? Why was no one troubled by the threat of a child rape lawsuit? How was the "pussy" thing not fatal? What about the mountain of extant lawsuits—75 open cases, according to some reports—for offenses ranging from simple nonpayment for services to sex discrimination? Why did no one care?

Incredibly, the popular explanation floated inside the NY-Washington-LA corridor was that this was the media's fault, that reporters were "not calling Trump out" while simultaneously overfocusing on issues like Hillary Clinton's emails.

But this explanation itself was a continuation of the same original misread of the public. Here was this massive new revolutionary movement rising out of the population, and the first instinct of the establishment was to turn to other members of the establishment for an explanation of why this was being allowed to happen. As in, where's the Seal of Death? Why haven't you vaporized this guy yet?

But we not only couldn't draw blood against Trump, we actually helped him every time we tried and failed to knock him out.

In his speeches, Trump would rip into the "crooked people in the press" for criticizing him and inevitably follow up with a tale of how well he was doing in the polls in spite of us.

Sometimes he'd call us "bloodsuckers" and "dishonest people" or even "highly paid," a dig that seemingly makes no sense coming from a Richie Rich real estate scion like Trump, unless you've listened to a lot of his voters talk.

These are the voters who've never met a New York billionaire, but they've sure met a lot of corporate middle managers and divorce lawyers and professors and other such often-overcompensated members of the intellectual class.

Trump voters almost uniformly don't begrudge someone for being an entrepreneurial success ("If the guy pulls his own weight, I don't care how much he makes" was a typical comment I heard). But they can't stand the book-smart college types who make cushy livings pushing words around in what these voters see as competition-averse professions that reward people who in real life need to call AAA to change a tire.

Trump tapped into all of this. His speeches were visual demonstrations of his power over us. We in the press, obediently clustered inside our protective rope line and/or standing mute on a riser in the middle of the hall, would sit looking guilty, like the pampered, narrow-shouldered, overgroomed hypocrites we are, while Trump blasted us as the embodiment of the class that had left regular America behind.

Then he'd point to our very presence following him in such huge numbers as proof of our defeat and moral lassitude. Even as we dismissed his campaign in print, we kept flocking to it in ever-bigger numbers. No matter how much we sneered, he insisted, we were slaves to his success. Just as everyone else would be. The Mexicans. The Chinese. ISIS. Everybody.

"See all those cameras back there?" he'd say. "They've never driven so far to a location."

Very often this victory over us was the first thing I heard about when I went into crowds to talk to Trump supporters.

"What do I like about him? He's got all you assholes jumping through hoops," hissed an older Trump supporter in Wisconsin, before launching into an impressively obscene tirade about *Rolling Stone* and the UVA rape case.

"He's gonna be his own man," a Trump supporter named Jay Matthews told me in Plymouth, New Hampshire. "He's proving that now with how he's getting all the media. He's paying nothing and getting all the coverage. He's not paying one dime."

This was part of the reason Trump's supporters seemed so stubborn in their lack of interest in "the facts." They were contemptuous of anything that came from us and our habit of trying to rub their noses in their mistake—well, it was just as off-putting as correcting their spelling, another thing educated liberal types tended to do a lot, especially on social media.

But the ineffectiveness of "facts" didn't stop there. The election of Trump was not just a political choice, a vote against minorities and foreigners, against intellectuals, a cry for better jobs, etc. This was also a metaphysical choice.

Sixty million people were announcing that they preferred one reality to another. Inherent in this decision was the revolutionary idea that you can choose your own set of facts.

Blue-state America could not wrap its head around this during election season. Facts, they protested, are facts! But Trump voters did not agree. They believed facts were a choice. We had made ours, choosing to ignore certain things, and they would make theirs, doing the same. No amount of "calling Trump out" would change that.

Once upon a time, if the three major commercial networks said a thing was a fact, everyone agreed it was a fact. That wasn't necessarily a good thing, because the three networks lied a lot, but still. Back in the day, when America argued with itself, it mostly argued over the same data.

News programs originally had little financial incentive to lie. They were designed to be loss leaders. Way back when, the Communications Act of 1934 set out the media business as a civic trade-off. The government would license out use of the public airwaves, but in exchange, private media companies would use those licenses for "public interest, convenience and necessity."

Eventually this morphed into a model where big media companies made money through sports and entertainment and satisfied the "public interest" portion of their mandate by creating news shows that had some degree of ethics and factual standards.

That worked relatively well, until the networks started to see that they could make very good money by altering the formula.

A key innovator was the new fourth major network, Fox,

which along with conservative talk radio began cleaving media consumers into two groups in the Eighties and Nineties.

For decades, CBS, ABC and NBC mostly told America the same story. But when Fox and figures like Rush Limbaugh came along, they preached an alternative political gospel with starkly different interpretations of the news. This new consumer choice often offered very different "facts" as well.

In 1997, Fox fired a husband-and-wife duo of TV investigative reporters named Jane Akre and Steve Wilson. They'd refused to water down a documentary about the potential hazards of bovine growth hormone.

In a lawsuit, it ultimately came out that the Fox station manager in Tampa had told the pair, "We paid $3 billion for these television stations. We will decide what the news is. The news is what we tell you it is."

Looking back, we should probably have paid more attention to moments like this. There was clearly an underserved market of reality-agnostic media consumers, and it was hardly invisible. It had already identified itself in the vast audiences for tabloid television news shows, lurid daytime talk shows, absurd televangelists, infomercials, home-shopping networks, and, of course, reality TV. Fox News decided it wasn't above picking its audience from this low branch of media consumers, and it became phenomenally successful.

The rise of CNN, the first 24-hour cable news network, was just an interesting business story to most when it first happened. Not many people really thought about the consequences of a news model in which TV stations were suddenly forced to fill oceans of airtime.

One immediate consequence was that live spectacles suddenly became crucially important to the commercial health of news programs. Something about being able to watch a "breaking" news story live was addictive for modern news audiences, even if the thing they were watching wasn't terribly remarkable.

The presidential campaign fit like a glove into the new demands of the news business. For nearly two years out of every four, some kind of live campaign event was usually happening somewhere.

If there were no speeches in places like Iowa or New Hampshire, then there were candidate appearances on TV, "Jefferson-Jackson Dinners," addresses to groups like AIPAC, straw polls, and 10,000 other ready-made news events. And you could fill the hours between those events with endless pre- and postelection analysis.

There are 8,760 hours in a year. During campaign season, you can fill nearly every one of them with campaign stuff if you really put your mind to it. But in the past, all those thousands of hours of coverage have always had to fit into the parameters of TV coverage generally, which like the campaign bubble is a world with very particular (and strictly policed) internal rules, mostly dictated by advertisers.

Donald Trump's innovation was to recognize what a bad TV show the campaign was. Any program that tried to make stars out of human sedatives like Scott Walker and Lindsey Graham needed new producers and a new script.

So here came Trump, bloviating and farting his way through his early campaign stops, saying outrageous things, acting like Hitler one minute and Andrew Dice Clay the next, and gee, what a surprise, TV couldn't take its eyes off him.

He dominated coverage and was more than happy to fill all 8,760 of those hours. Networks had long since abandoned their "public interest" mandate and now were financially dependent on anyone or anything that could revive their flagging ratings. They gave Trump as many hours as he could manage and he was narcissist enough to swallow all of them with a smile.

This part of Trump's rise really was the media's fault.

Trump was a legitimate news story. He had to be covered. He was leading a historic revolt against his own party, after all. But so was Bernie Sanders, who got nearly as many votes as Trump in the primaries. Yet Trump received something on the order of 23 times more television coverage than the Vermont senator.

Long segments of Trump's speeches were broadcast uninterrupted, which seldom if ever happened with Sanders, even on traditionally left-leaning cable networks. If we in the media asked ourselves why that was the case, we came up with some damning answers.

It wasn't just that Trump was outrageous and sensational and lurid, while Sanders dryly pushed substance over salesmanship. Nor was it just the car-wreck element to Trump's performances that kept audiences glued to the screen, wondering what crazy thing he might say next.

It was also the content. Trump sold hate, violence, xenophobia, racism, and ignorance, which oddly enough had long been permissible zones of exploration for American television entertainment. And the news media was becoming more and more indistinguishable from entertainment media.

Meanwhile, Bernie Sanders talked about poverty and

inequality, which are now and always have been taboo. On a level that is understood by news directors in their guts if not their minds, hate is sexy and sells, while the politics of Bernie Sanders were provocative in the wrong ways.

A news director who made the decision to run a Sanders speech in its entirety would worry about being accused of making a "political statement." Meanwhile, running Trump all day long would be understood as just business, just giving viewers what they want. Editorially the press denounced him, but it never turned the cameras off.

By February 2016, when Trump was already steaming toward the nomination, I began to realize the extent to which he'd conned all of us. He first used the media's financial desperation to secure free coverage, but when the attention became not just negative but condemnatory, he used that, too.

He converted the press's indignation toward him into street cred with ordinary people, cred that otherwise might have been out of reach for a coddled billionaire like himself. Perversely, the alienation of the political press from its audiences helped solve Trump's own accessibility problem.

The final insult to all of this is that when Trump secured the nomination, media companies looked down at their bottom lines and realized that, via the profits they made during his run—Trump is "good for business," CBS president Les Moonves infamously confessed—they had been made accomplices to the whole affair.

Covering the presidential campaign trail has been a staple of *Rolling Stone*'s political coverage dating back to the *Fear and Loathing* days. It's been my honor to uphold the tradition for the last four presidential races. Although some complicating factors kept me off the road this time more than I might perhaps have liked, I was still sent out regularly by the magazine to file reports during the 2015–16 campaign.

These long features from the trail, along with a selection of shorter dispatches and columns about the evolving catastrophe of this election season, form the basis of *Insane Clown President*. We didn't travel together, but illustrator Victor Juhasz and I collaborated from a distance. Victor and I went through a lot of the same struggles.

In his case, given that his first drawing about the 2016 campaign had a giant Trump emerging in clown face from an elephant's anus, the challenge was: where would he go for the next six pictures? We both ran up against the same problem of trying to find new ways to describe the worsening of a narrative that was pretty awful from day one.

The idea for his last illustration, done right after the "grab them by the pussy" scandal hit the news, came to him as he listened to Schubert's *Death and the Maiden*, which reminded him of a sculpture on that theme by a French artist named Hébert.

The substitution of the Statue of Liberty for the maiden, with Trump's hand creeping just a bit higher than Death had ventured in the original sculpture, made for an iconic image that captured everything appalling and frightening about what, in retrospect, was just about to go down.

For most of the 2015–16 race, I felt as certain as a journalist can be that I understood what I was seeing. I think it comes through in these pages that nothing about Trump's initial success came as a surprise to me, because I saw he was giving people a means to express their disgust at a campaign process that had long ago stopped working for voters.

Where I screwed up—and this is a glaring error in my coverage—was in dismissing Trump's chances in the general election. I fell for a lot of the popular myths about the invincibility of the multicultural consensus Barack Obama twice rode to victory. I thought Trump's legacy would be the destruction of the Republican Party. I couldn't have been more wrong.

During the Republican convention, I'd had what I thought was a moment of clarity. I was in the stands of the Quicken Loans Arena, watching Trump muddle through a horrible, violent, and racially loaded acceptance speech that was a transparent knockoff of Richard Nixon's infamous "law and order" address of 1968.

I remember looking around the stands at the thousands of faces staring in Trump's direction. They were all anxious and hopeful, almost childlike, even the older faces. They were expecting this man to finally vanquish the liberal enemy and restore their lost paradise of pre–Civil Rights Act America, whatever their idea of that was.

God only knew what fantasies were playing out behind those faces. Maybe it was cattle cars of Mexicans, maybe mushroom clouds over Mesopotamia, or maybe it was just one-family households with dinner cooked by Mom ready on the table when they came home.

Maybe it was a big beautiful wall and a million cops rounding up and sending to gleaming new prisons all those dope-slinging black "thugs" with their underpants showing who for years have been spilling out of the affordable housing high-rises Hillary Clinton types had spent decades sticking in their towns, lowering their property values. If anyone understood property values, it was this guy, Donald Trump! Trump would fix it!

What else were they were dreaming about? Maybe for some it was just a better job and lower taxes, with minorities and foreigners taking a bit of collateral damage (but that was OK because after all they'd had their eight years in the White House). Maybe others were secretly tired of having to watch what they said all day at work and were just living vicariously through this ribald, lecherous go-getter who defied the unwritten rules on the biggest stage and got away with it.

Who knew, but uniformly in the Q seats there was a look of breathless anticipation. Trump had promised a lot during campaign season. He said restoring America's greatness would be easy, no problem, that his America was going to be so great, you couldn't even imagine it.

"You're going to say, Mr. President, please, we can't take it anymore, we can't win anymore like this, Mr. President, you're driving us crazy, you're winning too much," he'd said, in the weeks before the convention. "And I'm going to say I'm sorry, we're going to keep winning!"

Wow. That sounded amazing! What would all that winning feel like? You could see in the crowd, they almost couldn't wait to start finding out.

But then I looked down at Donald Trump and I was sure I saw a con man who was just barely holding it together. His convention had been kind of a fiasco (Scott Baio as an opening-day speaker?), and his own speech now had none of his usual breezy bluster. He sounded like a politician. Instead of shooting from the hip, his every word was off a teleprompter.

"It is finally time for a straightforward assessment of the

state of our nation," he said, in painfully clean syntax that sounded like anyone in the world but Donald Trump.

The address he went on to deliver was a pathetic pastiche ripped off from the very Republican establishment he claimed to hate—five decades of dog-whistle clichés stolen from Nixon, Bush I, Jesse Helms, and countless others. He was going through the motions, trying to deliver a traditional boilerplate political scare speech about crime and terrorism. But Trump is an awful actor when not playing himself. He looked terrified, as if he was about to be found out.

In that moment I suddenly remembered the Archibald MacLeish poem "The End of the World." The poem is about a traveling circus. The audience is enthralled by the acrobats and lion tamers and freaks, until suddenly the top of the tent blows off:

And there, there overhead, there, there hung over
Those thousands of white faces, those dazed eyes,
There in the starless dark, the poise, the hover,
There with vast wings across the cancelled skies,
There in the sudden blackness the black pall
Of nothing, nothing, nothing—nothing at all.

To me this was a perfect metaphor for Trump. He had promised the world, but when we finally pulled the lid off him, there was not a Hitler or a Trujillo or even a Boss Tweed underneath, but just blackness, a void—nothing, nothing, nothing at all.

Trump was a cipher, a cheap fraud and TV showman who had gotten in way over his head and was now just gamely trying to play out the string. He seemed destined to be buried under a mountain of his outlandish promises, in the process leading these thousands of hoodwinked followers of his off the cliff of history.

I still believe this is true. For all the investigative energy focused on Trump, there was never much depth to discover underneath. A few scams maybe (well, more than a few), and possibly even some very serious crimes, philandering, sexual assault—a crook with money. But the only thing profound about the man was his level of self-absorption. The story might ultimately be that this preening idiot was brilliantly appropriated by forces that did harbor far-reaching revolutionary ideas, like Steve Bannon and the "alt-right" movement. But if Trump himself turns out to be a man of ideas, it will mean it's something he came to late in life—the same way George W. Bush didn't really get a job until he was around forty.

Who knows why he got in the race, or if he ever intended or even hoped to win. But the narrative in which this discombobulated bundle of urges was swept toward the presidency in spite of himself was an awesome and terrible black comedy.

Here was a figure of almost supernatural shallowness, who had almost certainly run for the presidency on some level out of boredom, who somehow became the vehicle for a collision of great and powerful historical trends in the world's last superpower.

There was the rise of a racist revanchist movement in the heartland on one side (merging with a distinctly upper-class, college-bred "alt-right" racist movement), and the collapse of the neoliberal consensus on the Democratic side. All of these movements took place against the backdrop of a splintering and collapsing of the media landscape that, en-

tering the 2016 race, left us without any real forum for a
national conversation, without a dependable way to communicate with one another.

America was so divided, so alienated from itself, so vulnerable, that even a zero like Trump could penetrate our
political system without breaking a sweat. To put it in terms
the casino-owning candidate would understand, he won the
presidency without so much as a pair of twos in hand.

It's impossible to say what kind of president Donald
Trump might be. The early returns are not good. His attorney general choice is Alabama senator Jeff Sessions, who
lost a judgeship because he apparently once jokingly said the
KKK was "OK" and called the NAACP "communist inspired." Steve Bannon, a conniving monster who looks a lot
like the late Chris Hitchens, only unhealthier and with a
worse case of neck bloat, ran a *Breitbart* site that is a sewer of
the foulest racist memes. He is set to be Trump's chief strategist, playing the David Axelrod role.

Who knows what will come next, but that's not really
what this story is about. *Insane Clown President* instead describes how we got here.

It's an *Alice in Wonderland* story, in which a billionaire
hedonist jumps down the rabbit hole of American politics
and discovers a surreal world where each successive barrier
to power collapses before him like magic. From a literary
standpoint it makes perfect sense that Trump would be the
grotesque and charmless protagonist that he is. His bellicose pussy-grabbing vulgarity and defiant lack of self-
awareness make him, unfortunately, the perfect foil for
reflecting the rot and neglect of the corrupted political system he conquers. A system unable to stop *this* must be very
sick indeed.

To return again to MacLeish's poem, we are all staring up at the same nothingness now. Who knows how it will be filled, but the real shock this past year was finding out how frail has been our illusion of stability all along. We were a shallow country, held together by stale rituals and muscle memory. And now it is a shallow man who will take us wherever he pleases.

Insane Clown President

1

The Great Derangement Redux

Ten years before Donald Trump, I wrote a book about Middle America's growing mistrust of government, the media and other mainstream forces. The thesis of the book was that we were moving toward a future in which facts would be increasingly irrelevant and people would gravitate more and more toward conspiratorial politics. This situation was fueled by the repeated failures of once-trusted institutions to respond to the frustrations of ordinary people.

I didn't exactly see Donald Trump coming. But there were a lot of signs that the conditions were set long ago for the rise of a truly postfactual candidate.

From the introduction to *The Great Derangement*:

WE WERE LIVING THROUGH* THE LAST STAGE OF THE AMERIcan empire. Historians consistently describe similar phe-

---

* Donald Trump's election occurred on the 99th anniversary of the Bolshevik seizure of power. The Winter Palace fell in Petrograd on November 8th, 1917.

nomena in past centuries. Great societies often collapse in the same way.

When the Bolsheviks finally broke through the gates of the Winter Palace,* they discovered tsarists inside obsessed with tarot cards. When the barbarians finally stormed Rome in its last days, they found the upper class paralyzed† by lethargy and inaction and addicted to the ramblings of fortune-tellers.‡

This, too, seemed to be the fate of America, viciously attacked by a serious enemy on 9/11 but unable to grasp the significance of this attack. Most of the country instead fled for consolation to the various corners of our vast media landscape, in particular seeking solace in the Internet,§ an escapist paradise for the informationally overwhelmed.¶

Trained for decades to be little more than good consumers, we had become a nation of reality shoppers, mixing and matching news items to fit our own self-created identities. We rejoiced in the idea that reality was not an absolute

---

* Steve Bannon, Donald Trump's chief strategist, is the latest and most faithful in a long line of recent hardcore conservatives, Grover Norquist being a prominent example, who claimed Lenin as a tactical model. Bannon's "alt-right" movement clearly drew upon Leninist principles, beginning with the concept of a "dangerously smart" college-educated vanguard leading a much larger "low-information" population. "Lenin wanted to destroy the state, and that's my goal, too," Bannon reportedly said. "I want to bring it all crashing down."

† The "Mannequin Challenge" will be the enduring image of the defeated Democrats.

‡ After the election, it was revealed that the Clinton campaign was relying upon a new computer program nicknamed Ada that simulated the responses of the population during an election season. Ada ran over 400,000 simulations a day of races against Trump. Decisions to deploy celebrities like Jay Z and Beyoncé came in part because of recommendations from Ada, who apparently failed to worry that the race might be close in Michigan or Wisconsin.

§ More people got their election news from social media, apps and Internet news sites (27 percent total) in 2016 than they did from cable television (23 percent).

¶ Donald Trump currently has 15.9 million followers on Twitter. One political operative called his tweets "a continuous political rally that happens at all hours."

but a choice, something we select to fit our own conception not of the world but of ourselves. We are Christians, therefore all world events have a Christian explanation. We hate George Bush, therefore Bush is the cause of it all.

And directly feeding into this madness was the actual, real failure of our own governmental system, reflected in a chilling new electoral trend. After two consecutive bitterly negative presidential elections and many years of what was turning into a highly deflating military adventure in Iraq, the American public had reached new levels of disgust with the very concept of elections.

People no longer voted for candidates they liked or were excited by. They voted against candidates they hated.* At protests and marches, the ruling emotions were disgust and rage. The lack of idealism, and especially the lack of any sense of brotherhood or common purpose with the other side (i.e., liberals and conservatives unable to imagine a productive future with each other, or even to see themselves as citizens of the same country†), was striking.

Politicians, with their automated speeches and canned blather about "hope" and "change"‡ and "taking the country

---

* 2016 was the first election in which majorities or near majorities of voters were more motivated by dislike of the other candidate than like of their own. In September 2016, 53 percent of Trump voters said they were motivated by dislike of Hillary Clinton, compared with 44 percent who said they were voting in favor of Trump. For comparison, 68 percent of Barack Obama's voters in 2008 were voting for him, while only 25 percent voted against McCain. Exit polls after the race showed that the levels of negative voting were three times the normal rate on the Republican side and double on the Democratic side.
† There were secessionist rumblings on both the left and the right in 2016, including rumors of a "Texit" after Britain's "Brexit" vote and calls for both California and Oregon to secede after Trump's win.
‡ One of the three main themes of Bill Clinton's 1992 campaign was "Change versus more of the same." ("The economy, stupid" was another.) Hillary Clinton's inability to use the word even as an empty slogan hurt her against Trump.

back," were now not only not believed by most ordinary people, but actively despised.*

A parallel phenomenon was a growing lack of faith in the mainstream media on both sides of the spectrum. Conservatives† and liberals‡ alike accepted unquestioningly the proposition that the stories put out by network news broadcasts and major daily newspapers amounted to little more than a stream of untrammeled, insidious deceptions.

In the 2006 senatorial primary contest between the would-be Jimmy Stewart–esque do-gooder millionaire Ned Lamont and the archetypal Washington whore Joe Lieberman,§ the fault lines were outlined with crystal clarity.¶

The "People" boosted Lamont with blogs and YouTube

---

* Polls consistently showed that Trump's biggest asset among voters was that he was "not a politician." As Trump supporter Trent Gower told me in Wilkes-Barre, Pennsylvania, "If we keep doing the same thing, it's just going to be the same old terrible result, so at least if we try something different with Donald, which he is completely different than all the other candidates."

† Both candidates and both voter bases believed the press had it in for them. Conservative pollsters after the race claimed that seven in ten voters did not believe the media to be honest and truthful, and eight in ten believed the media was biased in its coverage. Even Quinnipiac found that 55 percent of voters believed the media was biased against Trump.

‡ Meanwhile, there was an extensive movement among Democratic Party officials to blame the media for Trump's rise, with most focusing on two areas: the notion that the press gave Trump too much coverage and the idea that the press focused too much on Hillary's email scandals. Clinton campaign chief John Podesta, while refusing to accept responsibility for the electoral loss himself, explicitly blamed the press, saying, "The dominance of the way they covered the email" overshadowed revelations of Trump's corruption.

§ Lieberman showed his colors when he flirted with supporting Trump—"I'm one of those people, and there are a lot of us, who don't quite feel comfortable either way yet," he said after the conventions—before finally endorsing Clinton in August of 2016. This was despite that fact that Lieberman was a former chair of the Democratic Leadership Council, whose politics were essentially identical to Clinton's.

¶ Lamont-Lieberman was politically a preview of Sanders-Clinton and tactically a preview of Trump's Republican nomination run, in the sense that Lamont was a self-funded outsider who defied party wishes in the primary.

broadcasts, while the entrenched political mainstream circled the wagons around Lieberman.* The major news mags and dailies blasted the blogger phenomenon, and the likes of sanctimonious *New York Times* columnist David Brooks ascribed the antimedia bias to "moral manias" and a "Liberal Inquisition."[†]

On the right, similar fault lines were appearing. Whereas before conservative anger toward the "liberal media" had been usefully directed against the Democratic Party by Republican strategists, the failure of the Iraq war and also growing disillusionment on the part of Christians who had supported George W. Bush led more and more of those voters to seek out their own enthusiasms.[‡]

For the first time I started to see and hear people at Republican events who sounded very much like the dissidents on the fringes of American liberalism.[§] The Ron Paul supporters[¶] who began to collect around the rallies of assembly-

* The salient comparison here would be media coverage of Clinton vs. Sanders, but legacy media similarly galvanized almost entirely behind Clinton in the general election: she won 57 newspaper endorsements to Trump's 2, which shows how much people pay attention to newspaper endorsements.
† A punditry low point of the race was surely Brooks' February 2016 column railing against the "Danish dream" of Bernie Sanders, a column that warned that Sanders would usher in "dirigisme" and would result in people like Elon Musk not wanting to live in America.
‡ The massive rejection of traditional conservative media outlets by Trump voters was one of the more interesting (and, at times, amusing) storylines of 2016. The *National Review* recruited an all-star X-Men squad of 20 prominent conservatives, including Glenn Beck, to build a single unified punditry Maginot Line against Trump ("Conservatives Against Trump," January 21, 2016), and Trump voters basically didn't even notice.
§ There were a lot of ex-liberals, union members and other defectors from the Democratic Party at Trump rallies. "I grew up in a house full of FDR Democrats," Trump supporter Tim Kallas told me in Wisconsin, "but they just don't speak to me anymore." The numbers said as much as 20 percent of Democratic primary voters were prepared to defect to Trump, while there was also a significant (14 percent) number of Republicans moving to the Democratic ranks.
¶ Many conservatives place the beginning of Trump's rise in Ron Paul's original

line establishment-blowhard candidates like Mitt Romney were almost indistinguishable from the followers of liberal candidates like Dennis Kucinich.*

They were similarly against the war, similarly against the conspiracy of business interests that dominated Washington, similarly fed up with standard-issue campaign stumpery.

At these events I heard some of the same theories about "peak oil" and the nefarious influence of institutions like the Council on Foreign Relations and the Trilateral Commission that dominated 9/11 Truth rallies.†

But they weren't liberals. They were ex-Dittoheads‡ and dropouts from the Republican revolution. The Ron Paul candidacy was an extreme example of outsider politics on the left and right merging.

I spent time down in Texas with a group of churchgoers who were loyal to an apocalyptic theory of world events, one

---

"tea parties," which rallied around opposition to Bush-era deficit spending and foreign interventionism. This led to the larger Tea Party movement, which was more focused on Barack Obama, but also took aim at "establishment" Republicans like Mitch McConnell. Trump capitalized on the Tea Party theme of Republican establishment treachery, and incidentally appropriated many Ron Paul-ian themes on the stump, including ideas like "I don't think we should be nation-building."

* Dennis Kucinich's sister Teresa Sikorski voted for Trump. "His demeanor is a little out there," she said. "But he says what the working man says."

† No presidential candidate ever espoused as many Internet conspiracy theories as did Donald Trump. Apart from the Birther controversy, he pushed the notion that vaccines cause autism (this even became a debate question in primary season!), parroted white-power conspiracy stories about immigrants bringing in diseases, said Rafael Cruz was involved in the JFK assassination, called global warming "bullshit" and warned that the national election was "rigged" before he won it. Trump mainstreamed the conspiracy theory and even suggested that people vote for him so that we could find out "who really knocked down" the World Trade Center ("They have papers in there that are very secret"). This weirdly enough made him an ally of Rosie O'Donnell, who is on record wondering about the collapse of WTC-7: "It's the first time in history that fire has ever melted steel."

‡ Rush Limbaugh, who denounced "Barack Hussein Kardashian" for being "Celebrity of the United States," backed reality star Donald Trump.

in which 9/11 and the invasion of Iraq were part of an ongoing march toward a final battle between the forces of Satan and an army of God.

At the same time, I found myself involved, at times involuntarily, with the 9/11 Truth Movement.

The similarities between both of these groups is striking and should be clear to anyone who reads this book. Both groups were and are defined primarily by an unshakable belief in the inhumanity of their enemies on the other side.

The Christians seldom distinguished between Islamic terrorism and, say, Al Gore–style environmentalism. The Truthers easily believed that reporters for the *Washington Post*, the president, and the front-line operators of NORAD were equally capable of murdering masses of ordinary New York financial-sector employees.

Abandoned by the political center, both groups ascribed unblinkingly to a militant, us-against-them worldview, where only their own could be trusted.

What made them distinctly American was that, while actually the victims of an obvious, unhidden conspiracy of corrupt political power, they chose to battle bugbears that were completely idiotic, fanciful, and imaginary.

At a time when the country desperately needed its citizens to man up and seize control of their common destiny, they instead crawled into alleys and feverishly jacked themselves off* in frenzies of panicked narcissism.

Time and again during the research for this book, I encountered people who acted not like engaged citizens looking for solutions to real problems, but like frightened

* GOP strategist Rick Wilson blasted Trump's alt-right supporters, saying they are "childless single men who masturbate to anime."

adolescents, unaccustomed to the burdens of political power. People saw in the vacuum of governmental competence an opportunity not to take control of their lives, but to step in and replace the buffoons above with buffoon* acts of their own.

They made elaborate speeches to no one in particular, as though cameras were on them, they dressed in Washington and Jefferson costumes, they primped and preened like they were revolutionaries, modern-day Patrick Henrys and Thomas Paines. And they got nothing done.

I was struck particularly by a meeting of 9/11 Truthers[†] in Austin, Texas, in which a "discussion" of what to do about the conspiracy in Washington devolved into a speech-making session. A group of twenty-five to thirty Truthers filed into a little church on the outskirts of town and, led by a breezy, EST-counselorish moderator who enforced tolerance for the viewpoints of all, each participant got up and offered his or her own individual angry theory about the nature of The Conspiracy.

Some blamed the royals, others the bankers,[‡] others the Trilateral Commission, all blamed decades of Bush family iniquity, and one woman even talked about a conspiracy to hide the discovery of alien technologies at Area 51.[§]

* Colorado senator Cory Gardner called Trump a "buffoon," then voted for him.
† One of Trump's biggest allies is conspiracist and noted 9/11 Truther Alex Jones, about whom Trump said, "Your reputation is amazing." Jones countered on August 11th of 2016 by saying, "It is surreal to talk about issues here on air and then word-for-word hear Trump say it two days later." Jones politically represents the collision of lefty conspiracy theories and right-wing ideology.
‡ As a prominent critic of Goldman Sachs, I was pilloried on social media as a traitor to the anti-establishment cause because I criticized Trump, which led people to assume I was supporting Clinton, the "Goldman candidate."
§ In a nod to UFO enthusiasts, Hillary Clinton during the 2016 race promised to open up any files the U.S. government had on aliens, leading UFOlogists to dub her "the first E.T. president."

Everyone made his or her speech, and then the meeting was over with nothing accomplished except a decision to have another meeting.

Having seen all this, what I ended up trying to do in this book was describe the whole outline of the problem. Much of the book focuses on the insider game in Washington, from the corrupt response to Hurricane Katrina to both parties' absurdly transparent attempts to deflect popular opposition to the Iraq war.* At the same time I tried to describe the response to this nonfunctioning government across the country, on both the right and the left.

What I hope comes through is that the corruption of the system certainly has had consequences in the population, inspiring popular disgust and rage, with voters keenly understanding on some level anyway the depth of their betrayal.

But the form of the public response turns out to be a grotesquerie. It turns out that we've been split up and atomized for so long that real grassroots politics isn't really possible.

We don't respond to problems as communities, but as demographics. In the same way that we shop for cars and choose television programs, we pick our means of political protest. We scan the media landscape for the thing that appeals to us and we buy into it.

That it's the same media landscape these new dissidents often reject as a false and misleading tableau dominated by corrupt interests turns out not to be problematic for many.

In some cases, like that of those Christians I spent time

---

* The Beltway take on Iraq by 2016 had come all the way around to meeting the public's longtime opposition, to the point where Hillary Clinton finally admitted she was wrong to support the invasion, and accused Donald Trump of lying when he said he was against the war.

with in San Antonio, the trusted new figure, a preacher named John Hagee,* turns out to be every bit the establishment Washington insider these would-be religious revolutionaries think they're fleeing from.

In other cases, like that of the 9/11 Truthers, the radical canonical revolutionary tracts end up including thoroughly commercial mainstream entertainments like *V for Vendetta*[†] and *The Matrix*[‡] (at different times I would hear both radical conservatives and liberals describe their political awakenings using the phrase "taking the red pill").[§]

In short, what sounds on the surface like radical politics turns out to be just another fracturing of the media picture, one that ultimately will result in new groups of captive audiences that, if experience is any guide, will ultimately be assimilated[¶] and electorally coddled by a political mainstream in reality bent on ignoring both sides.

For now, however, the situation going into the 2008 election looks grim. We have a population more disgusted than ever with our political system, one inclined to distrust

* Hagee was an ardent supporter of Trump and warned his followers that there would be retribution for those who didn't vote for him. "God will not hold us harmless," he said. "I'm going to vote for the candidate that's going to make the U.S. military great again."
† The hacker Anonymous, dressed in a *V for Vendetta* mask, declared "total war" on Donald Trump in March 2016.
‡ The "Trump vs. Hillary" *Matrix* parody was one of the campaign's underappreciated viral efforts.
§ The Red Pill, a Reddit subforum dedicated to seeing "the world as it actually is," endorsed Donald Trump over Hillary, the "blue pill" candidate. "America is not a democracy, it is simply an illusion," the site reads. "George Soros has ties to 16 voting machines in different states."
¶ One of the first storylines of the Trump transition was his quickness in surrounding himself with the very establishment Republicans he had denounced during the campaign, with moves like naming Reince Priebus chief of staff particularly raising eyebrows. The *New Yorker* called it a "bait and switch."

the result no matter* who wins† the White House—and
should the national election end up being a contest between
a pair of full-of-shit establishment conservatives like Hillary Clinton and Rudy Giuliani, it will only confirm the
worst fears of both sides and result in an even further bon-
kerization of the population.

Gone will be the good old days of neat blue-state/
red-state hatred—a nicely symmetrical storyline that has
always appealed to the *Crossfire/American Gladiators* sports-
coverage mentality of the commercial media.

In its place, at least temporarily, will be a chaos of lunatic enthusiasms and dead-end political movements, with
calls for invasions of Babylon and, on the other side, congressional investigations‡ into nonexistent conspiracies . . . §

When a people can no longer agree even on the basic
objective facts of their political existence, the equation
changes. Real decisions, even in the approximate direction
of righteousness, eventually become impossible.

The Great Derangement is about a stage of our history
where politics has seemingly stopped being about ideology,
and has instead turned into a problem of information.

Are the right messages reaching our collective brain?

---

* Computer scientists quickly raced to encourage the Clinton camp to challenge
Trump's win, noting that Clinton performed significantly worse in counties with
electronic voting than in those with optical scanning or paper ballots.
† Trump of course famously refused to promise in advance to recognize the election results, essentially pre-rejecting their validity if he lost.
‡ Trump notoriously campaigned on slogans like "Lock her up!" but decided
against pursuing investigations of Hillary Clinton while in office, a move likely to
upset his base.
§ The so-called fake news movement blossomed on sites like Facebook, where
there was an explosion of phony stories. The owner of a Washington pizzeria
called Comet Ping Pong being implicated in a phony child sex ring with Hillary
Clinton and John Podesta was only one of the weirder ones, although even that
story became a disputed controversy known as "Pizzagate."

Are the halves of that brain even connected? Do we know who we are anymore? Are we sane? It's a hell of a problem for a nuclear power.

From Chapter One:

OUT THERE, IN STATES BOTH BLUE AND RED, THE PEOPLE were boarding the mothership, preparing to leave this planet for good.

The media had long ignored the implications of polls that showed that half the country believed in angels and the inerrancy of the Bible, or of the fact that the *Left Behind* series of books had sold in the tens of millions.

But on the ground the political consequences of magical thinking were becoming clearer.

The religious right increasingly saw satanic influences and signs of the upcoming apocalypse. Meanwhile, on the left, a different sort of fantasy was gaining traction, as an increasing number—up to a third of the country according to some polls—saw the "Bush crime family" in league with Al-Qaeda, masterminding 9/11.

Media outlets largely ignored poll results that they felt could not possibly be true. For instance, there was a CBS News survey that showed that only 16 percent believed that the Bush administration was telling the truth about 9/11, with 53 percent believing the government was "hiding something," and another 28 percent believing that it was "mostly lying."

Then there was a stunning Zogby poll taken just in advance of the 2004 Republican convention that showed that nearly half of New York City residents—49.3 percent—

believed that the government knew in advance that the 9/11 attacks were coming and purposely failed to act.

Voters didn't just distrust the government's words and actions. By 2007 they also had very serious doubts about their government's legitimacy.

Successive election cycles foundering on voting-machine scandals had left both sides deeply suspicious of election results. A poll in Florida taken in 2004 suggested that some 25 percent of voters worried that their votes were not being counted—a 20 percent jump from the pre-2000 numbers.*

Even more damning was a Zogby poll conducted in 2006 that showed only 45 percent of Americans were "very confident" that George Bush won the 2004 election "fair and square."

The most surprising thing about that last poll was the degree to which the distrust was spread wide across the demographic spectrum. That 71 percent of African Americans distrusted the 2004 results was perhaps not a surprise, given that black voters in America have been victims of organized disenfranchisement throughout this country's history.

But 28 percent of NASCAR fans? Twenty-five percent of born-again Christians? Thirty-two percent of currently serving members of the armed forces?

These are astonishing numbers for a country that even in its lowest times—after Watergate, say, or during Reconstruction—never doubted the legitimacy of their leaders to such a degree.

And if distrust of the government was at an all-time

---

* Before the election, 41 percent of voters believed the election would be stolen away from Donald Trump.

high, that was still nothing compared to what the public thought of the national media. Both the left and the right had developed parallel theories about the co-opting of the corporate press, imagining it to be controlled by powerful unseen enemies, and increasingly turned to grassroots Internet sources for news and information.

In the BBC/Reuters/Media Center's annual Trust in the Media survey in 2006, the United States was one of just two countries surveyed—Britain being the other—where respondents trusted their government (67 percent) more than they trusted national news reporters (59 percent). A Harris poll that same year showed that some 68 percent of Americans now felt that the news media were "too powerful."*

The country, in other words, was losing it. Our national politics was doomed because voters were no longer debating one another using a commonly accepted set of facts. There was no common narrative, except in the imagination of a daft political and media elite that had long ago lost touch with the general public.

What we had instead was a nation of reality shoppers, all shutting the blinds on the loathsome old common landscape to tinker with their own self-tailored and in some cases highly paranoid recipes for salvation and/or revolution.

They voted in huge numbers, but they were voting out of loathing, against enemies and against the system in general, not really for anybody. The elections had basically become a forum for organizing the hatreds of the population.

---

* The BBC/Reuters survey no longer exists, but Gallup does a trust-in-media survey as well, and 2016 marked its lowest numbers ever, with only 32 percent saying they have a "great deal" of faith and trust in the media.

And the worst thing was that the political parties at some level were complicit in this and understood what was going on perfectly. That's why they collectively spent $160 million on negative advertising in this cycle, as opposed to just $17 million on positive ads.*

There were no longer any viable principles in play. Just hate. And distrust.

The system had nothing left to offer the People, so the People were leaving the reservation. But where were they going?

---

* All the data aren't in yet, but 2016 certainly set records for volume of election ads, and to take one example, about 61 percent of Hillary Clinton's ads were negative.

2

August 12, 2015: Inside the GOP Clown Car

On the campaign trail in Iowa, Donald Trump's antics have forced the other candidates to get crazy or go home

T HE THING IS, WHEN YOU ACTUALLY THINK ABOUT IT, IT'S not funny. Given what's at stake, it's more like the opposite, like the first sign of the collapse of the United States as a global superpower. Twenty years from now, when we're all living like prehistory hominids and hunting rats with sticks, we'll probably look back at this moment as the beginning of the end.

In the meantime, though, the race for the Republican Party presidential nomination sure seems funny. The event known around the world as hashtagGOPClownCar is improbable, colossal, spectacular and shocking; epic, monumental, heinous and disgusting. It's like watching 17 platypuses try to mount the queen of England. You can't tear your eyes away from it.

It will go down someday as the greatest reality show ever conceived. The concept is ingenious. Take a combustible mix of the most depraved and filterless half-wits, scam artists and asylum Napoleons America has to offer, give them all piles of money and tell them to run for president. Add Donald Trump. And to give the whole thing a perverse gravitas, make the presidency really at stake.

It's Western civilization's very own car wreck. Even if you don't want to watch it, you will. It's that awesome of a spectacle.

But what does it mean? Or to put it another way, since we know it can't mean anything good: Is this enough of a disaster that we shouldn't laugh?

I went to Iowa to see for myself.

Rockwell City, Iowa, evening, July 30th. I've just rushed up from Des Moines to catch my first event on the Clown Car tour, a stump speech by TV personality Mike Huckabee, whom the Internet says was also once governor of Arkansas.

Traditionally, in these early stages of a presidential campaign, very little happens. Candidates treat their stump work like comedians practicing new material between the lunch and dinner hours. In the old days, they tiptoed their positions out before small audiences in little farm towns like this in an effort to see what minor policy tweaks might play better later on in the race, when the bullets start flying for real.

That's what one normally expects. But 2016 is very different, as I found out in Rockwell City right away.

Two factors have combined to make this maybe the

most unlikely political story of our times. The first is the campaign's extraordinary number of entrants. As the *Washington Post* noted last fall, this is the first time in recent memory that there is no heir-apparent candidate (like a Bob Dole). For some reason, during the last years of the Obama presidency, the national Republican Party chose not to throw its weight behind anyone, leading a monstrous field of has-beens and never-weres to believe that they had a real shot at winning the nomination.

So throughout this spring and summer, a new Human Punchline seemingly jumped into the race every week. There were so many of these jokers, coming so fast, that news commentators quickly latched onto the image of a parade of clowns emerging from a political Volkswagen, giving birth to the "clown car" theme.

But the more important factor has been the astounding presence of Donald Trump as the front-runner. The orangutan-haired real estate magnate entered the race in mid-June and immediately blew up cable and Twitter by denouncing Mexicans as rapists and ripping 2008 nominee John McCain for having been captured in war.

Both moves would have been fatal to "serious" candidates in previous elections. But amid the strange Republican leadership void of 2016, the furor only gave Trump further saturation among the brainless nativists in his party and inexplicably vaulted him to front-runner status. The combination of Trump constantly spewing crazy quotes and the strategy *actually working* turned his campaign into a veritable media supernova, earning the Donald more coverage than all of the other candidates combined.

This led to a situation where the candidates have had to resort to increasingly bizarre tactics in order to win press attention. Add to this the curious dynamic of the first Republican debate, on August 6th, in which only the top 10 poll performers get on the main stage, and the incentive to say outlandish things in search of a poll bump quickly reached a fever pitch. So much for the cautious feeling-out period: For the candidates, it was toss grenades or die.

Back in the Rockwell City library, the small contingent of reporters covering the day's third "Huckabee Huddle" was buzzing. A local TV guy was staring at his notes with a confused look on his face, like he couldn't believe what he read. "Weirdest thing," he said. "I was just in Jefferson, and Huckabee said something about invoking the 14th and 5th amendments to end abortion. I'm really not sure what he meant."

A moment later, Huckabee sauntered into the library for an ad-hoc presser, and was quickly asked what he meant. "Just what I said," he quipped. "It is the job of the federal government to protect the citizens under the Constitution."

He went on to explain that even the unborn were entitled to rights of "due process and equal protection." The attendant reporters all glanced sideways at one another. The idea of using the 14th Amendment, designed to protect the rights of ex-slaves, as a tool to outlaw abortion in the 21st century clearly would have its own dark appeal to the Fox crowd. But it occurred to me that Huckabee might have had more in mind.

"Are we talking about sending the FBI or the National Guard to close abortion clinics?" I asked.

"We'll see when I get to be president," he answered.

Huckabee smiled. Perhaps alone among all the non-Trump candidates, Huckabee knows what kind of fight he's in. This GOP race is not about policy or electability or even raising money. Instead, it's about Nielsen ratings or trending. It's a minute-to-minute contest for media heat and Internet hits, where positive and negative attention are almost equally valuable.

Huckabee launched his campaign on May 5th, running on a carefully crafted and somewhat unconventional Republican platform centered around economic populism, vowing to end "stagnant wages" and help people reach a "higher ground."

But emphasizing economic populism is the kind of wonky policy nuance that doesn't do much to earn notice in the Twitter age. After an early bump pushed him briefly up to fourth place, Huckabee began a steady slide in the polls as the unrestrained lunacy of Trump began seizing control of the race. By late July, Huckabee's numbers had fallen, and he had to be worrying that he would land out of the top 10.

But then, on July 25th, Huckabee gave an interview to *Breitbart News* in which he shamelessly invoked Godwin's Law, saying that Barack Obama's deal with Iran "would take the Israelis and basically march them to the door of the oven."

The quote hit the airwaves like a thunderclap. Virtually everyone in the English-speaking world with an IQ over nine shrieked in disgust. The Huckster's "ovens" rant brought MSNBC host Mika Brzezinski to near-tears on air. Huckabee even prompted an Israeli transportation minister to exclaim, *Dirty Dancing*–style, "Nobody marches the Jews to ovens anymore."

Even in Huckabee's own party, he was denounced. Jeb Bush, anxious to cast himself as the non-crazy, *Uncola* Republican in a field of mental incompetents, called on everyone to "tone down the rhetoric." Wisconsin Gov. Scott

Walker, known as one of America's most dickishly unscrupulous hate merchants, said, "You're not hearing me use that sort of language."

But far from being deterred by all of the negative attention, Huckabee shrewdly embraced it. Much like the Donald, Huckabee swallowed up the negative press energy like a Pac-Man and steamed ahead, and was soon climbing in the polls again.

Huckabee had stumbled into the truth that has been driving the support for the Trump campaign: That in this intensely media-driven race, inspiring genuine horror and disgust among the right people is worth a lot of votes in certain quarters, irrespective of how you go about it. If you're making an MSNBC anchor cry or rendering a coastal media villain like Anderson Cooper nearly speechless (as Trump has done), you must be doing something right.

In Rockwell City, it seemed like Huckabee was consciously trying to repeat his "ovens" stunt. He smiled as the media in attendance filed out of the presser, surely knowing we would have the "we'll see" quote up on social media within minutes.

At the event, he was glowingly introduced by Iowa Republican Congressman Steve King, who revved the crowd by bashing the Supreme Court ruling clearing the way for gay marriage. King had apparently been told on good authority by a lawyer friend that *Obergefell v. Hodges* meant that only one party in a marriage had to be a human being. "What that means," he said, "is you can now marry my lawn mower."

A reporter next to me leaned over. "King's lawn mower is gay?"

I shrugged. In the modern Republican Party, making

sense is a secondary consideration. Years of relentless propaganda combined with extreme frustration over the disastrous Bush years and two terms of a Kenyan Muslim terrorist president have cast the party's right wing into a swirling suckhole of paranoia and conspiratorial craziness. There is nothing you can do to go too far, a fact proved, if not exactly understood, by the madman, Trump.

Huckabee's speech tossed plenty of red meat into the grinder, explaining that America was divinely created by "providence of almighty God," which is the only explanation for the extreme longevity of the Constitution. He stepped down to hearty applause, giving way to a performance by a group of Rockwell City Republican women, who sang what they called a "rap song." There was no beat and each of the 10-odd singers was off from the next by a word or two:

> *People want the freedom*
> *To make medical and personal choices!*
> *And we want representatives*
> *To listen to our voices!*

Listening, I suddenly worried that the International Federation of Black People would detect this "rap" performance from afar and call in an air strike. Sneaking out the front door, I checked my phone to see how Huck's abortion-clinic play was doing: He'd already set off a media shitstorm.

Within 24 hours, he was being denounced across the blogosphere, but he was soon riding up in the polls again, one of the few shoo-ins to get on the main stage of the August 6th debate.

It was astounding, watching the other entrants try to

duplicate Huckabee's feat. Former Texas Gov. Rick Perry was last seen on the national stage choking on his own face in an infamous 2011 debate performance, when he was unable to name the three federal agencies he himself had promised to do away with. He returned to the race this year basically the same gaffe-spewing yutz he was four years ago, only dressed in preposterous "smart" glasses, a deadly error in a fight with a natural schoolyard bully like Donald Trump.

"He put glasses on so people will think he's smart," Trump croaked. "And it just doesn't work!"

Perry was so grateful to even be mentioned by Trump that he refocused his campaign apparatus on an epic response, apparently in an attempt to draw the Donald into a Drake/Meek Mill–style diss war. He tossed off a 3,000-word speech denouncing "Trumpism" as the modern incarnation of the Know-Nothing movement (one could almost hear Trump scoffing, "What the fuck is a Know-Nothing?"). He decried Trump himself as a "barking carnival act" and a "cancer" that the party should "excise" for its own sake—and, one supposes, for Rick Perry's.

Trump, too busy being front-runner to notice Perry's desperate volleys, basically blew the Texan off. A week later, Perry was in a tie for 10th place in the polls. Asked if his campaign was finished if he didn't make the debate cut, Perry replied, in characteristically malaprop fashion, that making the debate was "not a one-shot pony." He ended up missing his shot, or his pony, or whatever, and was squeezed out of the debate.

Many of the entrants tried nutty media stunts to re-inject energy into the race. Kentucky Sen. Rand Paul attempted to revive his flagging libertarian-niche campaign by putting out a video. In it, the candidate appears dressed in shop goggles and jeans, curly hair flying, chain-sawing the tax code in half. He looks like Ryan Phillippe doing a Billy Mays ad.

Then there was South Carolina Sen. Lindsey Graham, one of the few candidates with a sense of humor about how much of a long shot he is. "I do bar mitzvahs, birthday parties, weddings, funerals—call me, I'll come," he cracked. Once in the race, though, Graham immediately trolled Trump by calling him a "jackass," then briefly enjoyed some press limelight when the furious front-runner gave out Graham's telephone number to the public.

Graham responded to the blessing of a Trump insult by putting out a video celebrating his Trump-victimhood. In it, the candidate chops up his cellphone Ginsu-style, mixes it in a blender in a foul-looking yellow liquid, and whacks it with a nine-iron, or maybe a wedge (note: the Graham camp says it was a nine).

All of this actually happened. Can we be that far from candidates putting out dueling cat videos?

In late July, in a cramped conference room of a Marriott in West Des Moines, Graham showed up to introduce himself to voters. In person, he's an odd character, like an oversize ventriloquist's dummy, with too-bright eyes and cheeks frozen in a half-grin.

He calls his event a "No Nukes for Iran" rally. Clearly gunning for a Cabinet post in Defense or Homeland Security, Graham is running almost a one-issue race, campaigning on being the candidate who most thinks Barack Obama's Iran deal sucks.

Of course, all 17 of the Republican candidates think Obama's Iran deal sucks, but Graham wants you to know he really thinks it sucks. Part of his stump speech is ripped straight from *Team America*: He thinks the Iran deal will result in "9/11 times a hundred." Actually in Graham's version, it's 9/11 times a thousand.

"The only reason 3,000 of us died on 9/11 and not 3 million," he said, "is they could not get the weapons."

Graham would seem to be perfectly suited for this Twitter-driven race, because he has a reputation in Washington for being a master of the one-liner and a goofball with boundaries issues who not infrequently crosses lines in his humor. "Did you see Nancy Pelosi on the floor?" he reportedly once quipped. "Complete disgust. If you can get through the surgeries, it's disgust."

But in person, Graham is a dud. His nasal voice and dry presentation make Alan Greenspan seem like Marilyn Manson. Still, it doesn't take too long for him to drift into rhetoric that in a normal political season would distinguish him as an unhinged lunatic, which is interesting because pundits usually call Graham one of the "sane" candidates.

First, he firmly promised to re-litigate the Iraq War. "I'm gonna send some soldiers back to Iraq," he said. "If I'm president, we're going back to Iraq."

Promising concretely to restart a historically unpopular war is a solid Trump-era provocation, but Graham then took it a step further. He pledged to solve the Syria problem by channeling Lawrence of Arabia and leading an Arab army in an epic campaign to unseat the caliphate.

Graham, a politician who reportedly once said that "everything that starts with 'al-' in the Middle East is bad news," insisted he was just the man to unite the Saudis, Egyptians, Jordanians, Turks and other peoples in battle, and also get them to pay for the invasion (getting dirty foreigners to pay for our policies is another Trump innovation). "We're going into Syria with the Arabs in the lead," Graham said. "They will do most of the fighting, and they're gonna pay for it because we paid for the last two."

I looked around the room. No reaction whatsoever. An old man in the rear of the hall was picking a cuticle off his middle finger, but otherwise, nobody moved. There were reporters, but Graham's hawkish bleatings don't rate much in an America obsessed with Caitlyn and Rachel Dolezal and the Donald.

Instead, later that same day, news leaked out that a Trump political adviser, Sam Nunberg, had once referred to Al Sharpton's daughter as a "n———" on Facebook. This is news. It virtually obliterated all other campaign information.

Within a day, polls showed Trump surging like never before. One Reuters poll released on August 1st showed him scoring nearly 30 percent of the vote. The second-highest contender, Jeb Bush, was now nearly 20 points off the lead. When Trump completed the news cycle by giving Nunberg an *Apprentice*-style firing, his triumph was total.

If the clowns who engaged Trump mostly came out looking awful, the ones who didn't engage him came out looking even worse, including several of the ostensible favorites.

Jeb Bush was supposedly the smarter Bush brother and also the presumptive front-runner in this race. But on July 4th, just a few weeks after entering the race, Trump basically ended the fight in one fell swoop with a single kick in the balls, retweeting that Bush has to like "Mexican illegals because of his wife."

With a wife's honor at stake, most self-respecting males

would have immediately stalked Trump and belted him in the comb-over. But Bush stayed true to his effete Richie Rich rep and turtled. He said nothing and instead meekly had an aide put out a statement that Trump's words were "inappropriate and not reflective of the Republican Party's views."

It was such a bad showing that the Beltway opinionators at *Politico* ran a story asking, "Is Jeb Bush turning into Michael Dukakis?" Game, set, match! Bush has been plunging in the polls ever since.

A similar fate befell Marco Rubio, the boy-wonder Republican. Rubio cruised through the early portion of the race, when voters were impressed by his sideswept, anal-retentive, Cuban-Alex-Keaton persona, rising as high as 14 percent in the polls. But then Trump entered the race and blasted the clearly less-than-completely-American Rubio for favoring a pro-immigration bill. "Weak on immigration" and "weak on jobs," Trump scoffed. "Not the guy."

He battered Rubio with tweet after tweet, one-liner after one-liner. Trump aides hit Rubio for having "zero credibility" and being a "typical politician" who favored a "dangerous amnesty bill." Rubio meanwhile defended Mexicans in general after Trump's "rapists" line, but has passed on engaging Trump's personal attacks. As a result, Rubio's support for a path to citizenship for the undocumented has stood out like a herpes sore, and he's plummeted to five percent in the polls.

The only candidate to really escape Trump's wrath has been Texas Sen. Ted Cruz, and that's because Cruz has spent the entire political season nuzzling Trump's ankles, praising the Donald like a lovesick cellmate. The Texas senator, whose rhetorical schtick is big doses of Tea Party crazy (his best line was that Obama wanted to bring "expanded Medicaid" to ISIS) mixed with constant assurances that he's the most Reagan-y of all the candidates, even reportedly had an hour-long "confab" with Trump. "Terrific," he said of the meeting, calling Trump "one of a kind."

The subterranean Cruz-Trump communiqués are a fantastic subplot to this absurdist campaign, hashtagClown-Car's very own Nazi-Soviet nonaggression pact. It could mean the two plan to run together, or it could mean Cruz will plead for Trump's votes if and when the party finds a way to beg, threaten or blackmail Donald out of the race. Whatever it means, it's a microcosm of the campaign: simultaneously disgusting and entertaining.

It's not surprising that Trump's most serious competition will likely come from Wisconsin's Walker, who is probably the only person in the race naturally meaner than Trump.

A central-casting Charmless White Guy who looks like a vice principal or an overdressed traffic cop, Walker traced a performance arc in the past year that was actually a signal of what was to come with Trump. Back in February, when addressing the Conservative Political Action Conference, Walker answered a question of how he would deal with Islamic terrorists by saying, "If I can take on 100,000 protesters, I can do the same across the world."

Like Trump's Mexican remarks, Walker's gambit comparing American union workers to head-chopping Islamic terrorists seemed like a bridge too far even for many Republicans. He was criticized by the *National Review* and future opponent Perry, among others. But instead of plummeting in the polls, Walker, like Trump, gained ground.

The irony is that this was supposed to be the year when

the Republicans opened the tent up, made a sincere play for the Hispanic vote, and perhaps softened up a bit on gays and other vermin. But then the lights went on in the race and voters flocked to a guy whose main policy plank was the construction of a giant *Game of Thrones*–style wall to keep rape-happy ethnics off our lawns. So much for inclusion!

Waterloo, Iowa, August 1st. New Jersey Gov. Chris Christie showed up at Lincoln Park downtown to attend the Cedar Valley Irish fest, a multiday fair with street cuisine, tents full of hand-made crafts, live music and a 5K road race. In a state where a more typical event is a stale VFW hall buffet or a visit to the world's largest truck stop (the I-80 meet-and-greet is a staple of Iowa campaigning), the Irish fest is a happening scene, featuring good food and sizable numbers of people under the age of 60.

Two years ago, Christie's arrival at an event like this would have been a major political event. Back then, Christie was a national phenomenon, a favorite to be dubbed presumptive front-runner for 2016.

Christie's the type of candidate political audiences have come to expect: Once every four years, commentators in New York and Washington will fall in love with some "crossover" politician who's mean enough to be accepted by the right wing, but also knows a gay person or once read a French novel or something. In the pre-Trump era, we became conditioned to believe that this is what constituted an "exciting" politician.

Christie was to be that next crossover hit, the 2016 version of McCain. Washington's high priest of Conventional Wisdom, Mark Halperin, even called him "magical," and *Time* called him a guy who "loves his mother and gets it done."

But two years later, Christie has been undone by "Bridgegate," and the buzz is gone. When he showed up at Cedar Falls, there were just a few reporters to meet him. One of the Iowa press contingent explained to me that with the gigantic field, some of the lesser candidates are falling through the cracks. "We just don't have enough bodies to cover the race," the reporter said. "It's never been like this."

Christie and his wife, Mary Pat, made their way patiently through the crowd, shaking hands and talking football and other topics with a handful of attendees. It was old-school politics, the way elections used to be won in this country, but it was hard not to watch this painstaking one-person-at-a-time messaging and wonder how it competes in the social-media age.

After the event, I asked Christie whether the huge field makes it difficult to get media attention. "Well, I've never had any trouble getting attention," he said. "I just think it's differentiating yourself. I think it plays to our strengths, because we've always worked really hard."

Right, hard work: that old saw. Later in the day, back across the state in Rockwell City, former Pennsylvania Sen. Rick Santorum played the same tune at the town's "Corn Daze" festival. Dressed in jeans, a blue oxford and a face so pious that Christ would be proud to eat a burrito off it, Santorum rushed through a speech explaining that it is in fact he who is the hardest-working man in politics.

"I just want to let you know that we've gone to about 55 counties," he said. "Last time, we went to 99. We'll probably have 99 done here in the next few weeks."

I asked how anyone can distinguish himself or herself in a field with so many entrants. "Win Iowa," he answered curtly.

Right, but how? "What happens in August stays in August," he said mysteriously, then vanished to his next event. He had, like, 11 events in three days, far more than most other candidates.

Santorum actually won the Iowa race four years ago with his overcaffeinated, kiss-the-most-babies approach. But watching both him and Christie put their chips on the shoe-leather approach to campaigning feels like watching a pair of Neanderthals scout for mammoth. In the Age of Trump, this stuff doesn't play anymore.

Not that the old guard will go down without a fight. The much-anticipated inaugural Clown Debate in Cleveland was an ambush. Fox kicked off the festivities by twice whacking Trump, Buford Pusser–style, asking him to promise not to make a third-party run (he wouldn't) and sandbagging him with questions about his history of calling women "fat pigs" ("Only Rosie O'Donnell," Trump quipped). After the show, Fox had Republican pollster Frank Luntz organize a focus group that universally panned Trump's performance. "A total setup," one of Trump's aides complained on Twitter.

Trump didn't seem to care. Hell, he didn't even prepare for the debate. "Trump doesn't rehearse," an aide told reporters. All he did was show up and do what he always does: hog everything in sight, including airtime. As hard as Fox tried to knock him out, the network couldn't take its eyes off him. He ended up with almost two full minutes more airtime than the other "contestants," as he hilariously called them on the *Today* show the morning after the debate. It's the scorpion nature of television, come back to haunt the "reality-makers" at Fox: The cameras can't resist a good show.

Politics used to be a simple, predictable con. Every four

years, the money men in D.C. teamed up with party hacks to throw their weight behind whatever half-bright fraud of a candidate proved most adept at snowing the population into buying a warmed-over version of the same crappy policies they've always bought.

Pundits always complained that there wasn't enough talk about issues during these races, but in reality, issues were still everything. Behind the scenes, where donors gave millions for concrete favors, there was always still plenty of policy. And skilled political pitchmen like Christie, who could deftly deliver on those back-room promises to crush labor and hand out transportation contracts or whatever while still acting like a man of the people, were highly valued commodities.

Not anymore. Trump has blown up even the backroom version of the issues-driven campaign. There are no secret donors that we know of. Trump himself appears to be the largest financial backer of the Trump campaign. A financial report disclosed that Trump lent his own campaign $1.8 million while raising just $100,000.

There's no hidden platform behind the shallow facade. With Trump, the facade is the whole deal. If old-school policy hucksters like Christie can't find a way to beat a media master like Trump at the ratings game, they will soon die out.

In a perverse way, Trump has restored a more pure democracy to this process. He's taken the Beltway thinkfluencers out of the game and turned the presidency into a pure high-school-style popularity contest conducted entirely in the media. Everything we do is a consumer choice now, from picking our shoes to an online streaming platform to a presidential nominee.

The irony, of course, is that when America finally wrested control of the political process from the backroom oligarchs, the very first place where we spent our newfound freedom and power was on the campaign of the world's most unapologetic asshole. It may not seem funny now, because it's happening to us, but centuries from this moment, people will laugh in wonder.

America is ceasing to be a nation, and turning into a giant television show. And this Republican race is our first and most brutal casting call.

3

August 21, 2015: Donald Trump Just Stopped Being Funny

Win or lose, Trump's campaign threatens to
unleash the Great American Stupid

So TWO YAHOOS FROM SOUTHIE IN MY HOMETOWN OF Boston beat up a Hispanic homeless guy earlier this week. While being arrested, one of the brothers reportedly told police that "Donald Trump was right, all of these illegals need to be deported."

When reporters confronted Trump, he hadn't yet heard about the incident. At first, he said, "That would be a shame." But right after, he went on:

"I will say, the people that are following me are very passionate. They love this country. They want this

country to be great again. But they are very passionate.
I will say that."

This is the moment when Donald Trump officially
stopped being funny.

The thing is, even as Donald Trump said and did horrible things during this year's incredible run at the White
House, most sane people took solace in the fact that he could
never win. (Although new polls are showing that Hillary's
recent spiral puts this reassuring thought into jeopardy.)

In fact, most veteran political observers figured that the
concrete impact of Trump's candidacy would be limited in
the worst case to destroying the Republican Party as a
mainstream political force.

That made Trump's run funny, campy even, like a
naughty piece of pornographic performance art. After all,
what's more obscene than pissing on the presidency? It
seemed even more like camp because the whole schtick was
fronted by a veteran reality TV star who might even be in
on the joke, although of course the concept was funnier if he
wasn't.

Trump had the whole country rubbernecking as this
preposterous Spaulding Smails caricature of a spoiled rich
kid drove the family Rolls (our illustrious electoral process
in this metaphor) off the road into a ditch. It was brilliant
theater for a while, but the ugliness factor has gotten out of
control.

Trump is probably too dumb to realize it, or maybe he
isn't, but he doesn't need to win anything to become the
most dangerous person in America. He can do plenty of
damage just by encouraging people to be as uninhibited in
their stupidity as he is.

Trump is striking a chord with people who are feeling the squeeze in a less secure world and want to blame someone—the government, immigrants, political correctness, "incompetents," "dummies," Megyn Kelly, whoever— for their problems.

Karl Rove and his acolytes mined a lot of the same resentments to get Republicans elected over the years, but the difference is that Trump's political style encourages people to do more to express their anger than just vote. The key to his success is a titillating message that those musty old rules about being polite and "saying the right thing" are for losers who lack the heart, courage and Trumpitude to just be who they are.

His signature moment in a campaign full of them was his exchange in the first debate with *Fox*'s Kelly. She asked him how anyone with a history of calling women "fat pigs, dogs, slobs, and disgusting animals" could win a general election against a female candidate like Hillary Clinton.

"I've been challenged by so many people," Trump answered. "I frankly don't have time for political correctness. And to be honest with you, the country doesn't have time either. . . . We don't win anymore. We lose to China. We lose to Mexico. . . . We lose to everybody."

On the surface, Kelly was just doing her job as a journalist, throwing Trump's most outrageous comments back at him and demanding an explanation.

But on another level, she was trying to bring Trump to heel. The extraction of the humiliating public apology is one of the media's most powerful weapons. Someone becomes famous, we dig up dirt on the person, we rub it in his or her nose, and then we demand that the person get down on bended knee and beg forgiveness.

The Clintons' 1992 joint interview on *60 Minutes* was a classic example, as were Anthony Weiner's prostration before Andrew Breitbart and Chris Christie's 107-minute marathon apologia after Bridgegate. The subtext is always the same: If you want power in this country, you must accept the primacy of the press. It's like paying the cover at the door of the world's most exclusive club.

Trump wouldn't pay the tab. Not only was he not wrong for saying those things, he explained, but holding in thoughts like that is bad for America. That's why we don't win anymore, why we lose to China and to Mexico (how are we losing to Mexico again?). He was saying that hiding forbidden thoughts about women or immigrants or whoever isn't just annoying, but bad for America.

It's not exactly telling people to get out there and beat people with metal rods. But when your response to news that a couple of jackasses just invoked your name when they beat the crap out of a homeless guy is to salute your "passionate" followers who "love this country," you've gone next-level.

The political right in America has been flirting with dangerous ideas for a while now, particularly on issues involving immigrants and minorities. But in the last few years the rhetoric has gotten particularly crazy.

Texas Congressman Louie Gohmert proposed using troops and ships of war to stop an invasion of immigrant children, whom he described as a *28 Days Later*–style menace. "We don't even know all of the diseases, and how extensive the diseases are," he said.

"A lot of head lice, a lot of scabies," concurred another Texas congressman, Blake Farenthold.

"I'll do anything short of shooting them," promised Mo

Brooks, a congressman from the enlightened state of Alabama.

Then there's Iowa's Steve King, who is unusually stupid even for a congressman. He not only believes a recent Supreme Court decision on gay marriage allows people to marry inanimate objects, but also believes the EPA may have intentionally spilled three million gallons of toxic waste into Colorado's Animas River in order to get Superfund money.

Late last year, King asked people to "surround the president's residence" in response to Barack Obama's immigration policies. He talked about putting "boots on the ground" and said "everything is on the table" in the fight against immigrants.

So all of this was in the ether even before Donald Trump exploded into the headlines with his "They're rapists" line, and before his lunatic, *Game of Thrones* idea to build a giant wall along the southern border. But when Trump surged in the polls on the back of this stuff, it caused virtually all of the candidates to escalate their anti-immigrant rhetoric.

For example, we just had Ben Carson—who seems on TV like a gentle, convivial doctor who's just woken up from a nice nap—come out and suggest that he's open to using drone strikes on U.S. soil against undocumented immigrants. Bobby Jindal recently came out and said mayors in the so-called "sanctuary cities" should be arrested when undocumented immigrants commit crimes. Scott Walker and Marco Rubio have both had to change their positions favoring paths to citizenship as a result of the new dynamic.

Meanwhile, Rick Santorum, polling at a brisk zero percent, joined Jindal and Lindsey Graham in jumping aboard with Trump's insane plan to toss the 14th Amendment out the window and revoke the concept of birthright citizen-ship, thereby extending the war on immigrants not just to children, but babies.

All of this bleeds out into the population. When a poli-tician says dumb thing *X*, it normally takes 'Murica about two days to start flirting publicly with *X + way worse*.

We saw that earlier this week, when Iowa radio host Jan Mickelson blew up Twitter by calling for undocumented immigrants to become "property of the state" and put into "compelled labor." When a caller challenged the idea, Mick-elson answered, "What's wrong with slavery?"

Why there's suddenly this surge of hatred for immi-grants is sort of a mystery. Why Donald Trump, who's probably never even interacted with an undocumented im-migrant in a non-commercial capacity, in particular should care so much about this issue is even more obscure. (Did he trip over an immigrant on his way to the Cincinnati hous-ing development his father gave him as a young man?)

Most likely, immigrants are just collateral damage in Trump's performance art routine, which is an absurd ritual-istic celebration of the coiffed hotshot endlessly triumphing over dirty losers and weaklings.

Trump isn't really a politician, of course. He's a strong-man act, a ridiculous parody of a Nietzschean superman. His followers get off on watching this guy with (allegedly) $10 billion and a busty mute broad on his arm defy every political and social convention and get away with it.

People are tired of rules and tired of having to pay lip service to decorum. They want to stop having to watch what they say and think and just get "crazy," as Thomas Fried-man would put it.

Trump's campaign is giving people permission to do

just that. It's hard to say this word in conjunction with such a sexually unappealing person, but his message is a powerful aphrodisiac. Fuck everything, fuck everyone. Fuck immigrants and fuck their filthy lice-ridden kids. And fuck you if you don't like me saying so.

Those of us who think polls and primaries and debates are any match for that are pretty naive. America has been trending stupid for a long time. Now the stupid wants out of its cage, and Trump is urging it on. There are a lot of ways this can go wrong, no matter who wins in 2016.

4

September 4, 2015: The Republicans Are Officially the Party of White Paranoia

The rise of Trump obliterates all other issues—
campaign 2016 is now almost entirely about race

ABC NEWS PUBLISHED AN INTRIGUING POLL THE OTHER day, one that spelled out a growing racial divide:

"Nonwhites see Trump negatively by a vast 17–79 percent. . . . That said, whites are the majority group—64 percent of the adult population—and they now divide evenly on Trump, 48–49 percent, favorable-unfavorable. Clinton, by contrast, is far more unpopular than Trump among whites, 34–65 percent. So while racial and ethnic polarization is on the rise in views of Trump, it remains even higher for Clinton."

The Republicans already lost virtually the entire black vote (scoring just 4 percent and 6 percent of black voters the last two elections). Now, by pushing toward the nomination a candidate whose brilliant plan to "make America great again" is to build a giant wall to keep out Mexican rapists, they're headed the same route with Hispanics. That's a steep fall for a party that won 44 percent of the Hispanic vote as recently as 2004.

Trump's supporters are people who are tired of being told they have to be part of some kind of coalition in order to have a political voice. They particularly hate being lectured about alienating minorities, especially by members of their own party.

Just a few weeks ago, for instance, establishment GOP spokesghoul George Will spent a whole column haranguing readers about how Trump was ruining his party's chances for victory. He noted that Mitt Romney might have won in 2012 if he'd pulled even slightly more than 27 percent of the Hispanic vote.

Will blasted Trump's giant wall idea and even ridiculed the candidate's deportation plan by comparing Trump to Hitler:

"The big costs, in decades and dollars (hundreds of billions), of Trump's project could be reduced if, say, the targets were required to sew yellow patches on their clothing to advertise their coming expulsion."

It's not clear how forcing 11 million people to wear yellow patches saves money, but whatever. However it was supposed to be taken, the shock argument didn't work.

A few days later, in a rare episode of *National Review*–on–*National Review* crime, blogger Ramesh Ponnuru blasted Will for his hysterics. He argued Romney wouldn't have won even with a 45 percent bump in the Hispanic vote. "He needed more votes, obviously," Ponnuru wrote, "but he didn't need more Hispanic votes in particular."

Ponnuru was echoing an idea already expressed by the conservative commentariat. Hack-among-hacks Byron York said the same thing in the *Washington Examiner* back in 2013. He argued that even 70 percent of the Hispanic vote wouldn't have helped Romney, whose more serious problem "was that Romney was not able to connect with white voters who were so turned off . . . that they abandoned the GOP."

Rush Limbaugh bought what York was selling, arguing that Romney didn't lose because he failed to convince Hispanic voters that Republicans "like 'em."

"The difference-maker was, a lot of white voters stayed home," Rush said.

Anyway, the night after Ponnuru ran his brief blog post a week and a half ago, Trump had Univision anchor Jorge Ramos tossed from a press conference in Dubuque, Iowa, sneering at him to "siddown" and "go back to Univision."

Conservative blogs and social media commentators cheered Trump's decision to have "butthurt" Jorge Ramos "deported" from the press conference, thereby turning the whole thing into another brilliant piece of symbolic political theater for the Donald.

Whether or not it's true that a Republican candidate can win the White House with a minus-51 percent net unfavorable rating among Hispanic voters (Trump's well-earned current number) is sort of beside the point. The point is that Trump clearly feels he can afford to flip off the Hispanic community and win with a whites-only strategy. And his supporters are loving the idea that he's trying.

The decision by huge masses of Republican voters to

defy D.C.-thinkfluencer types like George Will and throw in with a carnival act like Trump is no small thing. For the first time in a generation, Republican voters are taking their destiny into their own hands.

In the elaborate con that is American electoral politics, the Republican voter has long been the easiest mark in the game, the biggest dope in the room. Everyone inside the Beltway knows this. The Republican voters themselves are the only ones who never saw it.

Elections are about a lot of things, but at the highest level, they're about money. The people who sponsor election campaigns, who pay the hundreds of millions of dollars to fund the candidates' charter jets and TV ads and 25-piece marching bands, those people have concrete needs.

They want tax breaks, federal contracts, regulatory relief, cheap financing, free security for shipping lanes, antitrust waivers and dozens of other things.

They mostly don't care about abortion or gay marriage or school vouchers or any of the social issues the rest of us spend our time arguing about. It's about money for them, and as far as that goes, the CEO class has had a brilliantly winning electoral strategy for a generation.

They donate heavily to both parties, essentially hiring two different sets of politicians to market their needs to the population. The Republicans give them everything that they want, while the Democrats only give them mostly everything.

They get everything from the Republicans because you don't have to make a single concession to a Republican voter.

All you have to do to secure a Republican vote is show lots of pictures of gay people kissing or black kids with their pants pulled down or Mexican babies at an emergency room.

Then you push forward some dingbat like Michele Bachmann or Sarah Palin to reassure everyone that the Republican Party knows who the *real* Americans are. Call it the "Rove 1-2."

That's literally all it's taken to secure decades of Republican votes, a few patriotic words and a little over-the-pants rubbing. Policywise, a typical Republican voter never even asks a politician to go to second base.

While we always got free trade agreements and wars and bailouts and mass deregulation of industry and lots of other stuff the donors definitely wanted, we didn't get *Roe v. Wade* overturned or prayer in schools or balanced budgets or censorship of movies and video games or any of a dozen other things Republican *voters* said they wanted.

While it's certainly been fun laughing about the lunacies of people like Bachmann and John Ashcroft and Ted Cruz, who see the face of Jesus in every tree stump and believe the globalist left is planning to abolish golf courses and force country-dwellers to live in city apartments lit by energy-efficient light bulbs, the truth is that the voters they represented have been irrelevant for decades.

At least on the Democratic side there was that 5–10 percent of industry policy demands that voters occasionally rejected, putting a tiny dent in what otherwise has been a pretty smoothly running oligarchy.

Now that's over. Trump has pulled all of those previously irrelevant voters completely out of pocket. In a development that has to horrify the donors who run the GOP, the candidate Trump espouses some truly populist policy beliefs, including stern warnings about the dire consequences companies will face under a Trump presidency if they ship American jobs to Mexico and China.

All that energy the party devoted for decades telling middle American voters that protectionism was invented by Satan and Karl Marx during a poker game in Brussels in the mid-1840s, that just disappeared in a puff of smoke.

And all that money the Republican kingmakers funneled into Fox and Clear Channel over the years, making sure that their voters stayed focused on ACORN and immigrant-transmitted measles and the New Black Panthers (has anyone ever actually seen a New Black Panther? Ever?) instead of, say, the complete disappearance of the manufacturing sector or the mass theft of their retirement income, all of that's now backing up on them.

The party worked the cattle in their pen into such a dither that now they won't rest until they get the giant wall that real-life, as-seen-on-TV billionaire Donald Trump promises will save them from all those measles-infected rapists pouring over the border.

Not far under the surface of Trump's candidacy lurks a powerful current of Internet conspiracy theory that's a good two or three degrees loonier than even the most far-out Tea Party paranoia. Gone are the salad days when red-staters merely worried about Barack Obama inviting UN tanks to mass on the borders of Lubbock.

Trump supporters have gone next-level, obsessed with gooney-bird fantasies about "white genocide," a global plan to exterminate white people by sending waves of third-world immigrants across American and European borders to settle and intermarry.

The white-power nerds pushing this stuff don't like the term RINO (Republican In Name Only) and prefer "cuckservative," a term that's a mix of "cuckold" and "conservative." *Cuck* is also a porn term that refers to a white guy who gets off on watching his wife take it from (usually) a black man. A *cuck* is therefore a kind of desexualized race traitor.

So you can see why the Internet lights up when Donald Trump tosses Jorge Ramos from a presser and tells him "mine's bigger than yours" (Trump was referring to his heart, but again, whatever). All of Trump's constant bragging about his money and his poll numbers and his virility speaks directly to this surprisingly vibrant middle American fantasy about a castrated white America struggling to re-grow its mojo.

Republicans won middle American votes for years by taking advantage of the fact that their voters didn't know the difference between an elitist and the actual elite, between a snob and an oligarch. They made sure their voters' idea of an *elitist* was Sean Penn hanging out with Hugo Chavez, instead of a Wall Street bank financing the construction of Chinese factories.

Trump similarly is scoring points with voters who don't know the difference between feeling sorry for themselves and actually being victims. We live in a society that is changing for a lot of reasons, and some of those changes feel annoying to certain kinds of people, particularly older white folks who don't like language-policing and other aspects of political correctness.

But as basketball star turned pundit Kareem Abdul-Jabbar pointed out earlier this week, PC isn't a new thing, or even a thing at all. It's just an "emotional challenge every generation has had to go through." We get older, our kids correct our bad habits, it happens.

Not to Trump's supporters. They've turned some minor cultural changes into a vast conspiracy of white victimhood. They're eating up Trump's "Make America Great Again" theme (which one supporter hilariously explained must be his true goal, because "it's on his hat"), because it's a fantasy tale of a once-great culture ruined by an invasion of mongrel criminals.

For reasons that are, again, obvious to everyone but Republican voters, this "woe is us" narrative is never going to fly with the rest of the country, including especially (one imagines) the nonwhite population. Few sane people are going to waste a vote on a sob story about how rough things have gotten for white people. But Trump supporters are clinging to this fantasy far more fiercely than red-state voters were ever clinging to guns or religion.

That leaves us facing a future in which national elections will no longer be decided by ideas, but by numbers. It will be a turnout battle between people who believe in a multicultural vision for the country, and those who don't.

Every other issue, from taxes to surveillance to war to jobs to education, will take a distant back seat to this ongoing, moronic referendum on white victimhood. And there's nothing any of us can do about it except wait it out, and wonder if our politics only gets dumber from here.

5

September 8, 2015: Casting
Clown Car, the Movie

Jeff Garlin as Chris Christie, Kirk Cameron as Rick
Santorum, Justin Timberlake as Rand Paul—the
possibilities are thrilling

S TART WITH THE TITLE: *CLOWN CAR!* MAY SOUND LIKE
the movie someone will inevitably make about the 2016
presidential campaign, but how about evoking those great
Seventies wacky-journey films like *Death Race 2000*, *Vanishing Point* or *Smokey and the Bandit*?

When I raised the question on Twitter, suggestions included *All the President's Wanna-Bes*, *Every Which Way But Left*, *Cannonball Rug*, *A Kochwork Orange* and the subtly appropriate *Hair*.

All excellent ideas, and we may have to put the movie name to a separate vote. Right now, though, the more pressing question is this: If someone did make a movie about the

2016 presidential race, who would play the candidates? Wouldn't that be the most thrilling casting job ever?

There was a fiery debate on social media about all of the roles. In the end, though, this is something that has to go to a vote. What we need in this country, after all, is more democracy.

For the time being, we'll just ask people to vote in the comments section below, or tweet responses to me at @mtaibbi.

Without further ado:

Donald Trump
Donald Trump (as himself)
Gary Busey
Alec Baldwin
Will Ferrell
Gerard Depardieu
Gary Oldman
Val Kilmer
Gene Hackman

The biggest debate is going to be about who gets to play the leading man in the film. Trump probably ought to be the only "as himself" role in the cast. Figuratively speaking, it fits the narrative of the campaign to have him as the only Real Person, surrounded by a bunch of actors.

But there's also something to be said for the idea that Trump lacks the self-awareness to sell the humor of his role. Acting-wise the role clearly should belong to one of Hollywood's interpersonal train-wreck actors, someone you can imagine waking up in bed with a farm animal and a bottle of Southern Comfort.

The first name you think of there is probably Gary Busey, although someone like Gerard Depardieu also makes sense. Alec Baldwin fits from the abject-assholedom angle. And I'm sympathetic to the argument for Will Ferrell as Trump; you could take a Ferrell-as-Trump movie to many interesting places. But is he too PG for the part?

<u>Chris Christie</u>
Kevin James
John Goodman
Delaney Williams
Jeff Garlin
Steve Schirripa
Meat Loaf
Oliver Platt
Jon Favreau

The Christie role is probably a two-man race, between *Mall Cop* thespian Kevin James and Jeff Garlin of *Curb Your Enthusiasm* fame. But there was a lot of sentiment online for casting the affable Delaney Williams, last seen playing the porn-connoisseur homicide sergeant Jay Landsman in *The Wire*. Meat Loaf is an intriguing idea, especially if *Cannonball Rug* or whatever the film ends up being called has a musical component—we could have Christie singing his excuse for Bridgegate.

<u>Ted Cruz</u>
French Stewart
Bill Murray
Danny Trejo
Anjelica Huston

"Grandpa" Al Lewis
Maxwell Emmett "Pat" Buttram

French Stewart's qualifications here seem impeccable, right down to the distractingly squinty eyes. But Bill Murray would bring out the ham in Ted Cruz (think the "It just doesn't matter" speech, only delivered to Tea Partiers on the night before the UN invasion of Galveston).

But this could also be a breakout role for Danny Trejo, who'd bring grit and street cred to the part—French Stewart isn't leaping through a methane explosion onto a moving Harley to shoot Mitch McConnell with a 12-gauge. Anjelica Huston, meanwhile, is also an inspired idea for the role, among other things because it would infuriate Cruz. Curiously, a lot of readers nominated dead actors to play Cruz, including Al Lewis of *The Munsters* and Pat Buttram, last seen playing bug-eyed Mr. Haney on *Green Acres*.

CARLY FIORINA
Kristen Wiig
Peri Gilpin
Meg Ryan
David Bowie
Andy Dick
Christine Baranski

There was overwhelming support for Wiig as Fiorina online, although a few people felt she wasn't loathsome enough. I like the choices of David Bowie and the underrated Christine Baranski, who could simply reprise the role of her sneering party-crashing aristocrat Connie Chasseur from *The Ref*.

<u>Rick Santorum</u>
Kirk Cameron
Steve Carell
Judge Reinhold
Paul Reubens

There was some sentiment to have Santorum played by Michael Ontkean, the Canadian actor who resembles Santorum and is best known for his deft performance as Ned Braden in the Oscar-snubbed minor league hockey epic *Slap Shot*. But someone from a civilized place like Vancouver might not be able to grasp the darkness of Rick Santorum.

A Canadian might try to play Santorum's fundamentalist Christian persona as a passive, beatific dreamer, where what you really need here is a secret BDSM freak who gets aroused looking at *Know Your Bible* illustrations of the crucifixion. Kirk Cameron to me is the obvious choice, although the *Foxcatcher* version of Steve Carell is pretty close to being who Rick Santorum really is, right down to his inexplicable belief in his ability to win any contest that exists outside his own mind.

<u>Mike Huckabee</u>
Kevin Spacey
Jon Hamm
Stephen Root
Tom Hanks

Spacey, whose voice is very close to Huckabee's, is an obvious choice, particularly if Huckabee turns out to have a diabolical plan for winning this thing in the end (he gets up and walks into the presidential limo as we notice our coffee cups

were made by Kobayashi porcelain). With Hanks, you worry
he might take it seriously and screw up the whole movie.

BOBBY JINDAL
Aziz Ansari
Dev Patel
The corpse of Bob Denver
Jack McBrayer

The funniest suggestion I received for the role of Jindal
was the empty chair from Clint Eastwood's infamous convention speech. In my mind, if Bob Denver was alive, he'd
be a lock.

GEORGE PATAKI
Daniel von Bargen
James Caan
Victor Garber
Stephen Tobolowsky + wig

I realize von Bargen is dead, but the man who nailed the
role of lunkheaded Mr. Kruger on *Seinfeld* would have been
perfect for the role of Pataki ("My fellow Americans, our
budget this year just passed into the red . . . or the black . . .
whatever the bad one is"). Excellent instincts by @cptyesterday,
who ably picked out the wonderfully nondescript veteran Canadian character actor Victor Garber, but also wondered "if
he'd settle for such a small part."

SCOTT WALKER
Chris Parnell
Vincent Kartheiser

Steve Carell
John Cusack
Michael Sheen

Parnell was the overwhelming choice for this role on Twitter, although in Hollywood they always give the evil-douchebag role to a Brit, so that makes me think Michael Sheen.

JEB BUSH
Ed Begley Jr.
Jason Segel
Ed Helms
Beau Bridges
Jeffrey Tambor
Chevy Chase
Jane Lynch

Jeb is a tough one. Beau Bridges would bring that less-heralded-brother angst to the role, and he fits facially too. Begley Jr. is the right height, and would also do a great job cowering and peeing himself in Trump's presence. Tambor has the vast experience playing the sad-sack second banana. Both Lynch and another popular choice, Jamie Lee Curtis, are too manly for the role.

MARCO RUBIO
John Leguizamo
Danny Pino
Oscar Isaac
Fred Armisen
Santiago Cabrera

I'm torn here between Fred Armisen, who'd bring a goofy nuance to Rubio, and John Leguizamo, who could really sink his teeth into the psycho-moonbat angle. Pino and Cabrera are closer looks-wise. Isaac would be more appropriate if Rubio was a true contender.

RAND PAUL
Justin Timberlake
Neil Patrick Harris
Ryan Phillippe
The kid from Billy Madison
Vincent Cassel
Anthony Geary
Barry Williams
Hugh Laurie
Michael Cera

Justin Timberlake was born to play Rand Paul. I feel like he was training for it when he nailed the role of dry-humping substitute teacher Scott Delacorte in the underrated Cameron Diaz epic *Bad Teacher.* That said, Neil Patrick Harris is a strong contender, among other things because of his experience playing the cool-headed fascist psychic Carl Jenkins in *Starship Troopers.* Nobody is going to argue with the kid from *Billy Madison* as a choice, however, and strong arguments could be made for Barry "Greg Brady" Williams, Ryan Phillippe or even poor Vincent Cassel (I'd like to cast as many French people as possible in this movie, because it would annoy the citizens of both countries).

LINDSEY GRAHAM
Zach Galifianakis
Eddie Izzard
Carol Channing
Steve Buscemi
Ricky Gervais
Justin Bieber

Eddie Izzard could do a fabulously campy Graham—his impersonation of Church of Englanders singing, "Oh God, what on earth is my hairdo all about?" sounds uncannily like a Graham stump speech. Galifianakis could probably play Graham in his sleep, but the Judd Apatow factor in this movie is dangerously high as it is.

BEN CARSON
Don Cheadle
Robert Guillaume
Dennis Haysbert
Yasiin Bey (formerly known as Mos Def)
Tim Meadows
Cuba Gooding Jr.

Gooding Jr. has already played Carson, but I don't know . . . I'd almost rather have Gooding run for president and have Carson star in the movie. If we can't do that, I like Dennis Haysbert of *Heat*, *24*, and Allstate commercial fame. It's a different kind of role for Haysbert. He's got the wizened eyes and the deep voice, but he'd have to work at that just-struck-by-a-frying-pan look that voters in Iowa love so much. The former Mos Def is also a great choice because he's probably smoked just enough weed to make sense of Carson's candidacy.

JOHN KASICH
Glenn Close
Jon Bon Jovi
Chris Cooper
Kevin Costner
Christopher McDonald

Glenn Close, reprising the asset-hoovering Captain Monica Rawling character from *The Shield*, is a strong choice for Kasich, although the Twitter user who suggested the violently yellow-haired veteran character actor McDonald of *Happy Gilmore* and *Spy Kids 2* fame was definitely on to something. Costner, who dialed his screen presence almost all the way down to zero for another Ohio-themed role in the wretched *Draft Day*, might also be a low-energy fit at this stage of his career.

RICK PERRY
Josh Brolin
Tommy Lee Jones
Harry Hamlin
Gary Cole
Tyler Perry

Harry Hamlin is an interesting choice because as @ruckcohlchez pointed out, Perry probably got the idea for the smart glasses by *watching* Hamlin wear glasses on *Mad Men*. Cole could do it—Gary Cole could probably play anyone from Patty Hearst to Patrice Lumumba—and casting Tyler Perry to play Rick Perry would be a nice running homage to Dennis Miller in a Republican-themed movie. But in the end, it has to be Josh Brolin as

Perry, doesn't it? Between the resemblance and Brolin's demonstrated skill at playing dazed, mentally absent politicians, his feels like a drop-the-mic audition.

JIM GILMORE
John C. Reilly
Ed Hermann
Martin Clunes
Elias Koteas

As @writer614 pointed out, it doesn't matter who plays Gilmore, because "he doesn't have any lines anyway." Moreover you could cast anyone in the role—Peter Dinklage, Pete Postlethwaite, Forest Whitaker, Rooney Mara, anyone—because nobody knows what Gilmore looks like. If we must make a serious choice, I like the perpetually confounded Clunes of *Doc Martin* fame, although as an American and a veteran of many toxic-dumb-person roles, Reilly would have more of an instinct here.

MITT ROMNEY (WHEN HE ENTERS THE RACE)
Bruce Campbell
Michael Shannon
Fred Willard
Fred Ward

It will be an injustice if the great Bruce Campbell doesn't get to play Mitt Romney at some point in his life.

HILLARY CLINTON
Robert Redford
Rebecca De Mornay

Helen Mirren
Meryl Streep
Amy Poehler
Emma Thompson

I think Robert Redford would make a great Hillary—just imagine it for a minute—but there are a lot of people who wouldn't see the humor there. The studio heads will want Mirren or Streep if they can't convince Emma Thompson to do it again (did she have a sequel deal for *Primary Colors?*). Rebecca De Mornay would be interesting if she souped up her Mrs. Mott/evil nanny role from *The Hand That Rocks the Cradle.*

BERNIE SANDERS
Bruce Dern
Christopher Lloyd
Larry David
James Adomian
Austin Pendleton

Sanders is going to be an interesting and controversial casting decision. Adomian has of course already played Bernie, but it's hard not to imagine Larry David or especially Christopher Lloyd in the role. Veteran character actor Austin Pendleton did a great impersonation of a lefty politician in *Searching for Bobby Fischer,* although the actual role was an aging chessmaster obsessed with taking a pawn in a penny-ante tournament that matters only to other chess players.

Two final notes. One, I left out a few of the ancillary Dems, like O'Malley and Chafee, because, well, who cares?

Secondly, I have a strong belief that Chow Yun-Fat should be in every movie. Since he doesn't really fit as any of the candidates, I'm open to write-in suggestions for his part in the film. Could he be Frank Luntz? Anderson Cooper? Huma Abedin? Nate Silver? All ideas are welcome.

6

September 16, 2015: The Official GOP Debate Drinking Game Rules, Part 2

Get your liver ready: the second
GOP debate is upon us

So the second GOP debate is upon us, scheduled for 8 p.m. EST on CNN tonight. The moderators are Hugh Hewitt, Jake Tapper and Dana Bash. You'll be reading a lot more about those names within 24 hours.

The first debate was an epic piece of comic theater. It featured at least a half dozen laugh-out-loud moments, including: the now-infamous Megyn Kelly–Donald Trump imbroglio, Mike Huckabee accusing Planned Parenthood of selling baby parts like "parts of a Buick," Ben Carson bragging that he was the only candidate to remove half a brain, Chris Christie and Rand Paul trading hilariously cringe-worthy "hug" jokes, Trump bragging that he bought

Hillary Clinton with campaign contributions and many other choice exchanges.

It was salacious, pathetic, vapid, undignified, degrading, uninformative and compelling, making it a model for how Americans will consume politics going forward in the reality TV era.

This debate promises to be just as explosive. In fact, this affair is, quite frankly, a setup. All three moderators have tangled with Donald Trump before. The event seems like *Jerry Springer*–style tactics by CNN: putting people disposed to throw chairs at each other onstage, turning the cameras on and waiting for all hell to break loose.

Hewitt in particular is virtually guaranteed to get into a scrap with Trump. A former Nixon ghostwriter, Hewitt is one of the most vile people in America, a charmless, self-congratulating pedant whose fiendishly boring right-wing radio show might be called *Not as Smart as I Think I Am*.

Hewitt interviewed Trump earlier this month and fired a string of *gotcha*-style foreign policy questions at the Donald, daring him to name the leaders of Hezbollah, al-Qaeda and ISIS. Trump deflected as only he knows how, saying that he didn't know but that it didn't matter because by the time he made it to office, "they'll all be gone." Similar to the Kelly episode, he grew angry about the exchange overnight, and the next day told Joe Scarborough that Hewitt is a "third rate radio announcer."

Bash, meanwhile, did the interview with Trump where he blasted attorney Elizabeth Beck for being "disgusting" while breastfeeding. And Tapper went after Trump in his own interview for promoting "traditional" marriage when Trump himself has been married three times.

My guess is that the debate will play right into Trump's

hands. Hewitt, who was a Harvard housemate of Grover Norquist and was tutored by Alan Keyes, will act as a stand-in for the Republican Party bigwigs: he'll try to bloody Trump by exposing his lack of concrete knowledge, in the area of foreign affairs particularly. Expect questions along the lines of "Who is Hassan Nasrallah's favorite soccer player?" or "Name two countries in South America."

This will make for excellent theater, but what Trump's audiences will see is their candidate being pestered by one GOP puppet and two reporters from CNN, which in 'Murica is widely understood to be a wing of the Democratic Party.

Anyway, there will be 11 candidates at the grownup table tonight. It's newcomer Carly Fiorina along with the ten from the last debate: Donald Trump, Ben Carson, Jeb Bush, Ted Cruz, Marco Rubio, Scott Walker, Mike Huckabee, John Kasich, Chris Christie and Rand Paul.

In the *Friday the 13th* movie that is this campaign, Rick Perry is the first to be found with an axe in his head. He dropped out this week, blaming his inability to get into the first debate and the unfortunate fact of his being under indictment (for coercing a public servant)* as reasons for his failed campaign. One of Perry's megadonors is already asking for his $5 million back, to which Perry's camp says it's reviewing its options; fun stuff. All in all, a great showing by the former Texas governor, who will almost certainly run again in 2020, perhaps with a Japanese soldier who hasn't heard WWII is over as a running mate.

Not listed here is former Virginia Gov. Jim Gilmore, who will be watching the debate from the mythical religious territory of purgatory. Gilmore of course didn't make it to the grownup event, but CNN says you need 1 percent

* The indictment was later dismissed.

in the polls to make even the kiddie-table debate, making Gilmore a second-rater among second-raters: as Beavis and Butthead would say, the "ass of the ass."

Here are the official rules for the second GOP debate drinking game. After a lengthy discussion on Twitter, we're adding an almost entirely new lineup here, with a few hold-overs. The event is taking place in California at the Ronald Reagan library, which means we can't have people drinking every time a candidate tries to fellate the Gipper's memory: we'd have Guyana-level mass deaths. We thought about making people drink at the sight of Ted Cruz's first Reagan-inspired boner, but the podium will make that rule tough to enforce.

Please take small shots! And when watching politics, please make sure to have a designated driver.*

I'll be tweeting throughout the event. The rules:

Drink THE FIRST TIME and the FIRST TIME only:

1. A candidate invokes the memory of Saint Reagan.
2. A candidate mentions Hillary's emails.

Drink EVERY TIME:

3. Hugh Hewitt hurls a douchey *gotcha* question at Trump.
4. Trump—or any of the other candidates—insults or threatens one of the moderators. Beer chaser if it's Tapper or Bash, and the candidate rips liberal-ass CNN in the process.

---

* I ended up passed out at the 9th Street PATH train station, where a kindly old Chinese woman woke me long after midnight and told me I should take better care of myself.

5. Trump brags about his wealth or his poll numbers, or mocks the low poll numbers of an opponent.

6. A candidate pledges to stand with Israel.

7. Carly Fiorina makes a joke about her own face.

8. A candidate claims a positive relationship with a minority. We're keeping this rule in every debate. (So far we're one-for-one: Kasich said he had a gay friend in the first debate.)

9. Anyone mentions Kim Davis or the "War on Christians."

10. A candidate says he'll stand up to Putin.

11. Trump derides someone for being a "lightweight" or having "low energy" or "low enthusiasm."

12. Anyone mentions Tom Brady or Deflategate.

13. Anyone calls Black Lives Matter a "hate group," argues that BLM or Barack Obama has endangered the lives of police, or pulls a "What about black-on-black crime?" line.

14. A candidate mentions the founders. Double shot if it's Rand Paul.

15. Carson invokes the Bible as an authority for something that has nothing to do with the Bible, like tax policy.

16. A candidate says, "I'm the only person on this stage who . . ." Double shot if it's Carson saying something like, "I'm the only candidate who's had his hands inside a human thorax."

17. Anyone mentions Hitler, Nazis or Neville Chamberlain. Includes related imagery, e.g. "ovens."

18. A candidate stumbles over what to call ISIS/ISIL, or mispronounces the name of a world leader.

19. Anyone mentions the Governator or makes a

Terminator-themed joke, e.g. "To illegal immigrants, I say, *Hasta La Vista*."

Drink EVERY TIME you hear:

20. "Anchor babies."
21. "Thug."
22. "Leading from behind."
23. "All lives matter."
24. "Apologize for America."
25. "*Eye*-ran."

Take a shot of JAGERMEISTER if:

26. Anyone compares Kim Davis to Rosa Parks.
27. Any candidate is seen wearing a Blue Lives Matter bracelet.
28. A candidate offers an insincere paean to departed Rick Perry. Double shot if someone references his "smart glasses."

7

November 3, 2015: The Case for Bernie Sanders

His critics say he's not realistic—but they have it backward

THE *NEW YORK TIMES* PUBLISHED A PIECE OVER THE WEEK-end about the political prospects of Bernie Sanders, a politician who apparently does not kiss enough babies:

"[Sanders] rarely drops by diners or coffee shops with news cameras in tow, unlike most politicians. He hardly ever kisses babies, aides say, and does not mingle much at fund-raisers.

"His high-minded style carries risk. As effective as his policy-laden speeches may be in impressing potential supporters, Mr. Sanders is missing opportunities to lock down uncommitted voters face to face in Iowa and New Hampshire, where campaigns are highly personal."

The media response to the Sanders campaign has been alternately predictable, condescending, confused and condescending again.

The tone of most of the coverage shows reporters deigning to treat his campaign like it's real, like he has a chance. John Cassidy of the *New Yorker*, for instance, swore he wouldn't be patronizing about the Sanders run. "Indeed, I welcomed Sanders to the race!" Cassidy wrote recently.

But Cassidy's hokey "Welcome to the 2016 Race, Bernie Sanders!" piece from last spring had a small catch. It basically said that Sanders was welcome because he would be a boon to the real candidate, Hillary Clinton.

"[Sanders] can't win the primary," Cassidy wrote. "And he will occupy the space to the left of Clinton, thus denying it to more plausible candidates, such as Martin O'Malley." (!)

Noting that Sanders held positions that were "eminently defensible, if unrealistic," Cassidy nonetheless said he was glad Sanders was running, because he would "provide a voice to those Democrats who agree with him that the U.S. political system has been bought, lock, stock, and barrel."

This passage he wrote just after arguing that Sanders cannot win and was only useful insofar as he would help the bought-off candidate win.

So what Cassidy really meant is that the Sanders campaign was allowing people who are justifiably pissed about our corrupted system to blow off steam, before they ultimately surrender to give their support to the system candidate.

And he welcomed that! But he wasn't being condescending or anything.

Cassidy referred back to that old piece recently, after he became among the first of many pundits pronouncing Hillary the knockout winner of a debate that most actual human beings seemed to think Sanders handled quite well. Cassidy went so far as to ask, "Did the media get the Democratic debate wrong?"

He thought and thought on this, then decided he/it didn't.

"Based on Clinton's manner," he wrote, "and her deftness in *evading awkward questions*, I think she delivered the best performance."

Campaign-trail reporting is like high school: a brutish, interminable exercise in policing mindless social rules. In school, if someone is fat or has zits or wears the wrong clothes, the cool kids rag on that person until they run home crying or worse.

The Heathers of the campaign trail do the same thing. Sanders is just the latest in a long line of candidates— Howard Dean, Dennis Kucinich and Ron Paul, to name a few—whom my media colleagues decided in advance were not electable, and covered accordingly, with a sneer.

When we reporters are introduced to a politician, the first thing we ask ourselves is if he or she is acceptable to the political establishment. We don't admit that we ask this as a prerequisite, but we do.

Anyone who's survived without felony conviction a few terms as a senator, governor or congressperson, has an expensive enough haircut, and has never once said anything interesting will likely be judged a potentially "serious" candidate.

If you're wondering why no Mozarts or Einsteins ever end up running for president in America, but an endless succession of blockheads like Rick Perry are sold to us on the cover of *Time* magazine as contenders, it's because of this absurd prerequisite.

Ultimately, what we're looking for is someone who's enough of a morally flexible gasbag to get over with the money people, and then also charming enough on some politically irrelevant level to attract voters. ("I'm a war hero, and Sharon Stone's cousin" was Chris Rock's take on acceptable presidential self-salesmanship.)

Bernie Sanders bluntly fails the Rick Perry test. In fact he pretty much defines what it means to fail that test. It isn't just that he doesn't kiss babies or comb his hair or "deftly evade answers." He's also unapologetically described himself as a socialist, which makes him a giant bespectacled block of Kryptonite for Beltway donors and mainstream journalists alike.

If questioned, most reporters would justify this by noting that an effective president must be able to bridge the gap between powerful interests and populist concerns. So it makes some sense to interrogate candidates accordingly, to make sure they're acceptable to both sides.

The flaw in this reasoning is that it assumes that Wall Street and Silicon Valley and Big Pharma and the rest need the help of us reporters to weed out the undesirables.

They don't, of course. Big money already has a stranglehold on the process of government. It outright owns most of the members of Congress, and its lobbyists write much of our important legislation. With *Citizens United*, buying elections is now more or less legal. Big money even owns most of the media companies that employ those pundits who are all telling us now to worry about how "realistic" Sanders isn't.

Everybody knows this. In fact, this numbing reality of how completely corrupted the modern American political process is bends the brains of those whose job it is to cover it. What happens over time is that you lose hope, and you begin to view everything through the prism of the corruption to which you're so accustomed.

When you stop believing in the electoral process, then the only questions left to interest a professional observer are who wins, and how many laughs there will be along the way. We've gotten good at thinking about these things. Cassidy's bit about Sanders harmlessly occupying the left flank and blocking more "plausible" candidates from threatening Hillary is exactly the kind of sounds-smart observation we've been trained to believe passes for political journalism today.

Conversely, we've been trained not to care about which old ladies are freezing to death this week because some utility somewhere is turning the heat off, or who's having their furniture put on the street by a sheriff executing a foreclosure order, or who's losing a leg to diabetes because they didn't have the money for a simple checkup two years ago, etc.

None of those characters make it into campaign reporting. As good as we are at the horse-race idiocy, we suck that much at writing about these other things.

Watching Bernie slog forward to an audience of political gatekeepers who wish he would stop being a bummer and just kiss more babies shames me into a confession. I find myself giving up on this process all the time.

Donald Trump, a man whose idea of policy is a big wall, was the Republican front-runner for months, and ceded the lead to a man who wants to fight immigrants with drones. This whole thing is a joke. At times, the only thing you can take seriously about any of this is the gambler's question of who wins.

I got into the act a few weeks back, gushing about how Trey Gowdy's Benghazi hearing solved Hillary Clinton's voter-sympathy problem. Quite a development in the soap opera! But a million miles from anything that matters.

Successful politicians today on both sides of the aisle are sprawling celebrity franchises. They seem always to be making piles of money and hobnobbing with Beautiful People when they're finished moving the status quo in some incremental direction, which some hack somewhere will always be willing to call change.

Whether it's the Clintons with their foundations or Al Gore with his movies and his carbon-trading interests or the Bush/Cheney axis of hereditary politics and energy commerce, we expect the politicians who make it to the big time to cash in somewhere along the line because, hey, this is America. Donald Trump, if elected, would find a way to turn *being* the president into a moneymaking operation.

Sanders is a clear outlier in a generation that has forgotten what it means to be a public servant. The *Times* remarks upon his "grumpy demeanor." But Bernie is grumpy because he's thinking about vets who need surgeries, guest workers who've had their wages ripped off, kids without access to dentists or some other godforsaken problem that most of us normal people can care about for maybe a few minutes on a good day, but Bernie worries about more or less all the time.

I first met Bernie Sanders ten years ago, and I don't believe there's anything else he really thinks about. There's no other endgame for him. He's not looking for a book deal or a membership in a Martha's Vineyard golf club or a cameo in a Guy Ritchie movie. This election isn't a game to him; it's not the awesomely repulsive dark joke it is to me and many others.

And the only reason this attention-averse, sometimes socially uncomfortable person is subjecting himself to this asinine process is because he genuinely believes the system is not beyond repair.

Not all of us can say that. But that doesn't make us right, and him "unrealistic." More than any other politician in recent memory, Bernie Sanders is focused on reality. It's the rest of us who are lost.

8

November 17, 2015:
The Clown Car Rolls On

On the campaign trail with the most dishonest,
bumbling and underqualified pack of
presidential candidates in history

N OT ONE OF THEM CAN WIN, BUT ONE MUST. THAT'S THE
paradox of the race for the 2016 Republican presidential nomination, fast becoming the signature event in the
history of black comedy.

Conventional wisdom says that with the primaries and
caucuses rapidly approaching, front-running nuts Donald
Trump and Dr. Ben Carson must soon give way to the "real"
candidates. But behind Trump and Carson is just more
abyss. As I found out on a recent trip to New Hampshire,
the rest of the field is either just as crazy or as dangerous as
the current poll leaders, or too bumbling to win.

Disaster could be averted if Americans on both the left

and the right suddenly decide to be more mature about this, neither backing obvious mental incompetents, nor snickering about those who do. But that doesn't seem probable.

Instead, hashtagClownCar will almost certainly continue to be the most darkly ridiculous political story since Henry II of Champagne, the 12th-century king of Jerusalem, plunged to his death after falling out of a window with a dwarf.

Just after noon, Wednesday, November 4th. I'm in Hollis, New Hampshire, a little town not far from the Massachusetts border.

The Hollis pharmacy is owned by Vahrij Manoukian, a Lebanese immigrant who is the former chairman of the Hillsborough County Republican Committee. If you come into his establishment looking for aspirin, you have to first survive dozens of pictures of the cannonball-shape businessman glad-handing past and present GOP hopefuls like Newt Gingrich, Rick Santorum and Rudy Giuliani.

Primary season is about who most successfully kisses the asses of such local burghers, and the big test in Hollis today is going to be taken by onetime presumptive frontrunner Jeb Bush.

Despite its ideological decorative scheme, the Manoukian pharmacy has some charming small-town quirks you wouldn't find in a CVS. There's a section of beautiful handmade wooden toys, for instance. There's also a pair of talkative parrots named Buddy and Willy perched near the cash registers.

While waiting for the candidate to arrive, I try to make conversation.

"Who are you voting for this year?"

"Hello," says Willy.

"Is Jeb Bush going to win?"

"*Rooowk!*" the bird screeches, recoiling a little.

It seems like a "no." Bush comes in a moment later and immediately hears the birds squawking. A tall man, he smiles and cranes his head over the crowd in their direction.

"Whose dog is that?" he cracks.

Technically, that is the correct comic response, but the room barely hears him. For Bush, Campaign 2016 has been a very tough crowd.

It's hard to recall now, but a year ago, it appeared likely that Bush would be the Republican nominee. He had a lead in polls, and some Beltway geniuses believed Republican voters would favor "more moderate choices" in 2016, pushing names like Mitt Romney, Chris Christie and this reportedly "smarter" Bush brother to the top of the list.

Moreover, the Bush campaign was supposed to be a milestone in the history of post–*Citizens United* aristocratic scale-tipping. The infamous 2010 Supreme Court case that deregulated political fundraising birthed a monster called the Super PAC, also known as the "independent-expenditure-only committee." This new form of slush fund could receive unlimited sums from corporations, billionaires and whomever else, provided it didn't coordinate with an active presidential campaign.

Decrying the "no-suspense primary" and insisting, "It's nobody's turn," Bush announced his candidacy on June 15th. But he and his Super PAC, Right to Rise, had been raising money all year long.

Fifteen days after his announcement, on July 1st, the books closed on the first six months of Right to Rise's backroom cash-hoovering. Bush was already sitting atop an astonishing $103 million. That was about 10 times the amount of the next-biggest GOP Super PAC, Christie's America Leads fund.

A hundred million bucks, a name that is American royalty, and the apparent backing of the smoke-filled room. What could go wrong?

Only everything! Before his official announcement even, Bush iceberged his candidacy when he crisscrossed the country in mid-May tying his face in knots in a desperate attempt to lay out a cogent position on his brother's invasion of Iraq.

During a remarkable five days of grasping and incoherent answers, in which Bush was both for and against the invasion multiple times, it became clear that this candidate: (a) doesn't understand the meaning of the phrase "knowing what we know now," and (b) doesn't know how to cut his losses and shut up when things go bad. People began to wonder out loud if he really was the smarter brother.

The real disaster was the second debate, when he decided to go after the other "plausible" establishment candidate, Florida Sen. Marco Rubio, and ended up getting beaten to gristle onstage. He was reduced after that episode to admitting, "I'm not a performer." He headed into his New Hampshire trip with reporters pronouncing his campaign "on life support."

The operating theory of the Bush campaign is that there's still a massive pot of donor cash, endorsements and support the Republican Party elders must throw to someone. But can Bush remake his candidacy in time to reestablish himself as a plausible vessel for all of that largesse?

In Hollis, there is little evidence of a remade Bush candidacy. His stump presentation is surprisingly half-assed. He tries to get over with lines like "We've had a divider-in-chief—we need a commander-in-chief," which are so plainly canned that they barely register, even with a crowd jacked up for any put-down of Obama.

Worse, he issues one of the odder descriptions of the American dream you'll ever hear from a Republican.

"We need to create a society," he says, "where we create a safety net for people, and then we say, 'Go dream the biggest possible dreams.'"

I look around. Did a Republican candidate just try to sell a crowd full of New Hampshire conservatives on a government safety net?

He has one near-excellent moment, when answering a question about Syria and Russia. "I don't want to sound bellicose," he says. (Why not? This is the Republican race.) "But my personal opinion is, we're the United States of f— of America. They should be more worried about us than we are about them."

Bush could have become an instant YouTube sensation if he'd completed his thought and said, "We're the United States of Fucking America," but he couldn't do it. That's just not who he is.

Who is he? Minus the family imperative, Bush is easily imagined as a laid-back commercial lawyer in some Florida exurb, the kind of guy who can crack dirty jokes while he runs a meeting about a new mixed-use development outside Tallahassee.

He doesn't seem at all like a power-crazed, delusionally self-worshipping lunatic, and that's basically his problem. He doesn't want this badly enough to be the kind of effortless sociopathic liar you need to be to make it through this part of the process.

Toward the end of his speech, for instance, the pharmacist Manoukian puts the Jebster on the spot. The local apothecary has a proposal he's been trying to make state law that would give drug dealers special status.

"They would be like child molesters, always being registered," he says. He wheezes excitedly as he details his plan to strip dealers of all social services. I don't think the plan involves using hot irons to brand them with neck tattoos, but that's the spirit.

The reporters all flash bored looks at one another. People like Manoukian are recurring figures on the campaign trail, particularly on the Republican side. There's always some local Junior Anti-Sex League chief who asks the candidate in a town hall to endorse a plan for summary executions of atheists or foreigners or whoever happens to be on the outs that election cycle.

Bush absorbs the pharmacist's question and immediately launches into a speech about the dangers of addiction—to prescription drugs! Through the din of screeching parrots, Bush talks, movingly, I think, about his "precious daughter" Noelle's problems with prescription pills.

"There are some bad actors," he says. "You have people who overprescribe, people who are pharmacy shopping, doctor shopping . . ."

Everything he just said is true, but Manoukian, as he listens to this diatribe, looks like someone has hit him with a halibut. Does Bush know he's talking to a pharmacist?

Trump would have killed a moment like this, delivering some dog-whistle-ready line about gathering up all the dealers by their hoodies and shooting them into space with all of the child molesters. Who cares if it makes sense? This is the Clown Car.

But Bush has no feel for audience. He doesn't know how

to play down to a mob. Nor does he realize how absurd he sounds when a Lucky Spermer scion like himself tries to talk about his "small-business" experience (his past three "jobs" were all lucrative gigs with giant companies that had done business with Florida when he was governor). Despite all this, Bush doesn't seem crazy, nor even like a particularly disgusting person by presidential-campaign standards, which probably disqualifies him from this race.

Lynn Cowan, a Hollis resident, agrees. She thinks Bush comes across as a reasonable guy, but she also thinks his reasonableness is probably crippling in the current political environment.

"It's to his detriment," she says. "And it's sad that we've reached a point where these politicians can't even be on the level."

A few hours later, Nashua, New Hampshire. Rubio strides onstage to a roaring young crowd at the Dion Center of Rivier University. He is like a cross of Joel Osteen and Bobby Kennedy, jacketless with a red tie and shirtsleeves. He is short but prickishly good-looking, all hair and teeth and self-confidence. He's the kind of guy that no group of men wants to go to a bar with, both because he spoils the odds and because he seems like kind of an asshole generally.

There are young women in the crowd looking up at him adoringly, like a Beatle. It's a sight one doesn't often see in presidential politics, but even more seldom on the Republican side, where most candidates are either 500 years old or belong to religions barring nonprocreative use of the wiener. Rubio plainly enjoys being an exception to the rule.

His speech is a total nothingburger, full of worn clichés about America being an "exceptional country," where people are nonetheless living "paycheck to paycheck" and wondering if "achieving [the American dream] is still possible."

But he's so slick, he could probably sell a handful of cars at every speech. His main pitch is his Inspirational Personal Tale™. As he's told it, he's the son of refugees from Fidel Castro's Cuba (actually, they left Cuba before Castro, but whatever) who rose from nothing to reach the U.S. Senate, where he was eventually able to draw a $170,000 paycheck despite a brilliant *Office Space*–style decision to not quit, exactly, but simply not go to work anymore. Which is pretty sweet.

Actually, that last bit isn't openly part of his stump speech. But if you listen hard enough, you can hear it. Rubio has announced that he isn't going to run for re-election to the Senate, where he recently cast his first vote in 26 days and spoke for the first time in 41. He said he didn't hate the work but was "frustrated" ("He hates it," a friend more bluntly told the *Washington Post*).

In addition to the stories about laying down in the Senate, old tales about Rubio's use of an American Express card given to him by the Republican Party when he was in the Florida House began swirling again. The stories are complex, but the upshot is that Rubio once used party credit cards upfront to spend $10,000 on a family vacation, $3,800 on home flooring, $1,700 on a Vegas vacation and thousands more on countless other absurdities.

Couple those tales with the troubling stories about his financial problems—the *Times* learned that he cashed in a retirement account and blew $80,000 on a speedboat he probably couldn't afford—and the subtext with Rubio is that he is probably both remaining in the Senate and running for president, at least partly, for the money.

A debt addict with a burgeoning Imelda Marcos shopping complex was pretty much the only thing missing from the top of this GOP field. Yet he looks like the party's next attempt at an Inevitable Candidate.

It's easy to see why. Rubio storms through his stump speech in Nashua, blasting our outdated infrastructure with perfect timing and waves of soaring rhetoric. We have outdated policies in this country, he says. "We have a retirement system designed in the 1930s. We have an immigration and higher-education system designed in the 1950s. Anti-poverty programs designed in the 1960s. Energy policies designed from the 1970s. Tax policies from the Eighties and Nineties . . ."

The punchline is something about needing to burn it all to the ground and remake everything into a new conservative Eden for the 21st century. "An economic renaissance, unlike anything that's ever happened," he gushes.

I raise an eyebrow. Any vet of this process will feel, upon seeing Rubio in person, a disturbance in the campaign-trail force. He checks all the boxes of what the Beltway kingmakers look for in a political marketing phenomenon: young, ethnic, good-looking, capable of working a room like a pro and able to lean hard on an inspirational bio while eschewing policy specifics.

A bitter Bush recently pegged Rubio as a Republican version of Obama, a comparison neither Rubio nor many Democrats will like, but it has a lot of truth to it. The main difference, apart from the policy inverses, is in tone. 2008 Obama sold tolerance and genial intellectualism, perfect for roping in armchair liberals. Rubio sells a kind of strident, bright-eyed dickishness that in any other year would seem tailor-made for roping in conservatives.

But this isn't any year. It isn't just our energy, education and anti-poverty systems that are outdated. So is our tradition of campaign journalism, which, going back to the days of Nixon, trains reporters to imagine that the winner is probably the slickest Washington-crafted liar, not some loon with a reality show.

But in 2016, who voters like and who the punditocracy thinks they'll swallow are continuing to be two very different things. In the Clown Car era, if reporters think you're hot stuff, that's probably a red flag.

Concord, New Hampshire, the Secretary of State's office, morning of November 6th. I'm waiting to see Ohio Gov. John Kasich officially register as a candidate for the New Hampshire primary.

In another election, Kasich might be a serious contender, being as he is from Ohio, a former Lehman Brothers stooge and a haranguing bore with the face of a dogcatcher. He exactly fits the profile of what party insiders used to call an "exciting" candidate.

At the moment, though, he's a grumpy sideshow to Trump and Carson whose main accomplishment is that he hogged the most time in the fourth debate (and also became the first non-Trump candidate to be booed). Kasich in person seems like a man ready to physically implode from bitterness at the thought that his carefully laid scheme for power might be undone by a flatulent novelty act like Trump.

Surrounded by reporters in the Concord state offices, Kasich seethes again about the tenor of the race. "I think there are some really goofy ideas out there," he says.

I've driven to Concord specifically for this moment. I want to ask Kasich if maybe this is the wrong time in American history for someone pushing cold realism as a platform.

It's a softball—I think he might enjoy expounding upon the issue of America's newfound fascination with "goofy" politicians.

"The people with the goofiest ideas are at the top of the polls," I say. "Do you think maybe being the sane candidate in this race is disqualifying?"

Kasich doesn't smile. Instead, he shoots me a look like I've just dented his Mercedes.

"No," he hisses.

The candidacy of Carly Fiorina, with its wild highs and lows, has exposed the bizarre nature of this primary season. She was in Nowheresville until midsummer, when she attracted the notice of Trump. At the time, reveling atop the polls in full pig glory, Trump told *Rolling Stone* that America wouldn't be able to take looking at Fiorina's face for a whole presidency. In the second debate, Fiorina responded, "I think women all over this country heard very clearly what Mr. Trump said."

Fiorina in the same debate implored Hillary Clinton and Obama to watch Planned Parenthood at work. "Watch these tapes," she said, staring hypnotically into the screen like a Kreskin or a Kashpirovsky. "Watch a fully formed fetus on the table, its heart beating, its legs kicking while someone says, 'We have to keep it alive to harvest its brain.' "

It was a brilliantly macabre performance, and, according to some, it won her the debate. Even by this race's standards, a tale of evil liberal women's-health workers ripping out the brains of live babies rated a few very good days of what they call "earned media," i.e., press you don't have to pay for.

Of course, Fiorina's claim that she had actually seen a video of someone trying to harvest the brain of a fetus with its legs kicking turned out to be false. Her story matched up vaguely with one video that included a description of a fetus having its brain removed, but no such footage existed, as fact-checkers immediately determined.

Called on her fib by Fox's Chris Wallace, Fiorina doubled down.

"I've seen the footage," she insisted. "And I find it amazing, actually, that all these supposed fact-checkers in the mainstream media claim this doesn't exist."

The week after that appearance with Wallace on *Fox News Sunday* was her best week in the polls, as she reached as high as 11 percent in some, tying for third with Rubio. She'd clued in to the same insight that drove the early success of Trump: that in the reality-show format of the 2016 race, all press attention is positive, and nobody particularly cares if you lie, so long as you're entertaining.

America dug Fiorina when she was a John Carpenter movie about bloodthirsty feminists harvesting baby brains. But when she talked about anything else, they were bored stiff.

On a Thursday night in Newport, New Hampshire, Fiorina is laboring through her monotone life story of corporate promotions and "solving problems." It's like watching a thermometer move. "Wouldn't it be helpful," she asks, "to reduce the 73,000-page tax code to three pages?"

I chuckle. Even by Clown Car standards, a three-page federal tax code is a hilarious ploy, right up there with Carson's 10-percent biblical tithe and a giant wall across the Central American isthmus. On the way out of the event, a few reporters are joking about it. "Three pages is good," one deadpans. "But I'd like to see her fit it on the label of a really nice local IPA."

Polls have suggested that Fiorina, Carson and Trump were all fighting over the same finite slice of Lunatic Pie (the Beltway press euphemistically calls it the "outsider vote"), a demographic that by late September comprised just north of half of expected Republican voters. That means that for Fiorina to rise, Trump or Carson must fall.

The problem is that after a late-summer swoon, Trump's support has stabilized. And Carson has taken campaign lunacy to places that a three-page tax code couldn't dent. Forget about winning a primary: Carson won the Internet.

Traditionally, we in the political media have always been able to finish off candidates once they start bleeding. The pol caught sending dick pics to strangers, lying about nannies, snuggling models on powerboats, concealing secret treatments for "exhaustion," or doing anything else unforgivably weird is harangued until he or she disintegrates. The bullying is considered a sacred tribal rite among the Beltway press, and it's never not worked.

Until this year. Trump should have been finished off half a dozen times—after the John-McCain-was-a-wuss-for-getting-captured line, after the "blood coming out of her wherever" bit, after the "Mexicans are rapists" episode, etc.

But we don't finish them off anymore. We just keep the cameras rolling. The ratings stay high, and the voters don't abandon their candidates—they just tune in to hate us media smartasses more.

Enter Ben Carson. Reporters early on in the summer thought he was a Jerzy Kosiński character, a nutty doctor who had maybe gotten lost on the way to a surgical convention and accidentally entered a presidential race. In the first debate, he looked like an amnesiac who might at any moment reach into his pocket, find a talisman reminding him of his true identity, and walk offstage.

Then he started saying stuff. First there was that thing about using drones on immigrants crossing the border. Then people began picking apart old stories he'd told, like that a Yale professor in a psych class called "Perceptions 301" had once given him $10 for being honest (nobody remembers that class), or that he'd helped hide frightened white high school students in a lab in Detroit during race riots (nobody remembers that, either).

Everyone who's ever been to an American megachurch recognizes the guy who overdoes the "before" portion of his evangelical testimony, telling tall tales about running with biker gangs or participating in coke orgies (this is always taking place somewhere like Lubbock or suburban Topeka) before discovering Jesus.

As some ex-evangelicals have pointed out, Carson fits this model. He claims in his autobiography, *Gifted Hands*, that he once tried to stab someone named "Bob," failing only because he accidentally hit a belt buckle. Also, he told reporters decades ago that as a youth he attacked people with "bats and bricks" and hammers. The hammer victim was apparently his mother.

In *Gifted Hands*, none of this stuff seems any more real than the book's other inspirational passages, like the one where as a college student he prays to God about being broke and gets immediate relief as he walks across campus. "A $10 bill lay crumpled on the ground in front of me," he wrote (the magical $10 bill is a recurring character in Carsonia).

Soon, reporters were interviewing childhood friends, who were revealing what is clear if you read between the lines of Carson's book, which is that he was probably never anything but a nerd with an overheated imagination. "He was skinny and unremarkable," a classmate named Robert Collier told CNN. "I remember him having a pocket saver."

Carson lashed out at reporters for doubting his inspirational tale of a homicidal, knife-wielding madman turned convivial brain surgeon. "I would say to the people of America: Do you think I'm a pathological liar like CNN does?" he said.

This bizarre state of affairs led to stories in the straight press that were indistinguishable from *Onion* fare. "Ben Carson Defends Himself Against Allegations That He Never Attempted to Murder a Child," wrote *New York* magazine, in perhaps the single funniest headline presidential politics has ever seen.

Next, *BuzzFeed* reporters unearthed an old speech of Carson's in which he outlined a gorgeously demented theory about the Egyptian pyramids: They were not tombs for Pharaohs, but rather had been built by the biblical Joseph to store grain. The latter idea he accepted after discarding the obvious space-aliens explanation.

"Various scientists have said, 'Well, you know there were alien beings that came down and they have special knowledge,'" he said. "[But] it doesn't require an alien being when God is with you."

Scientists were quick to point out all sorts of issues, like the pyramids not really being hollow and therefore really sucky places to store grain. Then there was the fact that the Egyptians wrote down what the pyramids were for in, well, writing.

The pyramid story sent the Internet, which specializes in nothing if not instant mockery, into overdrive. Carson quickly became perhaps the single funniest thing on Earth. *The Wrap* ran a piece about Carson being "mocked mercilessly" on social media, where other "Carson theories" quickly developed: that the Eiffel Tower was for storing French bread, brains were actually a fruit, and peanut butter can be used as spermicide, etc. The whole world was in on it. It was epic.

Poor Trump now had to concede that someone else in the race was even more ridiculous and unhinged than he was. The campaign's previously unrivaled carnival expert/circus Hitler was reduced to sounding like George Will as he complained somberly—and ungrammatically—about the attention the mad doctor was stealing away from him.

"With Ben Carson wanting to hit his mother on head with a hammer, stabb [sic] a friend and Pyramids built for grain storage," Trump tweeted sadly, "don't people get it?"

By the end of the first week of November, Carson did not experience, upon close scrutiny, an instant plunge in the polls, as previous front-runners-for-a-day like Rick Perry or Herman Cain had in years past. Instead, he remained atop the polls with Trump, having successfully convinced his followers that the media flaps were just liberal hazing of a black man who threatened leftist stereotypes. And so the beginning of the long-awaited "real race" stalled still another week.

Trump commented during a rally in Illinois: "You can say anything about anybody, and their poll numbers go up. This is the only election in history where it's better off if you stabbed somebody. What are we coming to?"

We are coming to the moment when Trump is the voice of reason, that's what.

9

November 25, 2015: America Is Too Dumb for TV News

Trump and others are proving it: we can't handle the truth

DONALD TRUMP SAID THIS TO SUPPORTERS AT AN ALA-bama rally: "Hey, I watched when the World Trade Center came tumbling down. And I watched in Jersey City, New Jersey, where thousands and thousands of people were cheering as that building was coming down. Thousands of people were cheering."

It was a hell of a revelation. Where did this witnessing take place? Was he standing on the Hoboken terminal clock tower? George Stephanopoulos challenged Trump on this on ABC's *This Week*, noting that police said nothing like that happened.

TRUMP: It did happen. I saw it.
STEPHANOPOULOS: You saw that . . .
TRUMP: It was on television. I saw it.

Until recently, the narrative of stories like this has been predictable. If a candidate said something nuts, or seemingly not true, an army of humorless journalists quickly dug up all the facts, and the candidate ultimately was either vindicated, apologized, or suffered terrible agonies.

Al Gore for instance never really recovered from saying, "I took the initiative in creating the Internet." True, he never said he invented the Internet, as is popularly believed, but what he did say was clumsy enough that the line followed him around like an STD for the rest of his (largely unsuccessful) political life.

That dynamic has broken down this election season. Politicians are quickly learning that they can say just about anything and get away with it. Along with vindication, apology and suffering, there now exists a fourth way forward for the politician spewing whoppers: Blame the backlash on media bias and walk away a hero.

This season has seen an explosion of such episodes. Carly Fiorina, in a nationally televised debate, claimed to have watched a nonexistent video of evil feminists harvesting fetal brains. Ben Carson has been through a half-dozen factual dustups, including furious debates over whether or not he stabbed someone and whether or not he once won $10 for being the only honest student in an (apparently nonexistent) Yale psychology class.

Trump, meanwhile, has been through more of these beefs than one can count, even twice blabbing obvious whoppers in live televised debates. Once he claimed the

Trans-Pacific Partnership was designed to help China, moving Rand Paul to point out that China isn't in the TPP. Another time he denied that he once called Marco Rubio "Mark Zuckerberg's personal senator." The line was on Trump's website as he spoke.

In all of these cases, the candidates doubled or tripled down when pestered by reporters and fact-checkers and insisted they'd been victimized by biased media. A great example of how candidates have handled this stuff involved Fiorina.

The former HP chief keeps using a roundly debunked line originally dug up by the Romney campaign, about how 92 percent of the jobs lost under Obama belonged to women. The Romney campaign itself ditched the line because it was wrong even in 2012. When confronted this year, Fiorina simply said, "If the liberal media doesn't like the data, maybe the liberal media doesn't like the facts."

This latest episode with Trump and the 9/11 "celebrations" was fascinating. When Trump started to take heat, he at first did something one journalist I know calls "panic-Googling." Panic-Googling is saying or writing something dumb, then frantically rushing to the Internet to see if you can luck out into evidence for what you've already blabbed in public.

Trump thought he lucked out, digging up a September 18, 2001, *Washington Post* article by reporters Serge Kovaleski and Frederick Kunkle. The old clip claimed a few people had been detained after allegedly being spotted celebrating in "tailgate-style" parties on rooftops in northern New Jersey.

Seizing upon this factoid, Trump tweeted, "I want an apology! Many people have tweeted that I am right!"

Forgetting that this didn't come close to being an affirmation that he'd seen "thousands" of people celebrating on television, Trump's supporters howled in outrage. Who were these biased witch-hunters to accuse him of lying? The Donald was right all along!

Other supporters referenced an article by Debbie Schlussel, Detroit's schlocky Ann Coulter knockoff, who long ago insisted in print that she once watched an MTV news report describing post-9/11 celebrations by Arabs in Paterson, New Jersey. It wasn't Jersey City, Schlussel said, and Trump got the numbers wrong, but aside from those minor issues, he was dead right.

Next in the progression came Rush Limbaugh, who came to Trump's defense by saying that "regardless of the specific details," Trump was right about Muslims on American soil celebrating the collapse of the towers on 9/11. "The bottom line is that a lot of Americans are well aware that Muslims were cheering," Rush said. "Maybe not in New Jersey in great numbers, but around the world they were because we saw the video."

As if the "regardless of the specific details" excuse wasn't weird enough, Trump spokesman Corey Lewandowski next went on Breitbart radio to explain that the campaign had in fact provided material about celebrating Muslims to mainstream news outlets, who were now collectively declining to run it because of an ongoing conspiracy against Trump.

"They want to try and discredit as many people as possible so they can have an establishment candidate come in," he said. "Because they are all controlled by special interests and all controlled by the media."

This is a horrible thing to have to say about one's own country, but this story makes it official. America is now too dumb for TV news.

It's our fault. We in the media have spent decades turning the news into a consumer business that's basically indistinguishable from selling cheeseburgers or video games. You want bigger margins, you just cram the product full of more fat and sugar and violence and wait for your obese, over-stimulated customer to come waddling forth.

The old Edward R. Murrow, eat-your-broccoli version of the news was banished long ago. Once such whiny purists were driven from editorial posts and the ad people over the last four or five decades got invited in, things changed. Then it was nothing but murders, bombs, and panda births, delivered to thickening couch potatoes in ever briefer blasts of forty, thirty, twenty seconds.

What we call right-wing and liberal media in this country are really just two different strategies of the same kind of nihilistic lizard-brain sensationalism. The ideal CNN story is a baby down a well, while the ideal Fox story is probably a baby thrown down a well by a Muslim terrorist or an ACORN activist. Both companies offer the same service, it's just that the Fox version is a little kinkier.

When you make the news into this kind of consumer business, pretty soon audiences lose the ability to distinguish between what they think they're doing, informing themselves, and what they're actually doing, shopping.

And who shops for products he or she doesn't want? That's why the consumer news business was always destined to hit this kind of impasse. You can get by for a long time by carefully selecting the facts you know your audiences will like, and calling that news. But eventually there will be a truth that displeases your customers. What do you do then?

In this case, as Rush said, "Americans are well aware Muslims were cheering" after 9/11. Because America "knows" this, it now expects the news media to deliver that story. And if reporters refuse, it can only be out of bias.

What this 9/11 celebrations story shows is that American news audiences have had their fantasies stroked for so long that they can't even remember stuff that happened not that long ago. It's like an organic version of *1984*, with audiences constantly editing even their own memories to fit their current attitudes about things.

It was preposterous from the start to think that there could have been contemporaneous broadcasts of "thousands" of people in New Jersey celebrating the 9/11 attacks. Does nobody remember how people felt that day? If there had been such broadcasts, there would have been massacres—angry Americans would have stormed Jersey City.

In fact, police had to be deployed to places like Paterson anyway to protect immigrants from exactly that sort of mob violence. This is one of the reasons we know Muslims weren't dancing en masse in the streets, because police were parked on those streets in huge numbers to keep people *out*.

The *Newark Star-Ledger* did a report in the weeks after the attacks from Paterson showing the city in "virtual lockdown," with police camped in Muslim neighborhoods for the protection of the locals.

"In this neighborhood, in South Paterson, we don't feel threatened," Samir Asmar, a Palestinian who became a U.S. citizen, told the paper. "But once we go outside, I fear for my wife and son."

Beyond all of that: if footage of such a celebration existed, it would have skyrocketed around the country, and not popped off ineffectually on some local broadcast for just Donald Trump to see and remember. The whole thing is nuts.

There are people of all political persuasions who insist

to this day they saw something like what Trump described, but nobody describes anything like the scale of the story Trump is spinning. To believe there was a mass demonstration of open, gloating defiance right across the river from Manhattan while the Towers smoldered, speaks to a powerfully crazy fantasy both about American impotence and about a brazen, homogenous evil in Muslim-American communities.

Maybe in the wake of Paris that's the way people feel, but it's not close to what happened. If we can't remember things correctly even in the video age, things are going to get ugly fast in this country.

10

December 9, 2015: It's Too Late to Turn Off Trump

We can't change the channel on the culture he's exposed

SOME PEOPLE IN THE NEWS BUSINESS ARE HAVING SECOND thoughts this week about their campaign strategy. They're wondering if they created a monster in Donald Trump.

The *LA Times* published a piece about how the tone of Trump's TV appearances has changed, now that's he's fully out of the closet as an aspiring dictator, with his plans to ban all Muslims and close the Internet and whatever else he's come up with in the last ten minutes.

The paper noted that the candidate had unusual trouble on *Morning Joe*, a show that usually doubles as Trump's weekly spa treatment:

"Typically, the billionaire TV personality is able to

bluster his way through morning talk shows. But Trump had an unusually contentious appearance Tuesday morning on MSNBC's 'Morning Joe,' where co-hosts Joe Scarborough and Mika Brzezinski grilled him on his proposals to keep Muslims out of the U.S. . . .

"'It certainly puts the burden on the people conducting the interviews to be tougher the more controversial his comments are,' Scarborough told *The Times* after the exchange."

The paper went on to dig in to the ethics of covering Trump:

"Trump represents something of a quandary for the media, especially TV networks. Privately, TV news producers acknowledge that Trump has turbocharged their ratings . . ."

Essentially, TV news producers are wondering: "How do we keep getting the great ratings without helping elect the Fourth Reich?"

In the same piece, Joe Scarborough said the problem was that Trump gives such great access to the media, just like John McCain did in 2000. "When John McCain was letting members of the press on his Straight Talk Express bus," Scarborough explained, "other Republicans always said he got the benefit of the doubt."

In other words, Trump is so open and accommodating with the press that it makes it hard for reporters to hammer his insane ideas. Scarborough doesn't seem to realize it, but that's a pretty damning admission.

There are some people now who are urging the media to ignore Donald Trump, and simply not cover him. But it's a little late for that.

The time to start worrying about the consequences of our editorial decisions was before we raised a generation of people who get all of their information from television, and who believe that the solution to every problem is simple enough that you can find it before the 21 minutes of the sitcom are over.

Or before we created a world in which the only inner-city black people you ever see are being chased by cops, and the only Muslims onscreen are either chopping off heads or throwing rocks at a barricades.

This is an amazing thing to say, because in Donald Trump's world everything is about him, but Trump's campaign isn't about Trump anymore. With his increasingly preposterous run to the White House, the Donald is merely articulating something that runs through the entire culture.

It's hard to believe because Trump the person is so limited in his ability to articulate anything. Even in his books, where he's allegedly trying to string multiple thoughts together, Trump wanders randomly from impulse to impulse, seemingly without rhyme or reason. He doesn't think anything through. (He's brilliantly cast this driving-blind trait as "not being politically correct.")

It's not an accident that his attention span lasts exactly one news cycle. He's exactly like the rest of America, except that he's making news, not following it—starring on TV instead of watching it. Just like we channel-surf, he focuses as long as he can on whatever mess he's in, and then he moves on to the next bad idea or incorrect memory that pops into his head.

Lots of people have remarked on the irony of this absurd caricature of a spoiled rich kid connecting so well with working-class America. But Trump does have something very much in common with everybody else. He watches TV. That's his primary experience with reality, and just like most of his voters, he doesn't realize that it's a distorted picture.

If you got all of your information from TV and movies, you'd have some pretty dumb ideas. You'd be convinced blowing stuff up works, because it always does in our movies. You'd have no empathy for the poor, because there are no poor people in American movies or TV shows—they're rarely even shown on the news, because advertisers consider them a bummer.

Politically, you'd have no ability to grasp nuance or complexity, since there is none in our mainstream political discussion. All problems, even the most complicated, are boiled down to a few minutes of TV content at most. That's how issues like the last financial collapse completely flew by Middle America. The truth, with all the intricacies of all those arcane new mortgage-based financial instruments, was much harder to grasp than a story about lazy minorities buying houses they couldn't afford, which is what Middle America still believes.

Trump isn't just selling these easy answers. He's also buying them. Trump is a TV believer. He's so subsumed in all the crap he's watched—and you can tell by the cropped syntax in his books and his speech, Trump is a watcher, not a reader—it's all mixed up in his head.

He surely believes he saw that celebration of Muslims in Jersey City, when it was probably a clip of people in Palestine. When he says, "I have a great relationship with the blacks," what he probably means is that he liked watching *The Cosby Show*.

In this he's just like millions and millions of Americans, who have all been raised on a mountain of unthreatening caricatures and clichés. TV is a world in which the customer is always right, especially about hard stuff like race and class. Trump's ideas about Mexicans and Muslims are typical of someone who doesn't know any, except in the shows he chooses to watch about them.

This world of schlock stereotypes and EZ solutions is the one experience a pampered billionaire can share with all of those "paycheck-to-paycheck" voters the candidates are always trying to reach. TV is the ultimate leveling phenomenon. It makes everyone, rich and poor, equally incapable of dealing with reality.

That's why it's so ironic that some people think the solution to the Trump problem is turning him off. What got us into this mess was the impulse to change the channel the moment we feel uncomfortable. Even if we take the man off the air, the problem he represents is still going to be there, just like poverty, corruption, mass incarceration, pollution and all of the other things we keep off the airwaves.

December 15, 2015: The Official GOP Debate Drinking Game Rules, Part 5

Wednesday morning is going to suck

LADIES AND GENTLEMEN, START YOUR LIVERS.
Onward we march, to the fifth Republican debate, held this time at the Venetian in Las Vegas, beginning Tuesday at 8:30 p.m. EST.

This one promises to be a lively affair, with some pundits predicting a brawl between onetime snuggle-bunnies Donald Trump and Ted Cruz. Trump recently called Cruz a "maniac," prompting Cruz, who has depressed us all with his repeated overenthusiastic Eighties pop culture references, to tweet back a link to Michael Sembello's "Maniac" song from *Flashdance*.

Ben Carson, returned from an extended trip abroad

taken in the wake of a string of bizarre and controversial public comments—the campaign version of taking a semester off to "find yourself"—will need to do something drastic to stop his freefall in the polls. Even Republican voters seemed freaked out at the lack of foreign policy knowledge he displayed in the last debate. So expect him to try to force-feed references to things he's recently learned about the Middle East, like that it is hot and you need a passport to visit it.

Marco Rubio was being set up in the press a month ago or so to be the establishment challenge to Trump, but his numbers have plateaued. Ted Cruz cunningly went after Rubio in the last debate with a passing mention of sugar subsidies. Expect Rubio to turn the tables this time and focus his blowdried boy-rage act at Cruz, who is his chief obstacle to winning Beltway support in the fight to dethrone the Donald.

My colleagues in the political media are lately trying to gin up a story suggesting that Chris Christie is making a run in the polls, but this has all the feel of a fake D.C.-concocted narrative—nobody actually likes Chris Christie. Nonetheless, look for the Gov to go out of his way to act like he's really the comer in this race. He'll probably interrupt people and pull his loud, hectoring moralist routine even more than usual.

As for the rest of them, God help us. Trump's continued success puts the onus on the field to try to out-crazy the frontrunner. Expect lots of rhetoric about the need to even more fully arm the populace (children included), put immigrants in camps, register all watchers of subtitled movies, carpet-bomb any country with sandy terrain, etc.

THE RULES:

Drink after every violation of:

1. The **doctor's note rule:** Self-explanatory. Drink after any riffing on Trump's latest stunt.
2. The **nuke 'em till they glow rule:** Drink after any promise to "carpet bomb" the Middle East, or after any attempt to one-up Ted Cruz's recent comments about how "I don't know if sand can glow in the dark, but we're going to find out."
3. The **Obama won't say "terrorism" rule:** Candidate complains that the president is afraid to use the words "radical Islam" or "Islamic terrorism."
4. The **climate change denial rule:** Complaint about the Paris climate change agreement. Shotgun a beer if it comes with a mention of how the nice local weather renders climate change talk meaningless.
5. The **War on Christmas rule:** Mention of "red cups," nativity controversies, etc.
6. The **Reince Priebus rule:** Mention of a brokered convention or use of the phrase "Let the people decide" in a discussion of RNC/Reince Priebus controversy. Double shot if the latter's name pronounced incorrectly.
7. The **George Lucas rule:** Gratuitous mention of *Star Wars.* Double shot if it comes with an impersonation or a sound effect (e.g., Cruz does a Yoda voice while threatening ISIS).
8. The **I'm just a simple caveman rule:** A candidate mentions that he/she is not a scientist, or generally derides higher education before proceeding to make a "common sense" point.

9. The **wet blanket rule:** Attempt by Kasich to implore his fellow candidates to be more realistic, followed by boos/catcalls from the audience.

10. The **Hitler had some really good ideas rule:** Salutary mention of Japanese internment, religious registries or other similar policies.

11. The **I don't just believe in the American dream, I'm a product of it rule:** Anyone talks about how they are the son/daughter/husband/wife of a humble bartender/maid/tow truck driver/whatever because dreams and opportunity.

12. The **good guy with a gun rule:** Self-explanatory.

13. The **empty God platitudes rule:** An anti-gun-control candidate extends "thoughts and prayers" to the victims of Paris, San Bernardino or whatever other mass shooting we'll have in the next ten minutes.

14. The **we're not racist rule:** A candidate complains that people with "traditional values" are being accused of being bigots. Double shot if it's Rubio.

15. The **Carly, interrupted rule:** Carly Fiorina interrupts someone and/or uses a bogus statistic. Double shot if it's that "73,000-page tax code" line she continues to send out there at every opportunity.

THE EVERGREEN RULES

ALWAYS drink, in every debate, when:

16. Trump brags about how much money he makes.
17. Anyone says, "I'm the only one on this stage who . . ."

18. Someone says, "Any one of us onstage is better than Hillary Clinton . . ."

19. The crowd breaks into uncomfortable applause at a racist/sexist statement.

20. Any candidate evokes Nazis, the Gestapo, Neville Chamberlain, concentration camps, etc.

21. Anyone force-feeds an Israel reference into a question where it doesn't belong. Also known as the **Ann Coulter rule.**

22. Anyone pledges to "take our country back."

23. The **Jim Webb rule:** Candidate complains about not getting enough time.

24. Any candidate illustrates the virtue of one of his/her positions by pointing out how not PC it is.

25. Someone invokes Saint Reagan. Beware, people, this is an *every time* rule again.

12

February 5, 2016: The Vampire Squid Tells Us How to Vote

———

Lloyd Blankfein charges for investment advice—
but his political wisdom is free

Lloyd Blankfein, Chief Executive Cephalopod of Goldman Sachs, issued a warning about the Bernie Sanders campaign this week.

"This has the potential to be a dangerous moment," he said on CNBC's *Squawk Box*.

The Lloyd was peeved that Sanders, whom he's never met, singled him out in a debate last week. "Another kid from Brooklyn, how about that," he lamented.

He ranted about how frightening it is that a candidate like Sanders, who seems to have no interest in "compromising" with Wall Street, could become so popular.

"Could you imagine," he asked, "if the Jeffersons and

Hamiltons came in with a total pledge and commitment to never compromise with the other side?"

The slobbering *Squawk Box* hosts went on to propose firing all the academics in the country, because clearly it is their fault that so many young people are willing to support a socialist.

"I'm ready," said co-host Joe Kernen, "to send my daughter to Brigham Young or Liberty or something."

Then Kernen, Becky Quick and Blankfein all made jokes about how socialism doesn't work and how all those Berniebots should take a trip to Cuba.

"The best real-time experiment is, I went to Cuba," said Lloyd.

"I haven't been," Kernen said proudly.

"You should go," said Lloyd. "You go there, stop in Miami and you just see the Cuban community and how much wealth they've generated."

Of course the politics of Sanders is closer to what you'd find in Sweden or Denmark than Cuba, but they were rolling by then.

Lloyd added that the current popular discontent with Wall Street was just something that happens randomly, like the weather. "There's a pendulum that happens in markets and it happens in political economy as well," he said.

He added that he didn't want to pick a candidate because "I don't want to help or hurt anybody by giving an endorsement."

For people who are so very pleased with themselves for ostensibly being so much smarter than everyone else, people like Blankfein are oddly uncreative when it comes to deflecting criticism.

The people who don't like them are always overemotional communists. All those young people who are flock-ing to the Sanders campaign? Dupes, misled by dumb professors who've never been to Cuba.

And their anger toward Wall Street? Causeless and ran-dom, just a bunch of folks riding an emotional pendulum that brainlessly swings back and forth. Don't take it person-ally, people are just moody that way.

Bill Clinton apparently agrees. A story about the former president's thoughts on the subject appeared in *Stress Test*, the vile battle memoir of the financial crisis penned by infa-mous Wall Street toady and former treasury secretary Tim Geithner.

In the book, Timmy goes on at length about how sad it made him that the public was so upset about the bailouts and other policies he engineered to make the Blankfeins of the world whole again. Looking for a way to not feel so hated, he went to Clinton to "discuss the politics of popu-lism with the master practitioner."

It's an important detail. Geithner's instinct for figuring out how to deal with ordinary people was not to go talk to any, but instead to talk to someone who'd had success mar-keting himself to them.

This squares with accounts I heard after 2008, about the Treasury Department in the Geithner years. In one story I remember, it took a presentation from a major retail com-pany about expected lower holiday spending levels to en-lighten Geithner's staff as to the level of economic pain in the population. Until they saw the graphs from executives, they had no clue.

Anyway, according to his book, Geithner got good ad-vice from Clinton. The former president advised him to press for tax hikes on the rich, but to "make sure I didn't look like I was happy about it." Then Clinton added that Timmy shouldn't take the public-anger thing too hard:

"You could take Lloyd Blankfein in an alley and slit his throat, and it would satisfy them for about two days," Clinton said. "Then the blood lust would rise again."

Ordinary people aren't just overemotional and dumb, they're also zombies! They don't have grievances, just blood lusts.

The attitude shared by Lloyd and Geithner and Bill Clinton is that the mindless quality of public discontent means that there's no point in worrying about it, or negotiating with it. This is funny because Blankfein is the one complaining that people like Sanders and his followers don't want to compromise with him.

Lloyd thinks politicians should naturally reside in a state of more or less constant accommodation with Wall Street. Thomas Jefferson would have compromised with us, he says!

One can assume that his model of a "compromising" politician is Hillary Clinton, who took $675,000 to give three speeches to his company. "Look, I make speeches to lots of groups," Hillary explained. "I told them what I thought."

Asked by Anderson Cooper if she needed to take $675,000 to tell Goldman what she "thought," Hillary shrugged. "I don't know," she said. "That's what they were offering."

Even more significant than the $675,000 Hillary took from Goldman, or the $30 million in speaking income she and her husband received combined in the last 16 months, is the account of what Hillary apparently told Goldman she "thought" during those speeches.

According to *Politico*, who spoke to several attendees, Hillary used the opportunity to tell the bankers in attendance that the "banker-bashing so popular within both parties was unproductive and indeed foolish."

She added that the proper attitude should be, "We all got into this mess together, and we're all going to have to work together to get out of it."

This squares with Geithner's account of what Bill Clinton said. The former president told Geithner that slitting Lloyd's throat would only satisfy "them" for about two days. *Them* was all those pissed-off regular people, and the *we* or *us* were politicians like himself and Geithner.

In her speech, Hillary's *we* included the executives in her audience. Her message was basically that It Takes a Village to create a financial crisis. This was the Robin Williams breakthrough scene in *Good Will Hunting*, with Hillary putting a hand on the Goldmanites' shoulders, telling them, "It's not your fault. It's not your fault."

But it was their fault. The crash was caused by a tiny handful of people who spent years hogging fortunes through a criminal scheme in the home lending markets. The FBI warned back in 2004 of an "epidemic" of mortgage fraud that could have an "impact as big as the S&L crisis," but those warnings were ignored.

What the FBI was talking about back then mainly had to do with smaller local lending operations that were systematically creating risky home loans, falsifying credit applications to get unworthy borrowers into mortgages they couldn't afford.

What they didn't understand back then is that the impetus for that criminal activity was the willingness of massive banking institutions on Wall Street to buy up those bad loans in bulk. They created a market for those fraudulent loans, bought billions' worth of them from local lenders, and then chopped up and resold those bad loans to pension funds, unions and other suckers.

The "village" didn't do this. Lloyd Blankfein and his buddies did this. (Goldman just a few weeks ago reached a deal to pay a $5.1 billion settlement to cover its history of selling bad loans to unsuspecting investors, joining Bank of America, Citi, JP Morgan Chase and others.)

People aren't pissed just to be pissed. They're mad because a tiny group of crooks on Wall Street built themselves beach houses in the Hamptons through a crude fraud scheme that decimated their retirement funds, caused property values in their neighborhoods to collapse and caused over four million people to be put in foreclosure.

And they're particularly mad that they got asked to pay for this criminal irresponsibility with bailouts funded with their tax dollars.

What the Clintons have done by turning their political careers into a vast moneymaking enterprise, it's not a value-neutral activity. The money isn't just about buying influence. The money also physically moves people, from one side of an imaginary line to another.

You will never catch Bernie Sanders standing in a room as a paid guest of a bank under investigation for ripping billions off pensioners and investors, addressing the audience in the first-person plural. He doesn't spend enough time with that kind of crowd to be so colloquial.

The Clintons meanwhile have by now taken so much money that when they stand in a room full of millionaires and billionaires, they can use the word "we" and not have it sound odd. The money has irrevocably moved them to that side of the rope line. On that side of the line, public anger isn't legitimate, but something to be managed and waited out, just as Lloyd suggests.

When people like Blankfein tell us they don't take criticism personally, what they're saying is that it's too brainless and irrational to be taken any other way. He means to be insulting. And we should all take it that way.

13

February 23, 2016: Morning Blow: How Mika and Joe Became Trump's Lapdogs

Joe Scarborough and Mika Brzezinski should be herded into a rocket and shot into space for their brown-nosing of Trump

ALL-TIME GREAT COMEDIAN HARRY SHEARER, THE MAN who brought us voices from *The Simpsons* and cucumber-hoarding bass player Derek Smalls in *This Is Spinal Tap*, has broken an embarrassing story about us journalists.

In his *Le Show* podcast, he released audio of off-camera dialogue between Donald Trump and ostensible news figures Joe Scarborough and Mika Brzezinski of the MSNBC program *Morning Joe*. The tape covers breaks in a town hall segment the trio filmed in South Carolina last week.

The embarrassing part starts when Brzezinski compliments Trump on his campaign stagecraft. She comments that it was a "wow" moment when Trump invited onstage two meatheads who tossed a protester from one of his South Carolina events.

A side note: The vigorous physical expulsion of loser-protesters has become a predictable scene at Trump events. Every time I've seen it in person, it's freaked me out—it's like a window into some future WWE-style dissident-beheading ritual—but Mika apparently thought the video of the South Carolina incident was inspiring.

"You know what I thought was kind of a wow moment, was the guy you brought up on stage," Mika says.

"We played it several times this morning!" adds a breathless Scarborough.

An approving Trump here verbally extends his ring to be kissed. "I watched your show this morning," he says. "You have me almost as a legendary figure, I like that."

If any politician ever said that to me, I would eat a cyanide capsule on the spot. Mika and Joe both seemed undisturbed.

Joe went on to apologize to Trump for having called the South Carolina debate wrong (he thought Trump lost). Next, Brzezinski thanked Trump for being on the show. Trump jokingly replied that he gets nothing out of their relationship, while she will get "great ratings and a raise."

Trump goes on to say, "Just make us all look good."

"Exactly," says Scarborough.

In another moment, someone in studio suggests a question to ask Trump through Scarborough's earpiece. "That's a great question," Scarborough says.

"What, the China?" Trump says. Trump had just been talking about China, so naturally he assumed that when Scarborough used the word "great," he was referring to something he'd said.

"No, they're telling me what to ask you," Scarborough explains. He then pretends that the prospect of a tough question scares The Donald.

"Look at you. I see, he's shaking," Joe says.

"Yeah. Whatever," Trump answers, with humorously obvious sincerity.

Scarborough, being playful, goes on to ask his mystery question: "When was the last time you golfed?"

Trump doesn't get that Scarborough is play-asking him a "tough" question and instead gives a serious answer right out of a textbook on Narcissistic Personality Disorder.

Trump explains that he played four days ago, but had to bow out of his outing with gorgeous 20-year-old pro Lexi Thompson because he was thinking too much about the whole running-for-president thing. "I played nine holes, I didn't even want to play anymore," he says sadly.

So I was playing nine holes with a famous golfer who is also a bikini model, but I had to cut it short because being the most talked-about (and soon most powerful) man on earth is so tiring . . .

Scarborough takes in this ridiculous story without comment. The only surprise is that he doesn't ask Trump for putting tips.

But the worst exchange is about the questions in the segment. Brzezinski at one point tries to check with Scarborough if it's OK to ask a tough question.

"Do you not want me to do, the um, the ones with, um, deportation?" she says.

Scarborough's answer is hilarious. "We really do have to go to some questions," he says. Though it's audio only, you can almost hear his brow furrowing with concern.

Trump at this point interjects. "Nothing too hard, Mika," he says.

"OK," she replies.

It goes without saying that there were no questions about deportation or immigration at the town hall.

Nobody who's covered the Trump run could fail to notice the increasingly hot-and-sweaty *ménage à trois* between the candidate and Mika and Joe. After hearing Trump give the duo chummy shout-outs at multiple campaign-trail events, I wrote about them in an upcoming piece for *Rolling Stone*. My idea is that they would be the royal media under the upcoming Trump monarchy/dictatorship. It's easy to imagine Joe in an official state journalist uniform, with epaulettes and a flying Trump-mane insignia.

Even their on-air performance at the town hall last Wednesday was such a craven display of bumlicking and softballing that media critics all over the country denounced them for it.

Erik Wemple of the *Washington Post* ripped Scarborough and Brzezinski for letting Trump squirm out of fact-checking problems (like his completely un-sourced, unconfirmed claim that he was against the Iraq invasion before 2003). He also blasted them for not asking him any questions about Trump's myriad crazy comments about women, minorities and the disabled.

To this, Mika and Joe responded that they had "humiliated" their competitors and that their critics were being hysterical. Scarborough's first defiant take recalled Bill Clinton's whiny observation that if you took Goldman CEO Lloyd Blankfein into an alley and "slit his throat," the rabble would still call you soft on Wall Street.

Said Scarborough of Trump: "If you don't stand on top of him with your knees on his chest and stab him in the side of the neck until he bleeds out, it's never going to be enough."

He added later that the rest of the press corps was just jealous that his show was the first to take Trump seriously. "You're really angry because we called this first," he said. "You're humiliated because this is your job."

Actually, guessing that Trump's campaign had a chance at success and shoving your tongue a foot and a half up the Trumpian orifice are two completely different journalistic acts. For the record, a lot of media people guessed early on that Trump's campaign was for real, and that group included many reporters who wouldn't sit within ten feet of Trump without a HazMat suit. (Even I put money on him to win the nomination way back in August.)

But Scarborough isn't really saying that he was the first pundit to call Trump a serious contender. What he's really bragging about is that he was the first media figure smart enough to strap on his kneepads in exchange for access once he saw that the Trump campaign was going places. He seems genuinely to think the rest of us are just jealous that we didn't think to do that first.

The reality, of course, is that Scarborough currently is winning the access battle with Trump because Donald Trump, like the Chinese emperors of yore who surrounded themselves with eunuchs as palace guards, refuses to interact with anyone who threatens him in any way.

Thus Trump's regular media contacts are exclusively a gang of supplicating ratings-whores like Bill O'Reilly, Sean Hannity, and especially Scarborough, who appears to be Trump's favorite lapdog. Trump seems to get a kick out of the fact that he now has an ex-congressman carrying his skirts for him in public, and he tosses Scarborough's name around at events like a war trophy.

Which, again, would normally be another reason to eat a cyanide capsule, but Joe seems pretty far from this.

Obviously Scarborough and Brzezinski aren't the only ostensibly neutral media figures to go in the tank for a candidate. They're not even the only ones at MSNBC.

Chris Matthews at *Hardball* seems to have become Hillary Clinton's unofficial campaign spokesman. The phenomenon is conspicuous enough that outlets on both the left and the right have chalked up Matthews' on-air prostrations to the fact that his wife Kathleen, who is running for Congress in Maryland, shares many campaign donors with Hillary.

The excuse parade for people like Scarborough is going to include the observation that he's not really a journalist but more like an entertainer or an "analyst." Even Callum Borchers of the *Washington Post*, in an otherwise critical article about the leaked audio, concluded that Scarborough and Brzezinski "shouldn't be held to the same standard of total neutrality" as straight-news reporters.

Maybe that's true, who knows. But even assuming that it's OK for someone like Scarborough to be something less than neutral, being an advocate is different from being a slobbering yes man.

There was a time in the journalism business when it was considered at least somewhat embarrassing to be caught openly shilling for a politician. Believe it or not, it was also once considered inappropriate to admit to being about nothing except ratings. Not that everyone has to be Seymour Hersh, but Jesus, have some pride.

14

February 24, 2016: How America Made Trump Unstoppable

———

He's no ordinary con man. He's way above average—and the American political system is his easiest mark ever

THE FIRST THING YOU NOTICE AT DONALD TRUMP'S RAL-
lies is the confidence. Amateur psychologists have
wishfully diagnosed him from afar as insecure, but in person the notion seems absurd.

Donald Trump, insecure? We should all have such
problems.

At the Verizon Giganto-Center in Manchester the night
before the New Hampshire primary, Trump bounds onstage to raucous applause and the booming riffs of the
Lennon-McCartney anthem "Revolution." The song is, hilariously, a cautionary tale about the perils of false prophets

peddling mindless revolts, but Trump floats in on its grooves like it means the opposite. When you win as much as he does, who the hell cares what anything means?

He steps to the lectern and does his Mussolini routine, which he's perfected over the past months. It's a nodding wave, a grin, a half-sneer, and a little U.S. Open–style applause back in the direction of the audience, his face the whole time a mask of pure self-satisfaction.

"This is unbelievable, unbelievable!" he says, staring out at a crowd of about 4,000 whooping New Englanders with snow hats, fleece and beer guts. There's a snowstorm outside and cars are flying off the road, but it's a packed house.

He flashes a thumbs-up. "So everybody's talking about the cover of *Time* magazine last week. They have a picture of me from behind, I was extremely careful with my hair . . ."

He strokes his famous flying fuzz-mane. It looks gorgeous, like it's been recently fed. The crowd goes wild. *Whoooo! Trump!*

It's pure camp, a variety show. He singles out a Trump impersonator in the crowd, tells him he hopes the guy is making a lot of money. "Melania, would you marry that guy?" he says. The future first lady is a Slovenian model who, apart from Trump, was most famous for a TV ad in which she engaged in a Frankenstein-style body transfer with the Aflac duck, voiced by Gilbert Gottfried.

She had one line in that ad. Tonight, it's two lines:

"Ve love you, New Hampshire," she says, in a thick vampire accent. "Ve, together, ve vill make America great again!"

As reactionary patriotic theater goes, this scene is bizarre—Melania Knauss didn't even arrive in America until 1996, when she was all of 26—but the crowd goes nuts anyway. Everything Trump does works these days. He steps to the mic.

"She's beautiful, but she's more beautiful even on the inside," he says, raising a finger to the heavens. "And, boy, is she smart!"

Before the speech, the PA announcer had told us not to "touch or harm" any protesters, but to instead just surround them and chant, "Trump! Trump! Trump!" until security can arrive (and presumably do the touching and/or harming).

I'd seen this ritual several times, and the crowd always loves it. At one event, a dead ringer for John Oliver ripped off his shirt in the middle of a Trump speech to reveal body paint that read "Eminent Domain This!" on his thorax. The man shouted, "Trump is a racist!" and was immediately set upon by Trump supporters, who yelled "Trump! Trump! Trump!" at him until security arrived and dragged him out the door to cheers. The whole Trump run is like a *Jerry Springer* episode, where even the losers seem in on the gags.

In Manchester, a protester barely even manages to say a word before disappearing under a blanket of angry boos: "Trump! Trump! Trump!" It's a scene straight out of *Freaks*. In a Trump presidency, there will be free tar and feathers provided at the executive's every public address.

It's a few minutes after that when a woman in the crowd shouts that Ted Cruz is a pussy. She will later tell a journalist she supports Trump because his balls are the size of "watermelons," while his opponents' balls are more like "grapes" or "raisins."

Trump's balls are unaware of this, but he instinctively likes her comment and decides to go into headline-making mode. "I never expect to hear that from you again!" he says, grinning. "She said he's a pussy. That's terrible." Then, the-atrically, he turns his back to the crowd. As the 500 or so reporters in attendance scramble to instantly make this the most important piece of news in the world—in less than a year Trump has succeeded in turning the USA into a massive high school—the candidate beams.

What's he got to be insecure about? The American electoral system is opening before him like a flower.

In person, you can't miss it: The same way Sarah Palin can see Russia from her house, Donald on the stump can see his future. The pundits don't want to admit it, but it's sitting there in plain view, 12 moves ahead, like a chess game already won:

President Donald Trump.

A thousand ridiculous accidents needed to happen in the unlikeliest of sequences for it to be possible, but absent a dramatic turn of events—an early primary catastrophe, Mike Bloomberg ego-crashing the race, etc.—this boor-ish, monosyllabic TV tyrant with the attention span of an Xbox-playing 11-year-old really is set to lay waste to the most impenetrable oligarchy the Western world ever de-vised.

It turns out we let our electoral process devolve into something so fake and dysfunctional that any half-bright con man with the stones to try it could walk right through the front door and tear it to shreds on the first go.

And Trump is no half-bright con man, either. He's way better than average.

It's been well-documented that Trump surged last sum-mer when he openly embraced the ugly race politics that, according to the Beltway custom of 50-plus years, is sup-posed to stay at the dog-whistle level. No doubt, that's been a huge factor in his rise. But racism isn't the only ugly thing he's dragged out into the open.

Trump is no intellectual. He's not bringing *Middlemarch* to the toilet. If he had to jail with Stephen Hawking for a year, he wouldn't learn a thing about physics. Hawking would come out on Day 365 talking about models and football.

But, in an insane twist of fate, this bloated billionaire scion has hobbies that have given him insight into the presidential electoral process. He likes women, which got him into beauty pageants. And he likes being famous, which got him into reality TV. He knows show business.

That put him in position to understand that the presidential election campaign is really just a badly acted, billion-dollar TV show whose production costs ludicrously include the political disenfranchisement of its audience. Trump is making a mockery of the show, and the Wolf Blitzers and Anderson Coopers of the world seem appalled. How dare he demean the presidency with his antics?

But they've all got it backward. The presidency is serious. The presidential electoral process, however, is a sick joke, in which everyone loses except the people behind the rope line. And every time some pundit or party spokesman tries to deny it, Trump picks up another vote.

The ninth Republican debate, in Greenville, South Carolina, is classic Trump. He turns these things into WWE contests, and since he has actual WWE experience after starring in Wrestlemania in 2007, he knows how to play these moments like a master.

Interestingly, a lot of Trump's political act seems lifted from bully-wrestlers. A clear influence is "Ravishing" Rick Rude, an Eighties champ whose schtick was to insult the audience. He would tell ticket holders they were "fat, ugly sweat hogs," before taking off his robe to show them "what a real sexy man looks like."

In Greenville, Donald "The Front-Runner" Trump started off the debate by jumping on his favorite wrestling foil, Prince Dinkley McBirthright, a.k.a. Jeb Bush. Trump seems to genuinely despise Bush. He never missed a chance to rip him for being a "low-energy," "stiff" and "dumb as a rock" weenie who lets his Mexican wife push him around. But if you watch Trump long enough, it starts to seem gratuitous.

Trump's basic argument is the same one every successful authoritarian movement in recent Western history has made: that the regular guy has been screwed by a conspiracy of incestuous elites. The Bushes are half that conspiratorial picture, fronts for a Republican Party establishment and whose sum total of accomplishments, dating back nearly 30 years, are two failed presidencies, the sweeping loss of manufacturing jobs, and a pair of pitiable Middle Eastern military adventures—the second one achieving nothing but dead American kids and Junior's re-election.

Trump picked on Jeb because Jeb is a symbol. The Bushes are a dissolute monarchy, down to offering their last genetic screw-up to the throne.

Jeb took the high road for most of the past calendar year, but Trump used his gentlemanly dignity against him. What Trump understands better than his opponents is that NASCAR America, WWE America, always loves seeing the preening self-proclaimed good guy get whacked with a chair. In Greenville, Trump went after Jeb this time on the issue of his brother's invasion of Iraq.

"The war in Iraq was a big f . . . fat mistake, all right?"

he snorted. He nearly said, "A big fucking mistake." He added that the George W. Bush administration lied before the war about Iraq having WMDs and that we spent $2 trillion basically for nothing.

Days earlier, Trump had gleefully tweeted that Bush needed his "mommy" after Jeb appeared with Lady Barbara on a morning show.

Jeb now went straight into character as the Man Whose Good Name Had Been Insulted. He defended his family and took exception to Trump having the "gall" to go after his mother.

"I won the lottery when I was born 63 years ago and looked up and I saw my mom," Jeb said proudly and lifted his chin. America loves Moms. How could he not win this exchange? But he was walking into a lawn mower.

"My mom is the strongest woman I know," Jeb continued.

"She should be running," Trump snapped.

The crowd booed, but even that was phony. It later came out that more than 900 of the 1,600 seats were given to local and national GOP officials. (Trump mentioned during the debate that he had only his wife and son there in comparison, but few picked up on what he was saying.) Pundits, meanwhile, lined up to congratulate Jeb for "assailing" Trump—"Bush is finally going for it," the *New York Times* wrote—but the exchange really highlighted many of the keys to Trump's success.

Trump had said things that were true and that no other Republican would dare to say. And yet the press congratulated the candidate stuffed with more than $100 million in donor cash who really did take five whole days last year to figure out his position on his own brother's invasion of Iraq.

At a time when there couldn't be more at stake, with the Middle East in shambles, a major refugee crisis, and as many as three Supreme Court seats up for grabs (the death of satanic quail-hunter Antonin Scalia underscored this), the Republican Party picked a strange year to turn the presidential race into a potluck affair. The candidates sent forth to take on Trump have been so incompetent they can't even lose properly.

One GOP strategist put it this way: "Maybe 34 [percent] is Trump's ceiling. But 34 in a five-person race wins."

The numbers simply don't work, unless the field unexpectedly narrows before March. Trump has a chokehold on somewhere between 25 and 40 percent of the Republican vote, scoring in one poll across every category: young and old, educated and less so, hardcore conservatives and registered Democrats, with men and with women, Megyn Kelly's "wherever" notwithstanding. Trump the Builder of Anti-Rapist Walls even earns an estimated 25 percent of the GOP Latino vote.

Moreover, there's evidence that human polling undercounts Trump's votes, as people support him in larger numbers when they don't have to admit their leanings to a live human being. Like autoerotic asphyxiation, supporting Donald Trump is an activity many people prefer to enjoy in a private setting, like in a shower or a voting booth.

The path to unseating Trump is consolidation of opposition, forcing him into a two- or three-person race. Things seemed headed that way after Iowa, when Ted Cruz won and Marco Rubio came in third.

Rubio's Iowa celebration was a classic. The toothy Floridian leaped onstage and delivered a rollickingly pretentious speech appropriate not for a candidate who just eked out wins in five Iowa counties, but for a man just crowned king of Jupiter.

"For months, they told us because we offered too much optimism in a time of anger, we had no chance," he thundered. Commentators later noted Rubio's language was remarkably similar to Barack Obama's florid "they said our sights were set too high" 2008 Iowa victory speech.

The national punditry predictably overreacted to Rubio's showing, having been desperate to rally behind a traditional, party-approved GOP candidate.

Why do the media hate Trump? Progressive reporters will say it's because of things like his being crazy and the next Hitler, while the Fox types insist it's because he's "not conservative." But reporters mostly loathe Trump because he craps on other reporters.

He called Fox's Kelly a period-crazed bias monster for asking simple questions about Trump's past comments about women, and launched a weirdly lengthy crusade against little-known *New Hampshire Union-Leader* publisher Joseph McQuaid for comparing Trump to *Back to the Future* villain Biff Tannen. He even mocked the neurological condition of *Times* reporter Serge Kovaleski for failing to ratify Trump's hilariously fictional recollection of "thousands" of Muslims celebrating after 9/11, doing an ad hoc writhing disabled-person impersonation at a South Carolina rally that left puppies and cancer kids as the only groups untargeted by his campaign. (He later denied the clearly undeniable characterization.)

But Trump's thin-skinned dealings with reporters didn't fully explain the media's efforts to prop up his opponents. We've long been engaged in our own version of the high school put-down game, battering nerds and outsiders like

Ron Paul and Dennis Kucinich while elevating "electable," party-approved candidates like John McCain and John Kerry.

Thus it was no surprise that after Iowa, columnists tried to sell the country on the loathsome "Marcomentum" narrative, a paean to the good old days when reporters got to tell the public who was hot and who wasn't—the days of the "Straight Talk Express," "Joementum," etc.

"Marco Rubio Was the Real Winner in Iowa," blared CNN. "Marco Rubio's Iowa Mojo," chimed in *Politico*. "Forget Ted Cruz, Marco Rubio Is the Real Winner of the Iowa Caucuses," agreed *Vanity Fair*.

Rubio, we were told, had zoomed to the front of the "establishment lane" in timely enough fashion to stop Trump. Of course, in the real world, nobody cares about what happens in the "establishment lane" except other journalists. But even the other candidates seemed to believe the narrative. Ohio Gov. John Kasich staggered out of Iowa in eighth place and was finishing up his 90th lonely appearance in New Hampshire when Boston-based reporters caught up to him.

"If we get smoked up there, I'm going back to Ohio," he lamented. Kasich in person puts on a brave face, but he also frequently rolls his eyes in an expression of ostentatious misanthropy that says, "I can't believe I'm losing to these idiots."

But then Rubio went onstage at St. Anselm College in the eighth GOP debate and blew himself up. Within just a few minutes of a vicious exchange with haranguing now-former candidate Chris Christie, he twice delivered the exact same canned 25-second spiel about how Barack Obama "knows exactly what he's doing."

Rubio's face-plant brilliantly reprised Sir Ian Holm's

performance in *Alien*, as a malfunctioning, disembodied robot head stammering, "I admire its purity." It was everything we hate about scripted mannequin candidates captured in a brief crack in the political facade.

Rubio plummeted in the polls, and Kasich, already mentally checked out, was the surprise second-place finisher in New Hampshire, with 15.8 percent of the vote.

"Something big happened tonight," Kasich said vaguely, not seeming sure what that thing was exactly. Even worse from a Republican point of view, Dinkley McBush somehow finished fourth, above Rubio and in a virtual tie with Iowa winner Ted Cruz.

Now none of the three "establishment lane" candidates could drop out. And the next major contest, South Carolina, was deemed by horse-race experts to have too tiny an "establishment lane" vote to decide which two out of that group should off themselves in time for the third to mount a viable "Stop Trump" campaign.

All of which virtually guarantees Trump will probably enjoy at least a five-horse race through Super Tuesday. So he might have this thing sewn up before the others even figure out in what order they should quit. It's hard to recall a dumber situation in American presidential politics.

"If you're Trump, you're sending flowers to all of them for staying in," the GOP strategist tells me. "The more the merrier. And they're running out of time to figure it out."

The day after Rubio's implosion, Trump is upstate in New Hampshire, addressing what for him is a modest crowd of about 1,500 to 2,000 in the gym at Plymouth State University. The crowd here is more full-blown New England townie than you'll find at his Manchester events: lots of work boots, Pats merch and f-bombs.

Trump's speeches are never scripted, never exactly the same twice. Instead he just riffs and feels his way through crowds. He's no orator—as anyone who's read his books knows, he's not really into words, especially long ones—but he has an undeniable talent for commanding a room.

Today, knowing the debate news is in the air, he makes sure to plunge a finger into Rubio's wound, mocking candidates who need scripts.

"Honestly, I don't have any teleprompters, I don't have a speech I'm reading to you," Trump says. Then he switches into a nasal, weenie-politician voice, and imitates someone reading tiny text from a crib sheet: "Ladies and gentlemen, it's so nice to be here in New Hampshire, please vote for me or I'll never speak to you again . . ."

The crowd laughs. Trump also makes sure to point a finger at the omnipresent Giant Media Throng.

"See all those cameras back there?" he says. "They've never driven so far to a location."

The crowd turns to gape and sneer at the hated press contingent, which seems glad to be behind a rope. Earlier, Trump had bragged about how these same reporters had begrudgingly admitted that he'd won the St. Anselm debate. "They hate it, but they gave me very high grades."

It's simple transitive-property rhetoric, and it works. The press went gaga for Rubio after Iowa because—why? Because he's an unthreatening, blow-dried, cliché-spouting, dial-surveying phony of the type campaign journalists always approve of.

And when Rubio gets exposed in the debate as a talking haircut, a political Speak n' Spell, suddenly the throng of journalists who spent the past two weeks trying to sell America on "Marcomentum" and the all-important "establishment lane" looks very guilty indeed. Voters were supposed to take this seriously?

Trump knows the public sees through all of this, grasps the press's role in it and rightly hates us all. When so many Trump supporters point to his stomping of the carpetbagging snobs in the national media as the main reason they're going to vote for him, it should tell us in the press something profound about how much people think we suck.

Jay Matthews, a Plymouth native with a long beard and a Trump sign, cites Trump's press beat-downs as the first reason he's voting Donald.

"He's gonna be his own man," he says. "He's proving that now with how he's getting all the media. He's paying nothing and getting all the coverage. He's not paying one dime."

Reporters have focused quite a lot on the crazy/race-baiting/nativist themes in Trump's campaign, but these comprise a very small part of his usual presentation. His speeches increasingly are strikingly populist in their content.

His pitch is: He's rich, he won't owe anyone anything upon election, and therefore he won't do what both Democratic and Republican politicians unfailingly do upon taking office, i.e., approve rotten/regressive policies that screw ordinary people.

He talks, for instance, about the anti-trust exemption enjoyed by insurance companies, an atrocity dating back more than half a century, to the McCarran-Ferguson Act of 1945. This law, sponsored by one of the most notorious legislators in our history (Nevada Sen. Pat McCarran was thought to be the inspiration for the corrupt Sen. Pat Geary in *The Godfather II*), allows insurance companies to share information and collude to divvy up markets.

Neither the Republicans nor the Democrats made a serious effort to overturn this indefensible loophole during the debate over the Affordable Care Act.

Trump pounds home this theme in his speeches, explaining things from his perspective as an employer. "The insurance companies," he says, "they'd rather have monopolies in each state than hundreds of companies going all over the place bidding. . . . It's so hard for me to make deals . . . because I can't get bids."

He goes on to explain that prices would go down if the state-by-state insurance fiefdoms were eliminated, but that's impossible because of the influence of the industry. "I'm the only one that's self-funding. . . . Everyone else is taking money from, I call them the bloodsuckers."

Trump isn't lying about any of this. Nor is he lying when he mentions that the big-pharma companies have such a stranglehold on both parties that they've managed to get the federal government to bar itself from negotiating Medicare prescription-drug prices in bulk.

"I don't know what the reason is—I do know what the reason is, but I don't know how they can sell it," he says. "We're not allowed to negotiate drug prices. We pay $300 billion more than if we negotiated the price."

It's actually closer to $16 billion a year more, but the rest of it is true enough. Trump then goes on to personalize this story. He claims (and with Trump we *always* have to use words like "claims") how it was these very big-pharma donors, "fat cats," sitting in the front row of the debate the night before. He steams ahead even more with this tidbit: Woody Johnson, one of the heirs of drug giant Johnson & Johnson (and the laughably incompetent owner of the New York Jets), is the finance chief for the campaign of whipping boy Jeb Bush.

"Now, let's say Jeb won. Which is an impossibility, but let's say . . ."

The crowd explodes in laughter.

"Let's say Jeb won," Trump goes on. "How is it possible for Jeb to say, 'Woody, we're going to go out and fight competitively'?"

This is, what—not true? Of course it's true.

What's Trump's solution? Himself! He's gonna grab the problem by the throat and fix it by force!

Throughout his campaign, he's been telling a story about a $2.5 billion car factory that a Detroit automaker wants to build in Mexico, and how as president he's going to stop it. Humorously, he tried at one point to say he already had stopped it, via his persistent criticism, citing an article on an obscure website that claimed the operation had moved to Youngstown, Ohio.

That turned out to be untrue, but, hey, what candidate for president hasn't impulse-tweeted the completely unprovable fact or two? (Trump will someday be in the Twitter Hall of Fame. His fortune-cookie mind—restless, confrontational, completely lacking the shame/veracity filter—is perfectly engineered for the medium.)

In any case, Trump says he'll call Detroit carmakers into his office and lay down an ultimatum: Either move the jobs back to America, or eat a 35 percent tax on every car imported back into the U.S. over the Mexican border.

"I'm a free-trader," he says, "but you can only be a free-trader when something's fair."

It's stuff like this that has conservative pundits from places like the *National Review* bent out of shape. Where, they ask, is the M-F'ing love? What about those conservative principles we've spent decades telling you flyover-country hicks you're supposed to have?

"Trump has also promised to use tariffs to punish companies," wrote David McIntosh in the *Review*'s much-publicized, but not-effective-at-all "Conservatives Against Trump" 22-pundit jihad. "These are not the ideas of a small-government conservative. . . . They are, instead, the ramblings of a liberal wanna-be strongman."

What these tweedy Buckleyites at places like the *Review* don't get is that most people don't give a damn about "conservative principles." Yes, millions of people responded to that rhetoric for years. But that wasn't because of the principle itself, but because it was always coupled with the more effective politics of resentment: Big-government liberals are to blame for your problems.

Elections, like criminal trials, are ultimately always about assigning blame. For a generation, conservative intellectuals have successfully pointed the finger at big-government-loving, whale-hugging liberals as the culprits behind American decline.

But the fact that lots of voters hated the Clintons, Sean Penn, the Dixie Chicks and whomever else, did not, ever, mean that they believed in the principle of Detroit carmakers being able to costlessly move American jobs overseas by the thousands.

"We've got to do something to bring jobs back," says one Trump supporter in Plymouth, when asked why tariffs are suddenly a good idea.

Cheryl Donlon says she heard the tariff message loud and clear and she's fine with it, despite the fact that it clashes with traditional conservatism.

"We need someone who is just going to look at what's best for us," she says.

I mention that Trump's plan is virtually identical to Dick Gephardt's idea from way back in the 1988 Democratic presidential race, to fight the Korean Hyundai import wave with retaliatory tariffs.

Donlon says she didn't like that idea then.

Why not?

"I didn't like him," she says.

Trump, though, she likes. And so do a lot of people. No one should be surprised that he's tearing through the Republican primaries, because everything he's saying about his GOP opponents is true. They really are all stooges on the take, unable to stand up to Trump because they're not even people, but are, like Jeb and Rubio, just robo-babbling representatives of unseen donors.

Back in Manchester, an American Legion hall half-full of bored-looking Republicans nurses beers and knocks billiard balls around, awaiting Iowa winner Ted Cruz. The eely Texan is presumably Trump's most serious threat and would later nudge past Trump in one national poll (dismissed by Trump as conducted by people who "don't like me").

But New Hampshire is a struggle for Cruz. The high point in his entire New England run has been his penchant for reciting scenes from *The Princess Bride*, including the entire Billy Crystal "your friend here is only mostly dead" speech for local station WMUR. The one human thing about Cruz seems to be that his movie impersonations are troublingly solid, a consistent B-plus to A-minus.

But stepping into the human zone for even a few minutes backfired. The actor Mandy Patinkin, who played Inigo Montoya in the film, reacted with horror when he learned Cruz was doing his character's famous line "You killed my father, prepare to die." He accused Cruz of deliberately leaving out the key line in Montoya's speech, after he finally slays the man who killed his father: "I've been in the revenge business for so long, now that it's over, I don't know what to do with the rest of my life."

Patinkin believed Cruz didn't do that line because Cruz is himself in the revenge business, promising to "carpet-bomb [ISIS] into oblivion" and wondering if "sand can glow."

Patinkin's criticism of Cruz cut deeply, especially after the Iowa caucuses, when Cruz was accused by Trump and others of spreading a false rumor that Ben Carson was dropping out, in order to steal evangelical votes and pad his lead.

The unwelcome attention seemed to scare Cruz back into scripted-bot mode, where he's a less-than-enthralling presence. Cruz in person is almost physically repellent. *Psychology Today* even ran an article by a neurology professor named Dr. Richard Cytowic about the peculiarly off-putting qualities of Cruz's face.

He used a German term, *backpfeifengesicht*, literally "a face in need of a good punch," to describe Cruz. This may be overstating things a little. Cruz certainly has an odd face—it looks like someone sewed pieces of a waterlogged Reagan mask together at gunpoint—but it's his tone more than anything that gets you. He speaks slowly and loudly and in the most histrionic language possible, as if he's certain you're too stupid to grasp that *he is for freedom*.

"The . . . Constitution . . . ," he says, "serves . . . as . . . chains . . . to . . . bind . . . the . . . mischief . . . of . . . government. . . ."

Four years ago, a candidate like this would have just continued along this path, serving up piles of euphuistic Tea Party rhetoric for audiences that at the time were still hot for the tricorner-hat explanation of how Comrade Obama ruined the American Eden.

But now, that's not enough. In the age of Trump, the Cruzes of the world also have to be rebels against the "establishment." This requirement makes for some almost unbelievable rhetorical contortions.

"Government," Cruz now ventures, "should not be about redistributing wealth and benefiting the corporations and the special interests."

This absurd Swiss Army cliché perfectly encapsulates the predicament of the modern GOP. In one second, Cruz is against "redistributionism," which in the Obama years was code for "government spending on minorities." In the next second, he's against corporations and special interests, the villains du jour in the age of Bernie Sanders and Trump, respectively.

He's against everything all at once. Welfare! Corporations! Special Interests! Government! The Establishment! He's that escort who'll be into whatever you want, for an hour.

Trump meanwhile wipes out Cruz in his speeches in a single, drop-the-mic line.

"They give Ted $5 million," he says, bringing to mind loans Cruz took from a pair of banks, Goldman Sachs and Citibank.

The total was closer to $1.2 million, but Trump's point, that even the supposed "outsider" GOP candidate is just another mindless payola machine, is impossible to counter.

The unexpectedly thrilling Democratic Party race between Hillary Clinton and Bernie Sanders, too, is breaking just right for Trump. It's exposing deep fissures in the Democratic strategy that Trump is already exploiting.

Every four years, some Democrat who's been a lifelong friend of labor runs for president. And every four years, that Democrat gets thrown over by national labor bosses in favor of some party lifer with his signature on a half-dozen job-exporting free-trade agreements.

It's called "transactional politics," and the operating idea is that workers should back the winner, rather than the most union-friendly candidate.

This year, national leaders of several prominent unions went with Hillary Clinton—who, among other things, supported her husband's efforts to pass NAFTA—over Bernie Sanders. Pissed, the rank and file in many locals revolted. In New Hampshire, for instance, a Service Employees International Union local backed Sanders despite the national union's endorsement of Clinton, as did an International Brotherhood of Electrical Workers chapter.

Trump is already positioning himself to take advantage of the political opportunity afforded him by "transactional politics." He regularly hammers the NAFTA deal in his speeches, applying to it his favorite word, "disaster." And he just as regularly drags Hillary Clinton into his hypothetical tales of job-saving, talking about how she could never talk Detroit carmakers out of moving a factory to Mexico.

Unions have been abused so much by both parties in the past decades that even mentioning themes union members care about instantly grabs the attention of workers. That's true even when it comes from Donald Trump, a man who kicked off the fourth GOP debate saying "wages [are] too high" and who had the guts to tell the *Detroit News* that Michigan autoworkers make too much money.

You will find union members scattered at almost all of Trump's speeches. And there have been rumors of unions nationally considering endorsing Trump. SEIU president Mary Kay Henry even admitted in January that Trump appeals to members because of the "terrible anxiety" they feel about jobs.

"I know guys, union guys, who talk about Trump," says Rand Wilson, an activist from the Labor for Bernie organization. "I try to tell them about Sanders, and they don't know who he is. Or they've just heard he's a socialist. Trump they've heard of."

This is part of a gigantic subplot to the Trump story, which is that many of his critiques of the process are the same ones being made by Bernie Sanders. The two men, of course, are polar opposites in just about every way—Sanders worries about the poor, while Trump would eat a child in a lifeboat—but both are laser-focused on the corrupting role of money in politics.

Both propose "revolutions" to solve the problem, the difference being that Trump's is an authoritarian revolt, while Sanders proposes a democratic one. If it comes down to a Sanders-Trump general election, the matter will probably be decided by which candidate the national press turns on first: the flatulent narcissist with cattle-car fantasies or the Democrat who gently admires Scandinavia. Would you bet your children on that process playing out sensibly?

In the meantime, Trump is cannily stalking the Sanders vote. While the rest of the GOP clowns just roll their eyes at Sanders, going for cheap groans with bits about socialism, Trump goes a different route. He hammers Hillary and compliments Sanders. "I agree with [Sanders] on two things," he says. "On trade, he said we're being ripped off. He just doesn't know how much."

He goes on. "And he's right with Hillary because, look, she's receiving a fortune from a lot of people."

At a Democratic town hall in Derry, New Hampshire, Hillary's strangely pathetic answer about why she accepted $675,000 from Goldman to give speeches—"That's what they offered"—seemed doomed to become a touchstone for the general-election contest. Trump would go out on Day One of that race and blow $675,000 on a pair of sable underwear, or a solid-gold happy-face necktie. And he'd wear it 24 hours a day, just to remind voters that his opponent sold out for the Trump equivalent of lunch money.

Trump will surely argue that the Clintons are the other half of the dissolute-conspiracy story he's been selling, representing a workers' party that abandoned workers and turned the presidency into a vast cash-for-access enterprise, avoiding scrutiny by making Washington into Hollywood East and turning labor leaders and journalists alike into starstruck courtiers. As with everything else, Trump personalizes this, making his stories of buying Hillary's presence at his wedding a part of his stump speech. A race against Hillary Clinton in the general, if it happens, will be a pitch right in Trump's wheelhouse—and if Bill Clinton is complaining about the "vicious" attacks by the campaign of pathological nice guy Bernie Sanders, it's hard to imagine what will happen once they get hit by the Trumpdozer.

The electoral roadshow, that giant ball of corrupt self-importance, gets bigger and more grandiloquent every four years. This time around, there was so much press at the Manchester Radisson, you could have wiped out the entire cable-news industry by detonating a single Ryder truck full of fertilizer.

Like the actual circus, this is a roving business. Cash flows to campaigns from people and donors; campaigns buy ads; ads pay for journalists; journalists assess candidates. Somewhat unsurprisingly, the ever-growing press corps tends in most years to like—or at least deem "most serious"— the candidates who buy the most ads. Nine out of 10 times in America, the candidate who raises the most money wins. And those candidates then owe the most favors.

Meaning that for the pleasure of being able to watch insincere campaign coverage and see manipulative political ads on TV for free, we end up having to pay inflated Medicare drug prices, fund bank bailouts with our taxes, let billionaires pay 17 percent tax rates, and suffer a thousand other indignities. Trump is right: Because Jeb Bush can't afford to make his own commercials, he would go into the White House in the pocket of a drug manufacturer. It really is that stupid.

The triumvirate of big media, big donors and big political parties has until now successfully excluded every challenge to its authority. But like every aristocracy, it eventually got lazy and profligate, too sure it was loved by the people. It's now shocked that voters in depressed ex-factory towns won't keep pulling the lever for "conservative principles," or that union members bitten a dozen times over by a trade deal won't just keep voting Democratic on cue.

Trump isn't the first rich guy to run for office. But he is the first to realize the weakness in the system, which is that the watchdogs in the political media can't resist a car wreck. The more he insults the press, the more they cover him: He's pulling 33 times as much coverage on the major networks as his next-closest GOP competitor, and twice as much as Hillary.

Trump found the flaw in the American Death Star. It doesn't know how to turn the cameras off, even when it's filming its own demise.

The problem, of course, is that Trump is crazy. He's like every other corporate tyrant in that his solution to most things follows the logic of Stalin: no person, no problem. You're fired! Except as president he'd have other people-removing options, all of which he likes: torture, mass deportations, the banning of 23 percent of the Earth's population from entering the United States, etc.

He seems to be coming around to the idea that having an ego smaller than that of, say, an Egyptian Pharaoh would be a sign of weakness. So of late, his already-insane idea to build a "beautiful" wall across the Mexican border has evolved to the point where he also wants the wall to be named after him. He told Maria Bartiromo he wanted to call it the "Great Wall of Trump."

In his mind, it all makes sense. Drugs come from Mexico; the wall will keep out Mexicans; therefore, no more drugs. "We're gonna stop it," he says. "You're not going to have the drugs coming in destroying your children. Your kids are going to look all over the place and they're not going to be able to find them."

Obviously! Because no one's ever tried wide-scale drug prohibition before.

And as bad as our media is, Trump is trying to replace it with a worse model. He excommunicates every reporter who so much as raises an eyebrow at his insanity, leaving him with a small-but-dependable crowd of groveling supplicants who in a Trump presidency would be the royal media. He even waves at them during his speeches.

"Mika and Joe are here!" he chirped at the MSNBC morning hosts at a New Hampshire event. The day after he won the New Hampshire primary, he called in to their show to thank them for being "supporters." To her credit, Mika Brzezinski tried to object to the characterization, interrupting Joe Scarborough, who by then had launched into a minute-long homily about how happy he was to be a bug on the windshield of the Trump phenomenon.

You think the media sucks now? Just wait until reporters have to kiss a brass Trump-sphinx before they enter the White House press room.

"He has all these crazy ideas, and [reporters] are so scared of him, they don't ask him any details," says Michael Pleyte, an Iraq vet who came all the way from Michigan to watch the New Hampshire primary in person. "Forget about A to Z, they don't even ask him to go A to Trump."

King Trump. Brace yourselves, America. It's really happening.

15

March 1, 2016: Revenge of the Simple: How George W. Bush Gave Rise to Donald Trump

Bush was just an appetizer—Trump would be the main course

To hear GOP insiders tell it, Doomsday is here. If Donald Trump scores huge tonight and seizes control of the nomination in the Super Tuesday primaries, it will mark the beginning of the end of the Republican Party, and perhaps the presidency.

But Trump isn't the beginning of the end. George W. Bush was. The amazing anti-miracle of the Bush presidency is what makes today's nightmare possible.

People forget what an extraordinary thing it was that Bush was president. Dubya wasn't merely ignorant when compared with other politicians or other famous people. No, he would have stood out as dumb in just about any setting.

If you could somehow run simulations where Bush was repeatedly shipwrecked on a desert island with 20 other adults chosen at random, he would be the last person listened to by the group every single time. He knew absolutely nothing about anything. He wouldn't have been able to make fire, find water, build shelter or raise morale. It would have taken him days to get over the shock of no room service.

Bush went to the best schools but was totally ignorant of history, philosophy, science, geography, languages and the arts. Asked by a child in South Carolina in 1999 what his favorite book had been growing up, Bush replied, "I can't remember any specific books."

Bush showed no interest in learning and angrily rejected the idea that a president ought to be able to think his way through problems. As Mark Crispin Miller wrote in *The Bush Dyslexicon*, Bush's main rhetorical tool was the tautology—i.e., saying the same thing, only twice.

"It's very important for folks to understand that when there's more trade, there's more commerce" was a classic Bush formulation. "Our nation must come together to unite" was another. One of my favorites was: "I understand that the unrest in the Middle East creates unrest throughout the region."

Academics and political junkies alike giddily compiled these "Bushisms" along with others that were funny for different reasons ("I'm doing what I think what's wrong," for instance).

But Bush's tautologies weren't gaffes or verbal slips. They just represented the limits of his reasoning powers: $A = A$. There are educational apps that use groups of images to teach two-year-olds to recognize that an orange is like an orange while a banana is a banana. Bush was stalled at that developmental moment. And we elected him president.

Bush's eight years were like the reigns of a thousand overwhelmed congenital monarchs from centuries past. While the prince rode horses, romped with governesses and blew the national treasure on britches or hedge-mazes, the state was run by Svengalis and Rasputins who dealt with what Bush once derisively described as "what's happening in the world."

In Bush's case he had Karl "Turd Blossom" Rove thinking out the problem of how to get re-elected, while Dick "Vice" Cheney, Donald "Rummy" Rumsfeld and Andrew "Tangent Man" Card took care of the day-to-day affairs of the country (part of Card's responsibilities involved telling Bush what was in the newspapers he refused to read).

It took hundreds of millions of dollars and huge armies of such behind-the-throne puppet-masters to twice (well, maybe twice) sell a voting majority on the delusion of George Bush, president. Though people might quibble with the results, the scale of this as a purely political achievement was awesome and heroic, comparable to a moon landing or the splitting of the atom.

Guiding Bush the younger through eight years of public appearances was surely the greatest coaching job in history. It was like teaching a donkey to play the Waldstein Sonata. It's breathtaking to think about now.

But one part of it backfired. Instead of using an actor like Reagan to sell policies to the public, the Svengalis behind Bush sold him as an authentic man of the people, the guy you'd want to have an O'Doul's with.

Rove correctly guessed that a generation of watching TV and Hollywood movies left huge blocs of Americans convinced that people who read books, looked at paintings and cared about spelling were either serial killers or scheming to steal bearer bonds from the Nakatomi building. (Even knowing what a bearer bond is was villainous.)

The hero in American culture, meanwhile, was always a moron with a big gun who learned everything he needed to know from cowboy movies. The climax of pretty much every action movie from the mid-Eighties on involved shotgunning the smarty-pants villain in the face before he could finish some fruity speech about whatever.

Rove sold Bush as that hero. He didn't know anything, but dammit, he was sure about what he didn't know. He was John McClane, and Al Gore was Hans Gruber. GOP flacks like Rove rallied the whole press corps around that narrative, to the point where anytime Gore tried to nail Bush down on a point of policy, pundits blasted him for being a smug know-it-all using wonk-ese to talk over our heads—as Cokie Roberts put it once, "this guy from Washington doing Washington-speak."

This is like the scene from the increasingly prophetic *Idiocracy* where no one can understand Luke Wilson, a person of average intelligence rocketed 500 years into America's idiot future, because whenever he tries to reason with people, they think he's talking "like a fag."

The Roves of the world used Bush's simplicity to win the White House. Once they got there, they used the levers of power to pillage and scheme like every other gang of rapacious politicians ever. But the plan was never to make ignorance a political principle. It was just a ruse to win office.

Now the situation is the opposite. Now GOP insiders are frantic at the prospect of an uncultured ignoramus winning the presidency. A group of major donors and GOP strategists even wrote out a memo outlining why a super PAC dedicated to stopping Trump was needed.

"We want voters to imagine Donald Trump in the Big Chair in the Oval Office, with responsibilities for worldwide confrontation at his fingertips," they wrote. Virginia Republican congressman Scott Ringell wrote an open letter to fellow Republicans arguing that a Trump presidency would be "reckless, embarrassing and ultimately dangerous."

Hold on. It wasn't scary to imagine George "Is our children learning?" Bush with the "responsibilities for worldwide confrontation" at his fingertips? It wasn't embarrassing to have a president represent the U.S. on the diplomatic stage who called people from Kosovo "Kosovians" and people from Greece "Grecians"?

It was way worse. Compared to Bush, Donald Trump is a Rutherford or an Einstein. In the same shipwreck scenario, Trump would have all sorts of ideas—all wrong, but at least he'd think of something, instead of staring at the sand waiting for a hotel phone to rise out of it.

Of course, Trump's ignorance level, considering his Wharton education, is nearly as awesome as what Bush accomplished in spite of Yale. In fact, unlike Bush, who had the decency to not even try to understand the news, Trump reads all sorts of crazy things and believes them all. From theories about vaccines causing autism to conspiratorial questions about the pillow on Antonin Scalia's face to Internet legends about Americans using bullets dipped in pigs' blood to shoot Muslims, there isn't any absurd idea Donald Trump isn't willing to entertain, so long as it fits in with his worldview.

But Washington is freaking out about Trump in a way

they never did about Bush. Why? Because Bush was their moron, while Trump is his own moron. That's really what it comes down to.

And all of the Beltway's hooting and hollering about how "embarrassing" and "dangerous" Trump is will fall on deaf ears, because as gullible as Americans can be, they're smart enough to remember being told that it was OK to vote for George Bush, a man capable of losing at tic-tac-toe.

We're about to enter a dark period in the history of the American experiment. The Founding Fathers never imagined an electorate raised on *Toddlers and Tiaras* and *Temptation Island*. Remember, just a few decades ago, shows like *Married With Children* and *Roseanne* were satirical parodies. Now the audience can't even handle that much irony. A lot of American culture is just dumb slobs cheering on other dumb slobs. It was inevitable, once we broke the seal with Bush, that our politics would become the same thing.

Madison and Jefferson never foresaw this situation. They knew there was danger of demagoguery, but they never imagined presidential candidates exchanging "mine's bigger than yours" jokes or doing "let's laugh at the disabled" routines. There's no map in the Constitution to tell us how to get out of where we're going. All we can do now is hold on.

16

March 25, 2016: Why Young People Are Right About Hillary Clinton

Listening to the youth vote doesn't always
lead to disaster

I WAS DISAPPOINTED TO HEAR THAT *ROLLING STONE* HAD
endorsed Hillary Clinton, but I also understood. In many
ways, the endorsement by my boss and editor, Jann Wenner,
read like the result of painful soul-searching, after this very
magazine had a profound influence on a similar race, back
in 1972.

Jann explains this eloquently in "Hillary Clinton for
President":

"*Rolling Stone* has championed the 'youth vote' since 1972,
when 18-year-olds were first given the right to vote. The
Vietnam War was a fact of daily life then, and Sen. George
McGovern, the liberal anti-war activist from South Dakota,

became the first vessel of young Americans, and Hunter S. Thompson wrote our first presidential-campaign coverage. We worked furiously for McGovern. We failed; Nixon was re-elected in a landslide."

The failure of George McGovern had a major impact on a generation of Democrats, who believed they'd faced a painful reality about the limits of idealism in American politics. Jann sums it up: "Those of us there learned a very clear lesson: America chooses its presidents from the middle, not from the ideological wings."

But it would be a shame if we disqualified every honest politician, or forever disavowed the judgment of young people, just because George McGovern lost an election four decades ago.

That '72 loss hovered like a raincloud over the Democrats until Bill Clinton came along. He took the White House using a formula engineered by a think tank, the Democratic Leadership Council, that was created in response to losses by McGovern and Walter Mondale.

The new strategy was a party that was socially liberal but fiscally conservative. It counterattacked Richard Nixon's Southern Strategy, a racially themed appeal to disaffected whites Nixon tabbed the "Silent Majority," by subtly taking positions against the Democrats' own left flank.

In 1992 and in 1996, Clinton recaptured some of Nixon's territory through a mix of populist positions (like a middle-class tax cut) and the "triangulating" technique of pushing back against the Democrats' own liberal legacy on issues like welfare, crime and trade.

And that was the point. No more McGoverns. The chief moral argument of the Clinton revolution was not about striving for an end to the war or poverty or racism or inequality, but keeping the far worse Republicans out of power.

The new Democratic version of idealism came in a package called "transactional politics." It was about getting the best deal possible given the political realities, which we were led to believe were hopelessly stacked against the hopes and dreams of the young.

In fact, it was during Bill Clinton's presidency that D.C. pundits first began complaining about a thing they called "purity." This was code for any politician who stood too much on principle. *The American Prospect* in 1995 derisively described it as an "unwillingness to share the burden of morally ambiguous compromise." Sometimes you had to budge a little for the sake of progress.

Jann describes this in the context of saluting the value of "incremental politics" and solutions that "stand a chance of working." The implication is that even when young people believe in the right things, they often don't realize what it takes to get things done.

But I think they do understand. Young people have repudiated the campaign of Hillary Clinton in overwhelming and historic fashion, with Bernie Sanders winning under-30 voters by consistently absurd margins, as high as 80 to 85 percent in many states. He has done less well with young African-American voters, but even there he's seen some gains as time has gone on. And the energy coming from the pre-middle-aged has little to do with an inability to appreciate political reality.

Instead, the millions of young voters that are rejecting Hillary's campaign this year are making a carefully reasoned, even reluctant calculation about the limits of the insider politics both she and her husband have represented.

For young voters, the foundational issues of our age have been the Iraq invasion, the financial crisis, free trade, mass incarceration, domestic surveillance, police brutality, debt and income inequality, among others.

And to one degree or another, the modern Democratic Party, often including Hillary Clinton personally, has been on the wrong side of virtually all of these issues.

Hillary not only voted for the Iraq War, but offered a succession of ridiculous excuses for her vote. Remember, this was one of the easiest calls ever. A child could see that the Bush administration's fairy tales about WMDs and Iraqi drones spraying poison over the capital (where were they going to launch from, Martha's Vineyard?) were just that, fairy tales.

Yet Hillary voted for the invasion for the same reason many other mainstream Democrats did: They didn't want to be tagged as McGovernite peaceniks. The new Democratic Party refused to be seen as being too anti-war, even at the cost of supporting a wrong one.

It was a classic "we can't be too pure" moment. Hillary gambled that Democrats would understand that she'd outraged conscience and common sense for the sake of the Democrats' electoral viability going forward. As a mock-Hillary in a 2007 *Saturday Night Live* episode put it, "Democrats know me. . . . They know my support for the Iraq War has always been insincere."

This pattern, of modern Democrats bending so far back to preserve what they believe is their claim on the middle that they end up plainly in the wrong, has continually repeated itself.

Take the mass incarceration phenomenon. This was pioneered in Mario Cuomo's New York and furthered under Bill Clinton's presidency, which authorized more than $16 billion for new prisons and more police in a crime bill.

As *The New Jim Crow* author Michelle Alexander noted, America when Bill Clinton left office had the world's highest incarceration rate, with a prison admission rate for black drug inmates that was 23 times 1983 levels. Hillary stumped for that crime bill, adding the Reaganesque observation that inner-city criminals were "super-predators" who needed to be "brought to heel."

You can go on down the line of all these issues. Trade? From NAFTA to the TPP, Hillary and her party cohorts have consistently supported these anti-union free trade agreements, until it became politically inexpedient. Debt? Hillary infamously voted for regressive bankruptcy reform just a few years after privately meeting with Elizabeth Warren and agreeing that such industry-driven efforts to choke off debt relief needed to be stopped.

Then of course there is the matter of the great gobs of money Hillary has taken to give speeches to Goldman Sachs and God knows whom else. Her answer about that—"That's what they offered"—gets right to the heart of what young people find so repugnant about this brand of politics.

One can talk about having the strength to get things done, given the political reality of the times. But one also can become too easily convinced of certain political realities, particularly when they're paying you hundreds of thousands of dollars an hour.

Is Hillary really doing the most good that she can do, fighting for the best deal that's there to get for ordinary people?

Or is she just doing something that satisfies her own definition of that, while taking tens of millions of dollars from some of the world's biggest jerks?

I doubt even Hillary Clinton could answer that question. She has been playing the inside game for so long, she seems to have become lost in it. She behaves like a person who often doesn't know what the truth is, but instead merely reaches for what is the best answer in that moment, not realizing the difference.

This is why her shifting explanations and flippant attitude about the email scandal are almost more unnerving than the ostensible offense. She seems confident that just because her detractors are politically motivated, as they always have been, that they must be wrong, as they often were.

But that's faulty thinking. My worry is that Democrats like Hillary have been saying, "The Republicans are worse!" for so long that they've begun to believe it excuses everything. It makes me nervous to see Hillary supporters like law professor Stephen Vladeck arguing in the *New York Times* that the real problem wasn't anything Hillary did, but that the Espionage Act isn't "practical."

If you're willing to extend the "purity" argument to the *Espionage Act*, it's only a matter of time before you get in real trouble. And even if it doesn't happen this summer, Democrats may soon wish they'd picked the frumpy senator from Vermont who probably checks his restaurant bills to make sure he hasn't been *under*charged.

But in the age of Trump, winning is the only thing that matters, right? In that case, there's plenty of evidence suggesting Sanders would perform better against a reality TV free-coverage machine like Trump than would Hillary

Clinton. This would largely be due to the passion and energy of young voters.

Young people don't see the Sanders-Clinton race as a choice between idealism and incremental progress. The choice they see is between an honest politician, and one who is so profoundly a part of the problem that she can't even see it anymore.

They've seen in the last decades that politicians who promise they can deliver change while also taking the money, mostly just end up taking the money.

And they're voting for Sanders because his idea of an entirely voter-funded electoral "revolution" that bars corporate money is, no matter what its objective chances of success, the only practical road left to break what they perceive to be an inexorable pattern of corruption.

Young people aren't dreaming. They're thinking. And we should listen to them.

17

May 18, 2016: RIP, GOP: How Trump's Campaign Is Killing the Republican Party

Donald Trump crushed 16 GOP opponents
in one of the most appalling, vicious campaigns
in history. His next victim? The entire
Republican Party

INDIANAPOLIS, INDIANA, MAY 3RD, 2016, A LITTLE BEFORE
8:30 p.m. Texas Sen. Ted Cruz strode onstage beneath a
gorgeous stained-glass relief in the city's Union Station.
The hall was doubling as a swanky bar for an upscale local
hotel, and much of the assembled press was both lubricated
and impatient. The primary had been called for Donald
Trump more than an hour before. What was the holdup?

"God bless the Hoosier State!" Cruz said to whoops and
cheers after he finally emerged. He was surrounded by a
phalanx of American flags, family members and his gimmick running mate of six and a half days, Carly Fiorina,

who stared out at the crowd with her trademark alien-abducted smile.

Cruz glanced back and forth across the room with that odd, neckless, monitor-lizard posture of his. He had to know the import of this moment. Nothing less than the future of the Republican Party had been at stake in the Indiana primary.

A Cruz loss effectively meant ceding control of the once-mighty organization to Trump, a seemingly unrepentant non-Republican more likely to read *Penthouse* than the *National Review*.

Before the vote, Cruz put it this way: "We are at the edge of a cliff, staring downward."

Now, Cruz was over that cliff, having been trounced 53 to 36 percent in his last-gasp effort to keep Trump from the nomination. In a detail the film-buff candidate Cruz would appreciate, he left Indiana with the same number of delegates as future senator John Blutarsky's grade-point average in *Animal House*: zero-point-zero.

Still, Cruz looked like he was ready for the "Was it over when the Germans bombed Pearl Harbor?" speech. He was going to fight.

"Will we hold fast to our founding values of rewarding talent, hard work and industry?" he asked. "Or will we continue on that path of creeping socialism that incentivizes apathy and dependency?"

The crowd roared.

"Will we keep America safe from the threats of nuclear war and atomic terrorism?" he thundered. "Or will we pass on to future generations a land devastated and destroyed by the enemies of civilization?"

More raucous cheers.

Cruz smiled. If he has a good quality, it is that he's not easily deterred by criticism. As he took the stage that night, he surely knew that former Speaker of the House John Boehner had recently called him "Lucifer in the flesh," and that fellow senator Lindsey Graham had said, "If you kill Ted Cruz on the floor of the Senate, and the trial was in the Senate, nobody could convict you." Likewise, when it was revealed Cruz once stated that one has no inherent right to "stimulate one's genitals," his college roommate Craig Mazin popped up to call him a hypocrite who'd whacked it plenty in college.

During the campaign, surprising numbers of Americans were even willing to believe Cruz might also be the Zodiac Killer. The infamous Bay Area murders began two years before Cruz was born, but 38 percent of Floridians at one point believed Cruz either was or might be the Zodiac.

Were they serious? In an age when Donald Trump is a presidential nominee, what does "serious" even mean? In any case, the cybercomics who fanned the flames of the Cruz-Zodiac meme will someday be first-ballot entrants in the Trolling Hall of Fame.

Finally, on the morning of the Indiana primary, Cruz woke up to hear opponent Trump babbling that Cruz's own father had been hanging out with Lee Harvey Oswald before the assassination of John F. Kennedy, a bizarre take on a ridiculous *National Enquirer* story that Trump, of course, believed instantly. Trump brought this up on *Fox and Friends*, which let him run the ball all the way to the end zone. "I mean, what was he doing with Lee Harvey Oswald, shortly before the death—before the shooting?" Trump asked. "It's horrible."

American politics had never seen anything like this: a presidential candidate derided as a haggardly masturbating incarnation of Satan, the son of a presidential assassin's accomplice, and himself an infamous uncaptured serial killer.

Despite the media humiliations, Cruz talked passionately of his supporters' resolve. "Just a few days ago, two young kids, ages four and six, handed me two envelopes full of change," he said. "All of their earnings from their lemonade stand. They wanted the campaign to have it."

The crowd cooed: *Awwww!* There was no way he could quit now and let those kids down. Except that moments later, Cruz did just that, announcing he was suspending his campaign because "the path to victory has been foreclosed." Then he fled the stage like he was double-parked.

The air vanished from the ballroom. Cruz supporters went nuts.

Nooooo! they screamed, hugging each other and crying. Many volunteers were from faraway states. They expected to be continuing on somewhere the next morning. Now they were all basically fired.

"What the fuck do we do now?" whispered one.

The pundits present were less emotional. "Does he get to use the lemonade money to pay campaign debts?" wondered one.

As ignominious an end as this was for Cruz, it was a million times worse for the Republican establishment.

The party of Nixon, Reagan and two Bushes had needed a win by Cruz, a man not just disliked but loathed by the party elite, to stave off a takeover by Trump.

And yet Cruz's main pitch to his voters had been that between himself and Trump, he was the one less connected to the Republican Party. "Cruz is the true outsider" was how one supporter put it in Indiana.

Cruz volunteer Dan Porter seemed stunned with grief

after the results came in, but his sadness was reserved for Cruz, not the Republican Party. He couldn't seem to wrap his head around the fact that so many people had voted for Trump, a man who'd "been a Democrat his whole life," while a dedicated constitutionalist like Cruz had been so roundly rejected.

So lost in thought that he stared at the carpet as he spoke, he gave just an incidental shake of the head when asked what the future of the GOP would be now. It was as if the question wasn't even that important.

"Oh, there won't be a Republican Party," he said. "It's basically over."

Cruz had at least won nearly 600 delegates and had passionate supporters shedding real tears for him at the end. But nobody anywhere was crying for the Republican Party. Even Custer had a less-lonely last stand.

Trump, meanwhile, spent the night basking in voluble self-admiration from Trump Tower in New York. This is becoming his victory ritual. The lectern from which he spoke said it all: TRUMP—VICTORY IN INDIANA—NEW YORK CITY.

Trump's naked disdain for the less-glamorous American flyover provinces he somehow keeps winning by massive margins continued to be one of the livelier comic subplots of the campaign.

From seemingly wondering if Iowans had eaten too much genetically modified corn to thanking the "poorly educated" after his Nevada win, Trump increasingly doesn't bother to even pretend to pander. This, too, is a major departure for the Republican Party, whose Beltway imageers for decades made pretending to sincerely prefer barns and trailers to nightclubs and spokesmodels a central part of their electoral strategy.

Not Trump. Hell, he went out of his way to brag about being pals with Tom Brady in the week before the Indiana primary, and still won by almost 20 points. Given the level of Colts-Patriots antipathy, this is a little like campaigning in Louisiana wearing a BP hat, or doing a whistle-stop tour through Waco with Janet Reno.

After his crushing win, Trump gave a breathless victory speech. It was classic Trump. "The people of Indiana have been incredible," he said. "I campaigned and I made lots of speeches and met lots of incredible people . . . You don't get better. The crowds got bigger and bigger . . . I didn't want to leave . . . We had a tremendous victory tonight . . . Boy, Bobby Knight was incredible."

He had a few choice words for the GOP leadership. "I want to thank and congratulate the Republican National Committee, and Reince Priebus," he croaked, as his heavily-made-up, Robert Palmer–chicks collection of wives and daughters twisted faintly in a deadpan chorus behind him.

"It is not an easy job, when you have 17 egos," Trump went on, smiling. "And now I guess he's down to one."

The crowd roared. The RNC had kissed Trump's ring. That was it, right there, the death of the modern Republican Party.

After 9/11, it felt like the Republicans would reign in America for a thousand years. Only a year ago, this was still a party that appeared to be on the rise nationally, having gained 13 Senate seats, 69 House seats, 11 governorships and 913 state legislative seats during the Obama presidency.

Now the party was effectively dead as a modern political force, doomed to go the way of the Whigs or the Free-Soilers.

After Indiana, a historic chasm opened in the ranks of the party. The two former President Bushes, along with

Mitt Romney, announced they wouldn't attend Trump's coronation at the convention in Cleveland. Additionally, House Speaker Paul Ryan refused to say he would support the nominee.

There were now two Republican Parties. One, led by Trump, was triumphant at the ballot, rapidly accruing party converts, and headed to Cleveland for what, knowing the candidate, was sure to be the *yuugest*, most obscene, most joyfully tacky tribute to a single person ever seen in the television age. If the convention isn't Liberace meets Stalin meets Vince McMahon, it'll be a massive disappointment.

From there, this Republican Party would steam toward the White House, which, who knows, it might even win.

The other Republican Party was revealed in the end to be a surprisingly small collection of uptight lawyers, financiers and Beltway intellectuals who'd just seen their chosen candidate, the $100 million Jeb Bush, muster all of four delegates in the presidential race. Meanwhile, candidates whose talking points involved the beheading of this same party establishment were likely to win around 2,000.

Like French aristocrats after 1789, those Republicans may now head into something like foreign exile to plot their eventual return. But whether they will be guillotined or welcomed back is an open question.

This was all because they'd misplayed the most unpredictable and certainly most ridiculous presidential-campaign season Americans had ever seen.

On the one hand, they'd been blindsided by Trump, a foulmouthed free-coverage magnet who impulsively decided to make mocking the Republican Party mullahs his pet project for the years 2015–2016.

But they were also undone by a surge of voter anger that

was in significant part their own fault. In recent years, the Koch brothers/Tea Party wing of the GOP had purged all moderates from the party, to the point where anyone who was on record supporting the continued existence of any federal agency, said Mexicans were people, or spoke even theoretically about the utility of taxes was drummed from the candidate rolls.

Their expected endgame here was probably supposed to be the ascension of some far-right, anti-tax, anti-government radical like Scott Walker, or even Cruz.

Instead, this carefully cultivated "throw the bums out" vibe was gluttonously appropriated by Trump, who turned the anger against the entire Republican Party before surging to victory on a strongman's platform of giant walls, mass deportation and extravagant job promises that made the moon landing or the Bernie Sanders agenda of free college look incrementalist in comparison.

One could say this was just a calamitous strategic misread on the part of the Koch-brothers types. But another way to look at it is that this was the inevitable consequence of the basic dynamic of the party, which by the end was little more than a collection plate for global business interests that were, if not foreign exactly, certainly nationless.

There was a time in this country—and many voters in places like Indiana and Michigan and Pennsylvania are old enough to remember it—when business leaders felt a patriotic responsibility to protect American jobs and communities. Mitt Romney's father, George, was such a leader, deeply concerned about the city of Detroit, where he built AMC cars.

But his son Mitt wasn't. That sense of noblesse oblige disappeared somewhere during the past generation, when the newly global employer class cut regular working stiffs loose, forcing them to compete with billions of foreigners without rights or political power who would eat toxic waste for five cents a day.

Then they hired politicians and intellectuals to sell the peasants in places like America on why this was the natural order of things. Unfortunately, the only people fit for this kind of work were mean, traitorous scum, the kind of people who in the military are always eventually bayoneted by their own troops. This is what happened to the Republicans, and even though the cost was a potential Trump presidency, man, was it something to watch.

If this isn't the end for the Republican Party, it'll be a shame. They dominated American political life for 50 years and were never anything but monsters. They bred in their voters the incredible attitude that Republicans were the only people within our borders who raised children, loved their country, died in battle or paid taxes. They even sullied the word "American" by insisting they were the only real ones. They preferred Lubbock to Paris, and their idea of an intellectual was Newt Gingrich. Their leaders, from Ralph Reed to Bill Frist to Tom DeLay to Rick Santorum to Romney and Ryan, were an interminable assembly line of shrieking, witch-hunting celibates, all with the same haircut—the kind of people who thought Iran-Contra was nothing, but would grind the affairs of state to a halt over a blow job or Terri Schiavo's feeding tube.

A century ago, the small-town American was Gary Cooper: tough, silent, upright and confident. The modern Republican Party changed that person into a haranguing neurotic who couldn't make it through a dinner without quizzing you about your politics. They destroyed the American character. No hell is hot enough for them. And when

Trump came along, they rolled over like the weaklings they've always been, bowing more or less instantly to his parodic show of strength.

In the weeks surrounding Cruz's cat-fart of a surrender in Indiana, party luminaries began the predictably Soviet process of coalescing around the once-despised new ruler. Trump endorsements of varying degrees of sincerity spilled in from the likes of Dick Cheney, Bob Dole, Mitch McConnell and even John McCain.

Having not recently suffered a revolution or a foreign-military occupation, Americans haven't seen this phenomenon much, but the effortless treason of top-tier Republicans once Trump locked up the nomination was the most predictable part of this story. Politicians, particularly this group, are like crackheads: You can get them to debase themselves completely for whatever's in your pocket, even if it's just lint.

That's why the first rule of any revolution is to wipe out the intellectuals. Trump is surely already dreaming of the vast logging camp he will fill with the Republican thinkfluencers who are at the moment making a show of being the last holdouts.

Not surprisingly, in the past weeks, there was an epidemic of Monday-morning quarterbacking among the Beltway punditocracy, as GOP cognoscenti struggled to cope with the reality of Trumpism.

There were basically two responses among the tie-and-glasses sect of Republicans to the prospect of kneeling before the philistine Trump: In the minority stood *New York Times* lonely-hearts moralist David Brooks, who took the remarkable step of looking at Trump's victories and wondering what part of this unraveling could be his own fault.

In Brooks-ian fashion, this essentially noble response came out as painful pretentious comedy. He concluded that the problem was that upper-crust conservatives like himself hadn't spent enough time getting to know the dirtier folks below decks.

Instead of "spending large chunks of my life in the bourgeois strata," Brooks promised to "go out into the pain" and "build a ladder of hope" by leaping across "chasms of segmentation."

Translated into English, this might have meant anything from trying the occasional domestic beer to actually hanging around the unemployed. But at least Brooks recognized that on some level, the rise of Trump pointed to a connection failure in the Republican kingmaking class.

No others among his conservative brethren saw it that way. Most Republican intellectuals recoiled in blameless horror from the Trumpening, blaming everything from media bias to the educational system for his rise. Some even promised to degrade themselves with a vote for Hillary Clinton before ever supporting Trump.

George Will of the *Washington Post* might have been the loudest objector. Will increasingly seems like a man who is sure history will remember him for his heroic opposition to Trump, and not for those 40-plus years of being an insufferable spinster who writes bad columns about baseball to prove his ties to the common man.

His diatribes against Trump, a "coarse character" who reads the *National Enquirer* and brags about the size of his "penis" (one could almost feel the pain it caused Will to have to commit this word to paper), took on an almost religious character.

Just before Indiana, Will began treating the nomina-

tion of Trump like a forest fire or a SARS outbreak, something that with the right spirit of sacrifice could be contained
with minimal loss of life, and perhaps only four years of a
Hillary presidency.

"If Trump is nominated," Will wrote, "Republicans
working to purge him and his manner from public life will
reap the considerable satisfaction of preserving the identity
of their 162-year-old party."

But the crowning effort on the right-wing snobbery
front came from none other than British blogging icon and
noted hairy person Andrew Sullivan. The aforementioned
came out of semiretirement to write a 7,000-word jeremiad
for *New York* magazine about how Trump was the inevitable
product of too much democracy.

The CliffsNotes summary of his monstrous piece, "Democracies End When They Are Too Democratic," might
go something like this: When I read Plato in grad school, I
learned that in free societies the mob eventually stops defer-
ring to the wisdom of smart people, and therefore must be
muzzled before they send Trump to wash the streets with
our blood.

Sullivan's analysis was a balm to the decades of butthurt that await the soon-to-be-ex-elite of the Republican
Party. It blamed Trump's rise on everyone but Republican
intellectuals: Obama, Black Lives Matter and even "the gay
left, for whom the word 'magnanimity' seems unknown."

"A struggling white man in the heartland is now told to
'check his privilege' by students at Ivy League colleges,"
Sullivan wrote, in a sentence that would probably be true
enough, if those two groups ever interacted. Sullivan was
right that white conservatives in places like Indiana hate Ivy

Leaguers and Black Lives Matter and the gay left and safe-spacers and feminists and all the other mocking, sneering, atheistic know-it-all types from cosmopolitan cities who scoff, as Obama famously did once, at their guns and their religion.

But they also hated all of those people eight years ago, 16 years ago, 30 years ago. What's new about the Year of Trump is that they have now also suddenly turned on their own party. Why?

Sullivan basically ignored this question. The closest he came to an explanation was a passage saying that "global economic forces" hurt blue-collar workers in particular, forcing them to compete with lots of other unskilled and basically fungible human beings around the world. Which made them, he guessed, pissed off.

This avalanche of verbose disgust on the part of conservative intellectuals toward the Trump voter, who until very recently was the Republican voter, tells us everything we need to know about what actually happened in 2016.

There never was any real connection between the George Wills, Andrew Sullivans and David Brookses and the gun-toting, Jesus-loving ex-middle-class voters they claimed to embrace. All those intellectuals ever did for Middle America was cook up a sales pitch designed to get them to vote for politicians who would instantly betray them to business interests eager to ship their jobs off to China and India. The most successful trick was linking the corporate mantra of profit without responsibility to the concept of individual liberty.

Into the heartland were sent wave after wave of politicians, each more strident and freedom-y than the last. They arrived draped in the flag, spewed patriotic bromides about God, guns and small-town values, and pledged to give the liberals hell and bring the pride back.

Then they went off to Washington and year after year did absolutely squat for their constituents. They were excellent at securing corporate tax holidays and tax cuts for the rich, but they almost never returned to voter country with jobs in hand. Instead, they brought an ever-increasing list of villains responsible for the lack of work: communists, bra-burning feminists, black "race hustlers," climate-change activists, Muslims, Hollywood, horned owls . . .

By the Tea Party era, their candidates were forced to point fingers at their own political establishment for votes, since after so many years of bitter economic decline, that was the only story they could still believably sell.

This led to the hilarious irony of Ted Cruz. Here was a quintessentially insipid GOP con man culled straight from the halls of Princeton, Harvard, the Supreme Court, the Federal Trade Commission and the National Republican Senatorial Committee to smooth-talk the yokels. But through a freak accident of history, he came along just when the newest models of his type were selling "the Republican establishment sucks" as an electoral strategy.

Cruz was like an android that should have self-destructed in a cloud of sparks and black smoke the moment the switch flipped on. He instead stayed on just long enough to win 564 delegates, a stunning testament to just how much Republican voters, in the end, hated the Republican kingmakers Cruz robotically denounced.

All of these crazy contradictions came to a head in Indiana, where Cruz succumbed in an explosion of hate and scorn. The cascade started the Sunday night before the primary, with a Cruz stump speech in La Porte that couldn't have gone worse.

Things went sideways as Cruz was working his way into a "simple flat tax" spiel, a standard Republican snake-oil proposal in which all corporate, estate and gift taxes would be eliminated, and replaced with a 10 percent flat tax and a 16 percent consumption tax. Not because the rich would pay less and the poor would pay more, but because America and fairness, etc. He was just getting to his beloved money line, claiming, "We can fill out our taxes on a postcard," when a 12-year-old boy interrupted with cries of "You suck!" and "I don't care!"

Cruz couldn't quite handle the pressure and stepped straight into the man-trap the moment presented. He lectured the kid about respecting his elders, then suggested the world might be a better place if someone had taught a young Donald Trump that lesson. It was a not-half-bad line of the type that the Harvard lawyer is occasionally capable. But Cruz couldn't help himself and added, "You know, in my household, when a child behaves that way, they get a spanking."

Boom! Within hours the Internet was filled with headlines about how Ted Cruz had suggested spanking someone else's 12-year-old for telling him he sucked.

This was on top of the ignominy of having already called a basketball hoop a "ring" while giving a speech on the gym floor in Knightstown, the home of the fictional Hickory team from *Hoosiers*. No American male would call a basketball hoop a ring, and even a French immigrant would know better than to do so in Indiana, but this was the kind of run he was on.

The rest of the race was a slapstick blowout. Carly Fiorina fell off a stage, and Cruz's wife, Heidi, actually had to answer a question from a Yahoo! reporter about her husband being called the Zodiac Killer. Heidi Cruz calmly responded that she'd been married to Ted for 15 years and "I know pretty well who he is." This, of course, was exactly what the wife of the actual Zodiac Killer would say, making for a perfectly absurd ending to a doomed campaign.

As anyone who's ever been to high school knows, there's no answer to "You suck!" When a bully pulls that line on you, it's because he can smell the weakness: the Jonas Brothers album in your closet, your good grades, your mantleful of band-camp participation trophies, whatever. When the mob smells unorthodoxy, there's no talking your way out of it. You just have to hold on for dear life.

Trump has turned the new Republican Party into high school. It will be cruel, clique-y and ruled by insult kings like himself and Ann Coulter, whose headline description of Cruz ("Tracy Flick With a Dick") will always resonate with Trump voters more than a thousand George Will columns.

And anyone who crosses the leader from now on will be fair game for the kind of brutal fragging Cruz and his circle experienced in Indiana. Dissenters will be buried under a cannonade of abuse coming from everywhere: Trump, other politicians, reporters, Internet memers, 12-year-olds, everyone. Add tough economic times to the Internet, and this is what you get: Nationalist High.

Indiana was the end of an era. As Fiorina moved through a pancake house on primary morning, her supporters meekly bowed and curtseyed as though she were the Queen Mother, calling her ma'am and showing off the small-town civility and churchy hospitality that was once a defining characteristic of Republican campaign-trail events. In the

Trump era, this seems likely to be replaced forever by the testosterone-fueled diss-fests that had undone Cruz in this state.

"People don't care about civility anymore," said Cruz supporter Julie Reimann with a sigh. "It's another sad state of affairs, and when you see it across the Midwest and in our small towns, it's like, 'What has happened to us? Why are we so mean?' "

The real question might be, "Why weren't we meaner before?"

Politics at its most basic isn't a Princeton debating society. It's a desperate battle over who gets what. But during the past 50 years, when there was a vast shift in the distribution of wealth in this country, when tens of millions of people were put out of good, dignified jobs and into humiliating ones, America's elections remained weirdly civil, Queensberry-rules reality shows full of stilted TV debates over issues like abortion, gay marriage and the estate tax.

As any journalist who's ever covered a miners' strike or a foreclosure court will report, things get physically tense when people are forced to fight for their economic lives. Yet Trump's campaign has been the first to unleash that menacing feel during a modern presidential race.

Some, or maybe a lot of it, is racial resentment. But much of it has to be long-delayed anger over the way things have been divvied up over the years. The significance of Trump's wall idea, apart from its bluntly racist appeal as a barrier to nonwhite people, is that it redefines the world in terms of a clear Us and Them, with politicians directly responsible for Us.

It's a plain rebuttal to the Sullivan explanation for why nobody between the coasts has a decent job anymore, i.e., that there are "global economic forces" at work that we can no more change than we can the weather. Trump's solutions are preposterous, logistically impossible and ideologically vicious, but he's giving people a promise more concrete than "tax cuts will stimulate growth that will eventually bring jobs back." He's peddling hope, and with hope comes anger.

Of course, Trump is more likely than not to crash the car now that he has the wheel. News reports surfaced that Donald Trump, unhinged pig, was about to be replaced by Donald Trump, respectable presidential candidate. No more schoolyard insults!

Trump went along with this plan for a few days. But soon after Indiana, he started public fights with old pal Joe Scarborough and former opponents Graham and Bush, the latter for backtracking on a reported pledge to support the Republican nominee. "Bush signed a pledge . . . while signing it, he fell asleep," Trump cracked.

Then he began his general-election pivot with about 10 million tweets directed at "crooked Hillary." With all this, Trump emphasized that the GOP was now mainly defined by whatever was going through his head at any given moment. The "new GOP" seems doomed to swing back and forth between its nationalist message and its leader's tubercular psyche. It isn't a party, it's a mood.

Democrats who might be tempted to gloat over all of this should check themselves. If the Hillary Clintons and Harry Reids and Gene Sperlings of the world don't look at what just happened to the Republicans as a terrible object lesson in the perils of prioritizing billionaire funders over voters, then they too will soon enough be tossed in the trash like a tick.

It almost happened this year, when the supporters of

Bernie Sanders nearly made it over the wall. Totally different politicians with completely different ideas about civility and democracy, Sanders and Trump nonetheless keyed in on the same widespread disgust over the greed and cynicism of the American political class.

From the Walter Mondale years on, Democrats have eaten from the same trough as Republicans. They've grown fat off cash from behemoths like Cisco, Pfizer, Exxon Mobil, Citigroup, Goldman and countless others, companies that moved jobs overseas, offshored profits, helped finance the construction of factories in rival states like China and India, and sometimes all of the above.

The basic critique of both the Trump and Sanders campaigns is that you can't continually take that money and also be on the side of working people. Money is important in politics, but in democracy, people ultimately still count more.

The Democrats survived this time, but Republicans allowed their voters to see the numerical weakness of our major parties. It should take an awful lot to break up 60 million unified people. But a few hundred lawyers, a pile of money and a sales pitch can be replaced in a heartbeat, even by someone as dumb as Donald Trump.

18

June 9, 2016: Democrats Will Learn All the Wrong Lessons from Their Brush with Bernie

Instead of a reality check for the party, it'll be smugness redoubled

Y EARS AGO, OVER MANY BEERS IN A D.C. BAR, A CONGRES-sional aide colorfully described the House of Representatives, where he worked.

It's "435 heads up 435 asses," he said.

I thought of that person yesterday, while reading the analyses of Hillary Clinton's victories Tuesday night. The arrival of the first female presidential nominee was undoubtedly a huge moment in American history and something even the supporters of Bernie Sanders should recognize as significant and to be celebrated. But the Washington media's assessment of how we got there was convoluted and self-deceiving.

This was no ordinary primary race, not a contest between warring factions within the party establishment, à la Obama-Clinton in '08 or even Gore-Bradley in '00. This was a barely quelled revolt that ought to have sent shock waves up and down the party, especially since the Vote of No Confidence overwhelmingly came from the next generation of voters. Yet editorialists mostly drew the opposite conclusion.

The classic example was James Hohmann's piece in the *Washington Post*, titled "Primary wins show Hillary Clinton needs the left less than pro-Sanders liberals think."

Hohmann's thesis was that the "scope and scale" of Clinton's wins Tuesday night meant mainstream Democrats could now safely return to their traditional *We won, screw you* posture of "minor concessions" toward the "liberal base."

Hohmann focused on the fact that with Bernie out of the way, Hillary now had a path to victory that would involve focusing on Trump's negatives. Such a strategy won't require much if any acquiescence toward the huge masses of Democratic voters who just tried to derail her candidacy. And not only is the primary scare over, but Clinton and the centrist Democrats in general are in better shape than ever.

"Big picture," Hohmann wrote, "Clinton is running a much better and more organized campaign than she did in 2008."

Then there was Jonathan Capehart, also of the *Post*, whose "This is how Bernie Sanders and Donald Trump are the same person" piece describes Sanders as a "stubborn outsider" who "shares the same DNA" as Donald Trump. Capehart seethes that both men will ultimately pay a karmic price for not knowing their places.

"In the battle of the outsider egos storming the political establishment, Trump succeeded where Sanders failed," he wrote. "But the chaos unleashed by Trump's victory could spell doom for the GOP all over the ballot in November. Pardon me while I dab that single tear trickling down my cheek."

If they had any brains, Beltway Dems and their clucky sycophants like Capehart would not be celebrating this week. They ought to be horrified to their marrow that the all-powerful Democratic Party ended up having to dig in for a furious rally to stave off a quirky Vermont socialist almost completely lacking big-dollar donors or institutional support.

They should be freaked out, cowed and relieved, like the Golden State Warriors would be if they needed a big fourth quarter to pull out a win against Valdosta State.

But to read the papers in the last two days is to imagine that we didn't just spend a year witnessing the growth of a massive grassroots movement fueled by loathing of the party establishment, with some correspondingly severe numerical contractions in the turnout department (though she won, for instance, Clinton received 30 percent fewer votes in California this year versus 2008, and 13 percent fewer in New Jersey).

The twin insurgencies of Trump and Sanders this year were equally a blistering referendum on Beltway politics. But the major-party leaders and the media mouthpieces they hang out with can't see this, because of what that friend of mine talked about over a decade ago: Washington culture is too far up its own backside to see much of anything at all.

In D.C., a kind of incestuous myopia very quickly becomes part of many political jobs. Congressional aides in particular work ridiculous hours for terrible pay and hang out almost exclusively with each other. About the only recreations they can afford are booze, shop-talk, and complaining about constituents, who in many offices are considered earth's lowest form of life, somewhere between lichens and nematodes.

It's somewhat understandable. In congressional offices in particular, people universally dread picking up the phone, because it's mostly only a certain kind of cable-addicted person with too much spare time who calls a politician's office.

"Have you ever called your congressman? No, because you have a job!" laughs Paul Thacker, a former Senate aide currently working on a book about life on the Hill. Thacker recounts tales of staffers rushing to turn on Fox News once the phones start ringing, because "the people" are usually only triggered to call Washington by some moronic TV news scare campaign.

In another case, Thacker remembers being in the office of the senator of a far-Northern state, watching an aide impatiently conduct half of a constituent phone call. "He was like, 'Uh huh, yes, I understand.' Then he'd pause and say, 'Yes, sir,' again. This went on for like five minutes," recounts Thacker.

Finally, the aide firmly hung up the phone, reared back and pointed accusingly at the receiver. "And you are from fucking *Missouri*!" he shouted. "Why are you calling me?"

These stories are funny, but they also point to a problem. Since The People is an annoying beast, young pols quickly learn to be focused entirely on each other and on their careers. They get turned on by the narrative of Beltway politics as a cool power game, and before long are way too often reaching for *Game of Thrones* metaphors to describe their jobs. Eventually, the only action that matters is inside the palace.

Voter concerns rapidly take a back seat to the daily grind of the job. The ideal piece of legislation in almost every case is a Frankensteinian policy concoction that allows the sponsoring pol to keep as many big-money donors in the fold as possible without offending actual human voters to the point of a ballot revolt.

This dynamic is rarely explained to the public, but voters on both sides of the aisle have lately begun guessing at the truth, and spent most of the last year letting the parties know it in the primaries. People are sick of being thought of as faraway annoyances who only get whatever policy scraps are left over after pols have finished servicing the donors they hang out with at Redskins games.

Democratic voters tried to express these frustrations through the Sanders campaign, but the party leaders have been and probably will continue to be too dense to listen. Instead, they'll convince themselves that, as Hohmann's *Post* article put it, Hillary's latest victories mean any "pressure" they might have felt to change has now been "ameliorated."

The maddening thing about the Democrats is that they refuse to see how easy they could have it. If the party threw its weight behind a truly populist platform, if it stood behind unions and prosecuted Wall Street criminals and stopped taking giant gobs of cash from every crooked transnational bank and job-exporting manufacturer in the world, they would win every election season in a landslide.

This is especially the case now that the Republican Party has collapsed under the weight of its own nativist lunacy. It's exactly the moment when the Democrats should feel free to become a real party of ordinary working people.

But they won't do that, because they don't see what just happened this year as a message rising up from millions of voters.

Politicians are so used to viewing the electorate as a giant thing to be manipulated that no matter what happens at the ballot, they usually can only focus on the Washington-based characters they perceive to be pulling the strings. Through this lens, the uprising among Democratic voters this year wasn't an organic expression of mass disgust, but wholly the fault of Bernie Sanders, who within the Beltway is viewed as an oddball amateur and radical who jumped the line.

Nobody saw his campaign as an honest effort to restore power to voters, because nobody in the capital even knows what that is. In the rules of palace intrigue, Sanders only made sense as a kind of self-centered huckster who made a failed play for power. And the narrative will be that with him out of the picture, the crisis is over. No person, no problem.

This inability to grasp that the problem is bigger than Bernie Sanders is a huge red flag. As Thacker puts it, the theme of this election year was widespread anger toward both parties, and both the Trump craziness and the near-miss with Sanders should have served as a warning. "The Democrats should be worried they're next," he says.

But they're not worried. Behind the palace walls, nobody ever is.

19

June 30, 2016: In Response to Trump, Another Dangerous Movement Appears

Fears of demagoguery are provoking a frightening swing in the other direction

THE "TOO MUCH DEMOCRACY" TRAIN ROLLS ON. Last week's Brexit vote prompted pundits and social media mavens to wonder aloud if allowing dumb people to vote is a good thing.

Now, the cover story in *The Atlantic* magazine features the most aggressive offering yet in an alarming series of intellectual-class jeremiads against the dangers of democracy.

In "How American Politics Went Insane," Brookings Institute Fellow Jonathan Rauch spends many thousands of words arguing for the reinvigoration of political machines, as a means of keeping the ape-citizen further from power.

He portrays the public as a gang of nihilistic loonies determined to play mailbox baseball with the gears of state.

"Neurotic hatred of the political class is the country's last universally acceptable form of bigotry," he writes, before concluding:

"Our most pressing political problem today is that the country abandoned the establishment, not the other way around."

Rauch's audacious piece, much like Andrew Sullivan's clarion call for a less-democratic future in *New York* magazine ("Democracies end when they are too democratic"), is not merely a warning about the threat posed to civilization by demagogues like Donald Trump.

It's a sweeping argument against a whole host of democratic initiatives, from increased transparency to reducing money in politics to the phasing out of bagmen and wardheelers at the local level. These things have all destabilized America, Rauch insists.

It's a piece that praises Boss Tweed's Tammany Hall (it was good for the Irish!), the smoke-filled room (good for "brokering complex compromises"), and pork (it helps "glue Congress together" by giving members "a kind of currency to trade").

Rauch even chokes multiple times on the word "corruption," seeming reluctant to even mention the concept without shrouding it in flurries of caveats. When he talks about the "ever-present potential for corruption" that political middlemen pose, he's quick to note the converse also applies (emphasis mine):

"Overreacting to the threat of corruption . . . is just as harmful. Political contributions, for example, look unseemly, but they play a vital role as **political bonding agents**."

The basic thrust is that shadowy back-room mechanisms, which Rauch absurdly describes as being relics of a lost era, have a positive role and must be brought back.

He argues back-room relationships and payoffs at least committed the actors involved to action. Meanwhile, all the transparency and sunshine and access the public is always begging for leads mainly to gridlock and frustration.

In one passage, Rauch blames gridlock on the gerrymandering that renders most congressional elections meaningless. In a scandal that should get more media play, Democrats and Republicans have divvied up territory to make most House districts "safe" for one party or another. Only about 10 to 20 percent of races are really contested in any given year (one estimate in 2014 described an incredible 408 of the 435 races as "noncompetitive").

As Rauch notes, meaningless general elections make primaries the main battlegrounds. This puts pressure on party candidates to drift to extremes:

"Walled safely inside their gerrymandered districts, incumbents are insulated from general-election challenges that might pull them toward the political center, but they are perpetually vulnerable to primary challenges from extremists who pull them toward the fringes.

"Everyone worries about being the next Eric Cantor, the Republican House majority leader who, in a shocking upset, lost to an unknown Tea Partier in his 2014 primary."

Most people would look at a problem like this and conclude that the solution, if one is needed (is the defeat of a supercilious reptile like Eric Cantor really a bad thing?), would be to end crooked gerrymandering.

Not Rauch. He leans more toward blaming the decision to allow direct-voting primary processes in the first place.

His piece longs for a time when party insiders were free to pick candidates without interference.

He gushes, for instance, over a passage in a biography of George H. W. Bush that describes how his daddy, Prescott Bush, got into politics:

"Samuel F. Pryor, a top Pan Am executive and a mover in Connecticut politics, called Prescott to ask whether Bush might like to run for Congress. 'If you would,' Pryor said, 'I think we can assure you that you'll be the nominee.'"

Commenting on this, Rauch writes, with undisguised sadness:

"Today, party insiders can still jawbone a little bit, but, as the 2016 presidential race has made all too clear, there is startlingly little they can do to influence the nominating process."

You see, we would never have to risk these Trump/ Bernie Sanders episodes at all, if only there was no voting and we turned over the process to insiders sipping highballs in a Pan Am executive's basement!

Rauch views Sanders as the flip side of the Trumpian coin. Both men, he says, "have demonstrated that the major political parties no longer have intelligible boundaries or enforceable norms."

So what does Rauch propose to do about these usurpers who come out of nowhere, and, without so much as the per- mission of a Pan Am executive, run for public office?

One of Rauch's solutions is to force candidates to get permission slips to go on the electoral field trip:

"There are all kinds of ways the parties could move in- siders back to the center of the nomination process. If they wanted to, they could require would-be candidates to get petition signatures from elected officials and county party chairs . . ."

Rauch compares "outsiders" and "amateurs" to viruses that get into the body, and describes the institutions that failed to prevent the likes of Trump from being nominated as being like the national immune system. Revolt against party insiders is therefore comparable to "abusing and attacking your own immune system."

This lurid metaphor is going to be compelling to a lot of people when Donald Trump is still moving in the direction of the nuclear football. But these "too much democracy" critics all leave out a key part of the story: It's all bull.

Voters in America not only aren't over-empowered, they've for decades now been almost totally disenfranchised, subjects of one of the more brilliant change-suppressing systems ever invented.

We have periodic elections, which leave citizens with the feeling of self-rule. But in reality people are only allowed to choose between candidates carefully screened by wealthy donors. Nobody without a billion dollars and the approval of a half-dozen giant media companies has any chance at high office.

People have no other source of influence. Unions have been crushed. Nobody has any job security. Main Street institutions that once allowed people to walk down the road to sort things out with other human beings have been phased out. In their place now rest distant, unfeeling global bureaucracies.

Has a health insurance company wrongly denied your sick child coverage? Good luck even getting someone on the phone to talk it over, much less get it sorted out. Your neighborhood bank, once a relatively autonomous mechanism for stimulating the local economy, is now a glorified ATM machine with limited ability to respond to a community's most basic financial concerns.

One of the underpublicized revelations of the financial crisis, for instance, was that millions of Americans found themselves unable to get answers to a simple question like "Who holds the note to my house?"

People want more power over their own lives. They want to feel some connection to society. Most particularly, they don't want to be dictated to by distant bureaucrats who don't seem to care what they're going through, and think they know what's best for everyone.

These are legitimate concerns. Unfortunately, they came out in this past year in the campaign of Donald Trump, who'd exposed a tiny flaw in the system.

People are still free to vote, and some peculiarities in the structure of the commercial media, combined with mountains of public anger, conspired to put one of the two parties in the hands of a coverage-devouring billionaire running on a "Purge the Scum"* platform.

But choosing a dangerous race-baiting lunatic as the vehicle for the first successful revolt in ages against one of the two major parties will have many profound negative consequences for voters. The most serious will surely be this burgeoning movement to describe voting and democracy as inherently dangerous.

Donald Trump is dangerous because as president, he'd

---

* Trump soon after would begin circulating a new slogan in his tweets: #draintheswamp. This was another Trumpism once popularized by Reagan, although the term was originally used by *Mother Jones* magazine as a socialist rallying cry against capitalists.

likely have little respect for law. But a gang of people whose metaphor for society is "We are the white cells, voters are the disease" is comparably scary in its own banal, less click-generating way.

These self-congratulating *cognoscenti* could have looked at the events of the last year and wondered why people were so angry with them, and what they could do to make government work better for the population.

Instead, their first instinct is to dismiss voter concerns as baseless, neurotic bigotry and to assume that the solution is to give Washington bureaucrats even more leeway to blow off the public. In the absurdist comedy that is American political life, this is the ultimate anti-solution to the unrest of the last year, the mathematically perfect wrong ending.

Trump is going to lose this election, then live on as the reason for an emboldened, even less-responsive oligarchy. And you thought this election season couldn't get any worse.

20

July 22, 2016: Trump's Appetite for Destruction: How Trump's Disastrous Convention Doomed the GOP

Republican National Convention made a joke of American democracy

HELL, YES, IT WAS CRAZY. YOU RUBBED YOUR EYES AT THE sight of it, as in, "Did *that* really just happen?"

It wasn't what we expected. We thought Donald Trump's version of the Republican National Convention would be a brilliantly bawdy exercise in Nazistic excess.

We expected thousand-foot light columns, a 400-piece horn section where the delegates usually sit (they would be in cages out back with guns to their heads). Onstage, a chorus line of pageant girls in gold bikinis would be twerking furiously to a techno version of "New York, New York" while an army of Broadway dancers spent all four days building a Big Beautiful Wall that read winning, the cere-monial last brick timed to the start of Donald's acceptance speech . . .

But nah. What happened instead was just sad and weird, very weird. The lineup for the 2016 Republican National Convention to nominate Trump felt like a fallback list of speakers for some ancient UHF telethon, on behalf of a cause like plantar-wart research.

Was one of the headliners really Ultimate Fighting chief Dana White, head all swollen and shouting into the microphone like a man having a road-rage dispute?

Was that really *General Hospital* star and Calvin Klein underwear model Antonio Sabato Jr. warning gravely that "our rights have been trampled and our security threat-ened" by President Obama's policies? And were there really two soap stars in the lineup, the second being Kimberlin Brown, of *The Young and the Restless*, who drove a spear through the grave of Henny Youngman with an agonizing attempt at warm-up humor?

"Many of you know me from one of your favorite soap operas," she said. "But since we only have one life to live . . . I decided to follow other dreams!" Punchline: She grows avocados now, and loves Donald Trump.

There were four categories of speakers. First, the Trump family members, including poor wife Melania, whose speechwriters pushed her into a media buzz saw on opening night.

Then, there were even a few Republican politicians who seemed to want to be there voluntarily, people like crazed Alabama Sen. Jeff Sessions, who came off like a shaved and slightly angrier version of Yosemite Sam. Ex-candidate Ben Carson emerged from a grain-storage chamber somewhere to connect Hillary Clinton to Lucifer and say things about transgender people so outrageous that even Orrin Hatch rushed to their defense.

The third group consisted of Republican officials who had no choice but to be there. People like Republican Party chief Reince Priebus and House Majority Leader Paul Ryan rarely spoke Trump's name and seemed pained throughout, aware they might spend eternity giving each other back rubs in hell as punishment for participating in this event.

The rest were basically personal friends of Trump's who owed him a favor.

The nominee seemed to mine the very bottom of his Rolodex for the exercise, to the point where we even heard a testimonial from Natalie Gulbis, the world's 492nd-ranked professional woman golfer.

"The first time I played golf with him, in 2005, I shared two things I had told countless CEOs, billionaires and politicians before him," said Gulbis. The two things sort of turned out to be one thing, i.e., that she wanted to open a Boys & Girls Club and she was tired of having such business ideas rejected.

"Those words previously fell on deaf, albeit well-intentioned ears," she went on. "But that day was different. They finally fell on ears that cared enough to take action." Trump funded her Boys & Girls Club!

"Trump's ears cared?" cracked a nearby reporter, stuffing his face with yogurt peanuts while Googling "Natalie Gulbis naked" on his cellphone.

Then there was Scott Baio. Scott Baio, ladies and gentlemen! Not the Fonz or Richie or even Pinky Tuscadero, but the man who played Chachi, a gimmick character in a show about an America that never existed, a time when there were no black people and the last gasps of our apart-heid state were called *Happy Days.*

Republicans have been selling a return to that mythical Fifties golden age for the past half-century, but it took Donald Trump for the sales pitch to come out as such extreme comedy. Make America's Days Happy Again!

Trump had Baio in the convention lineup just days after wired-on-Jesus former Congresskook Michele Bachmann described the nominee as a man with "1950s sensibilities," who grew up in an era when "even . . . Jews would say Merry Christmas." Why can't we go back to those days?

"Let's make America America again!" is how Baio put it in his speech.

The next day, Baio labored through a confused and contentious appearance on MSNBC with host Tamron Hall. The headline that emerged from that uncomfortable segment involved Hall confronting Baio over a tweet in which he appeared to call Hillary Clinton a "cunt." But the real shocker came at the beginning of the interview.

"Did you write your own speech?" Hall asked.

"I did," said Baio. "I was asked to do this Thursday. I wrote my speech in church on Sunday morning."

Donald Trump did not nail down Scott Baio, perhaps Earth's most conspicuously available actor, as a speaker for opening night of the Republican Party Convention until four days before it started!

It didn't get any better when the so-called professional politicians spoke. As if in one voice, they all repeated a mantra more appropriate for a megachurch full of Rapture-ready Christians than a political convention: We are not safe, the end is nigh, run for the hills and vote Trump on your way out.

"There's no next election—this is it," screeched Rudy Giuliani (or "9/11's Rudy Giuliani," as he is jokingly dubbed in the press section).

The former New York mayor's "there are terrorists trimming their beards under your bed as we speak" act has been seen a million times before by this political press corps, but even that jaded group was stunned by the hysterical heights—or depths?—to which he rose/sank in his appearance for Trump.

"To defeat Islamic extremist terrorists, we must put them on defense!" he shouted, with his usual bluster at first.

Then, suddenly, in a frenzy of violent hand gestures, Giuliani found another gear. *"We must commit ourselves to unconditional victory against them!"* he bellowed, with a flourish that could only be described as Hitlerian. It was a daring performance that met with some roars on the floor, but also plenty of murmuring.

The thing is, the convention crowd wasn't exactly the fevered revolutionary rally the press had been predicting for months. It was, in fact, a sadly muted affair, with many delegates quietly despairing at what had happened to the Grand Old Party.

The Republican Party under Trump has become the laughingstock of the world, and it happened in front of an invading force of thousands of mocking reporters who made sure that not one single excruciating moment was left uncovered.

So, yes, it was weird, and pathetic, but it was also disturbing, and not just for the reasons you might think. Trump's implosion left the Republican Party in schism, but it also created an unprecedented chattering-class consensus and a dangerous political situation.

Everyone piled on the Republicans, with pundits from George Will to David Brooks to Dan Savage all on the same side now, and nobody anywhere seeming to worry about the obvious subtext to Trump's dumpster-fire convention: In a two-party state, when one collapses, doesn't that mean only one is left? And isn't that a bad thing?

Day two of the Republican National Convention in Cleveland, a little after 6:30 p.m. Roll has been called, states are announcing their support for the Donald, and the floor is filled with TV crews breathlessly looking for sexy backdrops for the evolving train wreck that is the Republican Party.

Virtually every major publication in America has run with some version of the "Man, has this convention been one giant face-plant, or what?" story, often citing the sanitized, zero-debate conventions of the past as a paradise now lost to the GOP.

"The miscues, mistakes [and] mishandled dissent," wrote Elizabeth Sullivan in Cleveland's *Plain Dealer*, "did not augur well for the sort of smoothly scripted, expertly choreographed nominating conventions our mainstream political parties prefer."

The odd thing is that once upon a time, conventions were a site of fierce debates, not only over the content of the party platform but even the choice of candidates themselves. And this was regarded as the healthy exercise of democracy.

It wasn't until the television era, when conventions became intolerably dull pro-forma infomercials stage-managed for the networks to consume as fake shows of unity, that we started to measure the success of conventions by their lack of activity, debate and new ideas.

A Wyoming delegate named Rick Shanor shakes his

head as he leans against a wall, staying out of the way of the crews zooming to and fro. He insists dissent is always part of the process, and maybe it's just that nobody cared before.

"It's beautiful," he says. "You've got to have the discourse. You've got to have arguments about this and that. That's the way we work in the Republican Party. We yak and yak, but we coalesce."

The Republican Convention in Cleveland was supposed to be the site of revolts and unprecedented hijinks on the part of delegates. But on the floor of Chez LeBron, a.k.a. the Quicken Loans Arena, a.k.a. the "Q," it's the journalists who are acting like fanatics, buttonholing every delegate in sight for embarrassed quotes about things like Melania's plagiarism flap.

"The only safe place to stand is, like, in the middle row of your delegation," one delegate says, eyeing the media circling the edges of the floor like a school of sharks. "If you go out to get nachos or take a leak, they come after you."

A two-person crew, a camera and a coiffed on-air hack, blows through a portion of the Washington state delegation, a bunch of princely old gentlemen in zany foam tree-hats. The trees separate briefly, then return to formation.

Meanwhile, the TV crew has set up and immediately begun babbling still more about last night's story, Melania Trump's plagiarism, which *Esquire*'s Charlie Pierce correctly quipped was a four-hour story now stretching toward multiple days.

Nearby, watching the reporters, one delegate from a Midwestern state turns to another.

"This is like a NAMBLA convention," he says with a sigh. "And we're the kiddies."

Outside, it's not much better.

The vast demilitarized zone set up between the Q and anywhere in the city that contains people is an inert, creepy place to visit. Towering metal barricades line streets cleansed of people, with the only movement being the wind blowing the occasional discarded napkin or pamphlet excerpt of *The Conservative Heart* (the president of the American Enterprise Institute's hilarious text about tough-love cures for poverty first littered the floor of the Q, then the grounds outside it).

Thus the area around the convention feels like some other infamous de-peopled landscapes, like Hitler's paintings, or downtown New Orleans after Katrina. You have to walk a long way, sometimes climbing barriers and zigzagging through the multiple absurd metal mazes of the DMZ, to even catch a glimpse of anyone lacking the credentials to get into this most exclusive of clubs: American democracy.

Concepts like "free speech zones" or the idea that the general public may not come within a half-mile or so of the actual event seemed insane when they were first introduced years ago. But the public has since become inured to the notion, which perhaps is a reason the protests here have been far tamer than in years past.

In 2004, the first year that both parties were unembarrassed enough to actually use the Orwellian term "free speech zones," there were large demonstrations for and against issues like the Iraq War, and the zones themselves.

But this time around, it is only the press that turned out in massive numbers, apparently hoping to catch a repeat of 1968, when a violent street ruckus upended the Democratic Convention. But 1968 was exactly the sort of televisable show of dangerous dissent these zones are designed to preclude.

Eleven a.m., Day Three, Cleveland's Soldiers' and Sailors' Monument. Rumors had circulated that something big was going to happen here this morning, like thousands of Latinos building a human wall around the Q.

But at the appointed time, there are just a few dozen protesters wearing hand-painted burlap "Wall Off Trump" costumes . . . and about a million journalists.

The joke in the past few days had been that there were 10 cops for every reporter and 10 reporters for every protester. But under the monument at this moment, you can actually see the math.

"Welcome to the photographers' convention!" seethes videographer James Woods, a.k.a. JamesFromTheInternet (no relation to the unhinged actor).

An executive producer at the popular indie press outlet act.tv, the burly, bearded Woods is a fixture on the protest circuit, a one-man TV production unit who has been spotted chronicling everything from the Ferguson riots to antiwar marches to the unrest that rocked New York after the Eric Garner grand jury.

Woods came to the RNC on the off chance that some real anarchist craziness might finally happen. But he was quickly dispirited when it became a scene where everyone in America with a blog or an iPhone showed up to take selfies while "covering" the historic event, a kind of journo-tourism.

"It's like everyone who's been sitting around for four years decided to scrape the dust off their cameras and show up here," he says, shaking his head.

After a brief attempt at an interlocking-hand "wall" that stretches for perhaps 15 people, the anti-Trump group begins moving in a single row toward the Q, chanting, "Wall off Trump! Wall off Trump!"

They are followed, no joke, by groups of reporters six or

seven rows deep on both sides. And when a pair of pro-Trumpers show up quietly holding American flags along the street's edge, they are suddenly set upon by photographers in search of a confrontation.

One of the pro-Trumpers, a 31-year-old Los Angeleno named Shawn Witte, is walking in silence carrying a flag. "Just fucking walking," as he puts it. But the mass of reporters, detecting him, seem anxious to clear a lane between him and the human wall, perhaps hoping they will bite one another or something.

The day before, Witte says, the same thing had happened. When he went outside with his flag, reporters rushed back and forth between Witte and some Black Lives Matter protesters, pointing them out to each other.

"Everybody in Black Lives Matter, they were cool with it," Witte says. "They were like, 'Right on, man. I don't agree with what you're saying, but you have a personal right.' Media was trying to hype that shit up."

The 1968 narrative never materializes, much to the obvious chagrin of the monstrous press contingent (the "human centipede of bastards," as one sketch artist dubbed them). Handfuls of protesters do their thing peacefully, on the permitted side of the DMZ, and it is weak-beer TV no matter how you look at it.

That the press seemed let down by the lack of turmoil on the streets was odd, given that the Trump convention itself was, after all, a historic revolt.

Thirteen million and three hundred thousand Republican voters had defied the will of their party and soundly rejected hundred-million-dollar insider favorites like Jeb Bush to re-seize control of their own political destiny. That they made perhaps the most ridiculous choice in the history of democracy was really a secondary issue.

It was a tremendous accomplishment that real-life conservative voters did what progressives could not quite do in the Democratic primaries. Republican voters penetrated the many layers of money and political connections and corporate media policing that, like the labyrinth of barricades around the Q, are designed to keep the riffraff from getting their mitts on the political process.

But it wasn't covered that way. What started a year ago as an amusing story about a clown car full of bumbling primary hopefuls was about to be described to the world not as a groundbreaking act of defiance, but as a spectacular failure of democracy.

The once-divided media class now came together to gang-troll flyover America for its preposterous decision, turning the coverage of the convention into a parable on the evil of letting voters make up their own dumb minds. This was the *Fatal Attraction* of political coverage, a warning disguised as a story: Look what happens, you rubes, when you step outside the lines.

One of the great propaganda successes of the past few decades has been the myth of the liberal media. The idea that a monolithic herd of leftist snobs somehow controlled the news spread in part because of a seemingly key but really irrelevant demographic truth, i.e., that most individual reporters lean blue in their personal politics.

Moreover, from *All the President's Men* to *The Insider* to *Good Night, and Good Luck* to *Spotlight*, Hollywood portrayals of the media always involve prudish conservative villains upended by chain-smoking/disheveled/wisecracking lefty heroes, Robert Redford's amusingly hunky representation of then-Republican Bob Woodward notwithstanding.

But whatever their personal leanings, influential reporters mostly work in nihilistic corporations, to whom the news is a non-ideological commodity, to be sold the same way we hawk cheeseburgers or Marlboro Lights. Wars, scandals and racial conflicts sell, while poverty and inequality do not. So reporters chase one and not the other. It's just business.

Previously, at conventions like this, pundits always played up the differences between Republicans and Democrats (abortion, religion, immigration), while ignoring the many areas of consensus (trade, military spending, surveillance, the Drug War, non-enforcement of financial crime, corporate tax holidays, etc.).

Any halfway decent boxing promoter will tell you the public must be made to believe the fighters hate each other in order to sell the fight. The fighters also must be hyped as both having a good shot to win. Otherwise, why watch?

The same principle applies in politics. Or at least it did, until Donald Trump arrived in Cleveland.

Thanks to Trump, we in the media can no longer cast politics as a sports story, because the illusion that both sides have a compelling chance at victory is now a tougher sell.

Instead, we will sell it as a freak show, a tent full of bearded ladies and pinheads at which to gape. Next to sports, freak shows are what the media do best, so it'll be an easy switch. Shows like *Anderson Cooper 360°* will become high-tech versions of *Here Comes Honey Boo Boo* or *The Biggest Loser*, destinations for Americans to tune in for a bit to feel superior to the mutants debasing themselves onscreen.

And it's here that the irony of a reality-TV star like Donald Trump winning the nomination comes full circle.

Trump won because he grasped instinctively that the campaign trail was more TV show than democracy.

He rolled through primary season simply by being a better and more magnetic reality character than the likes of Scott Walker, Lindsey Graham and Jeb Bush. (You couldn't build a successful reality show around those pols even if you locked them in a hyena cage with Ryan Seacrest and Tila Tequila.)

Then he went to his convention, and his lineup of speakers, minus the handful of "real" politicians who held their noses through the thing, read suspiciously like an episode of *The Apprentice* or *Flavor of Love*. His celebrity guests were a bunch of D-listers ready to eat snails, walk on coals, swap wives or (in this case) publicly support Donald Trump to keep their fading celebrity alive.

The big exception was *Duck Dynasty*'s Willie Robertson, an actual huge star who scored cheers attacking the media.

"It's been a rough year for the media experts," he said. "They don't hang out with folks like us who like to hunt, and fish, and pray, and actually work for a living. I don't even know if they know how to talk to people from Middle America."

It was hard to listen to Robertson's defiant spiel and not wonder at the fact that both he and his most ardent fans probably still have no idea that he was put on TV to be laughed at. *Duck Dynasty* viewers think they're the experts on hunting, but actually they're the hunted ones, just another dumb demographic to be captured, laughed at and force-fed commercials for Geico and Home Depot by the Smart People in New York and L.A.

Trump's voters will almost certainly share the same

fate. They will be mined by cable news shows for their entertainment value before ultimately being held up as dangerous loons whose noisy little revolt will serve as the rationale for a generation of Democratic Party rule at the White House level.

Of course, the Republicans blew the one chance they had to save themselves. They could have turned the internal discord to their advantage and held an open convention of ideas, dispensing with the pretense of unity and presenting themselves instead as a big enough tent to embrace and accept many different viewpoints.

Trump should have invited his fiercest critics, the Mike Lees and George Wills of the world, to come onstage and explain why they so fervently disagreed with his tactics and rhetoric. He even should have stopped short of demanding endorsements from all of them. A smart Donald Trump—such a thing is difficult to imagine, but let's say—would have given his opponents a forum to just whale away at him, even removing time constraints. It would have helped make Trump look more like presidential material.

And this would have accomplished two other things.

First, and most important, it would have rescued the immediate future of the party in the highly likely event that Trump goes on to lose in November.

The Republican leadership from Ryan on down could have walked away from this convention with their pseudo-dignity intact, having spoken out against Trump's more naked and vulgar form of racism, standing instead on the principle of a more covert, more subterranean, more dog-whistle-y form of race politics—you know, like Mitt Romney lecturing the NAACP about black people wanting "free stuff."

Second, it would have made for a fascinating run-up to Trump's final address. Here was a man famous for being so thin-skinned that he stays up at night tweeting insults at judges and editors of New Hampshire newspapers, giving the world's biggest stage to his critics.

Then he could have ascended the podium on the concluding night and delivered his apocalyptic argument, which he'd describe as believing in so strongly he stacked it up against his fiercest critics. And he'd have plenty of fodder to swing back at, with decades of Republican inaction, corruption and failure to save American jobs to use in service of his case for a radical change of leadership.

Alas, exactly the opposite happened, and everybody, to the last speaker, came out looking smaller than before.

Priebus and Ryan hanged themselves at the start, endorsing Trump despite clearly not wanting to do so. If Trump loses, they go down the drain of history as pathetic quislings. In the unlikely event that Trump wins, a triumphant Donald would replace them at the first opportunity with horses or WWE ring doctors or anyone who didn't make such a big show of being reluctant supporters when the chips were down.

Some say Ted Cruz was the only winner, given that he came the closest to openly defying the nominee. Cruz refused to endorse Trump, giving a remarkably poisonous and self-serving speech in which he preened like a bully wrestler and told people to "vote your conscience, vote for candidates up and down the ticket," instantly drawing boos from the crowd. Chris Christie, another quisling whose career will soon be over, felt compelled to shake his head in disbelief, while Cruz went on to repulse the crowd with his 10 gazillionth recitation of his Inspirational Family History, including what trail reporters derisively call "the under-pants fable."

"Love of freedom has allowed millions to achieve their dreams," he said. "Like my mom, the first in her family to go to college, and my dad, who's here tonight, who fled prison and torture in Cuba, coming to Texas with just $100 sewn into his underwear . . ."

"Fuck your mom!" grumbled someone in the cheap seats.

"You suck!" shouted another.

Trump should have let this all play out, but instead he tried to screw with Cruz's rhythm by entering the hall mid-speech and giving a thumb's-up. Later, Cruz's wife, Heidi, was heckled by Trump supporters who yelled, "Goldman Sachs! Goldman Sachs!" at her, which was both amusing and kind of revolting. Why not yell it at her husband?

But even Cruz wasn't denouncing Trump's belittling of Mexicans, veterans, the Chinese, the disabled, Jewish people, Megyn Kelly's wherever, Carly Fiorina's face, Super Bowl 50 ("Boring!") or any of the hundreds of other groups, people and things targeted by the nominee in the past year.

Instead, the next day, Cruz said that he was not "in the habit" of supporting candidates who attacked his family. This was a sensible enough position but not one that partic-ularly marked him as having stood on principle, especially given that his politics are basically identical to Trump's, minus the oddball insults. If Cruz turns out to be the one Republican who survives this mess, that will be the cruelest blow of all.

By the time Cruz's speech was done, it felt as though an improbable collection of America's most obnoxious, vapid, mean-spirited creeps had somehow been talked into assembling at the Q for the sheer novelty of it ("like X-Men, but for assholes" is how one reporter put it).

As for the subsequent speech by VP hopeful Mike Pence, there's little to report beyond that it happened and he'll someday regret it. Pence redefines boring. He makes Al Gore seem like the Wu-Tang Clan. His one desperate attempt at a Hillary takedown—calling her "the secretary of the Status Quo"—was so painful that people visibly winced in the stands. And when it was all over, he left Trump hanging for an excruciating unexecuted air kiss that immediately became the most mocked thing on Twitter since anything ever. It was a mathematically inexpressible level of Awkward.

All of these awful happenings left only one possibility for salvation: Trump's speech. Unfortunately, by Thursday the multitudinous letdowns had already dented the TV ratings and all but wiped out the possibility of a saving last-night performance. But if anyone could make a bad situation worse, it was Trump. If only for that reason, it was worth attending.

The buzz in the hall on the final night was that Trump might screw things up—how could he not? On the primary trail we had never seen anything like him: impulsive, lewd, grandiose, disgusting, horrible, narcissistic and dangerous, but also usually unscripted and 10 seconds ahead of the news cycle.

We could never quite tell what he was: possibly the American Hitler, but just as possibly punking the whole world in the most ambitious prank/PR stunt of all time. Or maybe he was on the level, birthing a weird new rightist/populist movement, a cross of Huey Long, Pinochet and David Hasselhoff. He was probably a monster, but whatever he was, he was original.

Then came Thursday night.

With tens of millions of eyes watching, Trump the Beltway conqueror turtled and wrapped his arms around the establishment's ankles. He spent the entirety of his final address huddled inside five decades of Republican Party clichés, apparently determined to hide in there until Election Day.

And not just any clichés, either. Trump ripped off the Republican Party's last-ditch emergency maneuver, a scare-the-white-folks spiel used by a generation of low-charisma underdogs trailing in the polls.

Many observers called it the most terrifying speech they'd ever seen, but that had a lot to do with its hysterical tenor (the *Times* amusingly called it "almost angry"), the Mussolinian head-bobs, the draped-in-flags Caesarean imagery, and his strongman promises. It was a relentlessly negative speech, pure horror movie, with constant references to murder and destruction. If you bought any of it, you probably turned off the tube ready to blow your head off.

But it wasn't new, not one word. Trump cribbed his ideas from the Republicans he spent a year defaming. Trump had merely reprised Willie Horton, Barry Goldwater's "marauders" speech, Jesse Helms' "White Hands" ad, and most particularly Richard Nixon's 1968 "law and order" acceptance address, the party's archetypal fear-based appeal from which Trump borrowed in an intellectual appropriation far more sweeping and shameless than Melania's much-hyped mistake.

He even used the term "law and order" four times, and rehashed a version of Nixon's somber "let us begin by committing ourselves to the truth" intro, promising to "honor the American people with the truth, and nothing else."

In place of Nixon's "merchants of crime," Trump spoke of 180,000 illegal immigrants roaming the countryside like zombies, hungry for the brains of decent folk.

"The number of new illegal-immigrant families who have crossed the border so far this year already exceeds the entire total from 2015," he cried. "They are being released by the tens of thousands into our communities, with no regard for the impact on public safety or resources." The tragic story of Sarah Root, killed by a released immigrant, was just Willie Horton without the picture.

He mentioned cities in crisis, a rising crime rate, and an opponent who promised "death, destruction, terrorism and weakness" for America. His argument really came down to that: Vote for me or die.

As for his populist critiques of money in politics and the pay-for-play corruption in both parties that made up so much of his stump speeches, the same critiques that Bernie Sanders used to throw a scare into Hillary Clinton, they took a back seat in crunch time.

Trump was always just smart enough to see that the same money backs the Jeb Bushes and Hillary Clintons of the world. But he never had the vision or the empathy to understand, beyond the level of a punchline, the frustrations linking disenfranchised voters on both the left and right.

Presented with a rare opportunity to explain how the two parties stoke divisions on social issues to keep working people from realizing their shared economic dilemmas, Trump backed down. Even if he didn't believe it, he could have turned such truths into effective campaign rhetoric. But such great themes are beyond his pampered, D-minus mind. Instead, he tried to poach Sanders voters simply by chanting Bernie's name like a magic word.

In the end, Trump's populism was as fake as everything else about him, and he emerged as just another in a long line of Republican hacks, only dumber and less plausible to the political center.

Which meant that after all that we went through last year, after that crazy cycle of insults and bluster and wife wars and penis-measuring contests and occasionally bloody street battles, after the insane media tornado that destroyed the modern Republican establishment, Trump concluded right where the party started 50 years ago, meekly riding Nixon's Southern Strategy. It was all just one very noisy ride in a circle. All that destruction and rebellion went for nothing. Officially now, he's just another party schmuck.

Archibald MacLeish once wrote a poem called "The End of the World," about a circus interrupted when the big top blows away. The freaks and lion-tamers and acrobats are frozen mid-performance, and the "thousands of white faces" in the audience gasp as they look up at the vast sky to see, after all the fantastical performances in the ring, the ultimate showstopper: emptiness, an endless black sky, "nothing, nothing, nothing—nothing at all."

Trump's finale was like that. When we finally pulled the lid off this guy, there was nothing there. Just a cheap fraud and TV huckster who got in way over his head, and will now lead his hoodwinked followers off the cliff of history.

21

August 15, 2016: The Summer of the Media Shill

Campaign 2016 won't just have lasting
implications for American politics. It's obliterated
what was left of our news media

YEARS AGO, WHEN I WAS AN EXCHANGE STUDENT IN THE
Soviet Union, a Russian friend explained how he got
his news.

"For news about Russia, Radio Liberty," he said. "For
news about America, Soviet newspapers." He smiled.
"Countries lie about themselves, tell truth about others."

American media consumers are fast approaching the
same absurd binary reality. We now have one set of news
outlets that gives us the bad news about Democrats, and
another set of news outlets bravely dedicated to reporting
the whole truth about Republicans.

Like the old adage about quarterbacks—if you think you have two good ones, you probably have none—this basically means we have no credible news media left. Apart from a few brave islands of resistance, virtually all the major news organizations are now fully in the tank for one side or the other.

The last month or so of Trump-Hillary coverage may have been the worst stretch of pure journo-shilling we've seen since the run-up to the Iraq war. In terms of political media, there's basically nothing left on the air except Trump-bashing or Hillary-bashing.

Take last week's news cycle:

Red-state media obsessed over a series of emails about the Clinton Foundation obtained by Judicial Watch (a charter member of the "vast right-wing conspiracy") as part of a Freedom of Information lawsuit. The emails hinted that Foundation donors might have had special access to Hillary Clinton's State Department.

Meanwhile, the cable-news channels consumed by Democrat-leaning audiences, MSNBC and CNN, spent most of last week hammering Donald Trump's latest outrages, especially "the Second Amendment people" comments seeming to incite violence against Hillary Clinton or her judicial appointments.

Practically every story on non-conservative cable last week was a Democratic Party news flash: Reagan's daughter blasts Trump's comments! More Republicans defect to support Hillary! GOP, expecting Trump loss, shifts funds to down-ballot races! Khizr Khan challenges McCain to Dump Trump! Trump's worst offense was mocking disabled reporter, poll finds!

It's not that stations were wrong to denounce Trump's

comments. He deserves it all. But he's not the only stupid, lying, corrupt politician in the world, which is the impression one could easily get watching certain stations these days.

These all-Trump, all-the-time story lineups are like Fox in reverse. The commercial media has devolved, finally, into two remarkably humorless messaging platforms.

What's crucial to understand is that a great many commercial media outlets now are not so much liberal-leaning as Democratic-Party leaning.

There's a huge difference between advocacy journalism and electoral advocacy. Not just occasionally but all the time now, private news organizations are doing the work that political parties used to have to pay for in the form of ads.

In the same way that Fox used to (and probably still does) save on reporting and research costs by simply regurgitating talking points from the RNC, blue-leaning cable channels are running segments and online reports that are increasingly indistinguishable from Democratic Party messaging.

Trump really sent this problem into overdrive. He is considered so dangerous that many journalists are beginning to be concerned that admitting the truth of negative reports of any kind about the Democrats might make them complicit in the election of the American Hitler.

There's some logic in that, but it's flawed logic. When journalists start acting like politicians, we pretty much always end up botching things even more politically and crippling our businesses to boot.

Our job is to grope around promiscuously for stories on all sides, like dogs sniffing fire hydrants. Trying to fill any other role leads to trouble. It's the media version of the *Bull Durham* rule: "Don't think, it can only hurt the ball club."

Just look at the history of Fox and its satellite organizations.

Yes, the Murdoch empire has succeeded in accruing enormous power across the globe. In the United States, its impact on political affairs has been incalculable. It's led us into war, paralyzed Democratic presidencies, helped launch movements like the Tea Party and effectively spread so much disinformation that huge majorities of Republicans still doubt things like the birthplace of Barack Obama.

But Fox's coverage has been so overwhelmingly one-sided that it has lost forever the ability to convince non-conservatives of anything. Rupert Murdoch has turned into the Slime Who Cried Wolf. Even when Murdoch gets hold of a real story, he usually can't reach more than an inch outside his own dumbed-down audience.

Worse still, when you shill as constantly as his outlets have, even your most enthusiastic audience members very quickly learn to see through you.

This is a problem because if there ever comes a time when you want to convince your own audience of hard truths, you'll suddenly find them not nearly as trusting and loyal as you'd thought. Deep down, they'll have known all along you were full of it.

This happened to many Republican/conservative media figures in the past year.

The world may never have heard a yawn louder than the one evinced by flyover audiences in January, when the *National Review* gathered 20 prominent conservatives, headlined by Glenn Beck, to demand that Republican voters draw a line in the sand against Trump. It was an unprecedented show of media unity and determination.

Trump walked through the mighty phalanx of Republican pundits like they weren't there.

This was a powerful lesson. Media power comes from trust and respect, and both are eroded quickly if you only ever give people what they want to hear.

The formula for profits in the news business has grown stale. Commercial news shows now are subsisting on audiences of mostly older viewers who tend to enjoy programming that simply bashes whatever party it is they've grown to hate over the years, be they Republicans or Democrats. The median age of both Fox and MSNBC viewers is over 60.

But young audiences in particular tend to be incredibly turned off by the media-as-cheerleaders model of reporting. News audiences among the young have in recent years declined rapidly, mirroring a corresponding loss of trust in major-party politics.

"Garbage, lies, propaganda, repetitive and boring," is how a University of Texas researcher described the perceptions of young people vis-à-vis the news. Corporate news directors, much like the leaders of the Republican and Democratic Parties, seem blissfully unconcerned with the changing attitudes of their future customer base.

They'll be in for a huge shock five or 10 years from now when more people are getting their news from independent web content streamed to them through video games or online shopping platforms than they do from people like Wolf Blitzer.

Certainly that won't change if the "MSM" devolves completely into a McDonald's/Burger King situation where the major media splits into Trump Sucks or Hillary Sucks outlets. Forget about the fact that it's boring. From now on, how will we know if a real scandal hits?

The model going forward will likely involve Republican media covering Democratic corruption and Democratic media covering Republican corruption. This setup just doesn't work.

For one thing, if most of your staff is busy all day working up negative stories about Republicans, that dramatically lowers the likelihood that they'll develop sources with info about Democratic corruption.

Moreover, even if you do make an effort to look at both sides, stories usually must be picked up by outlets across the spectrum to have an impact. That happens less and less in the partisan age.

Last year, the *New York Times* dipped a toe into the "Clinton Cash" material and did its potentially damaging "Uranium One" story about a series of suspicious donations to the Clinton Foundation. The story was soundly reported and forced the Clinton campaign to admit to "mistakes" in its disclosures.

But the response of other non-conservative outlets was mostly silence and/or damage control. That left it to mostly circulate in the *Washington Times* and *Breitbart* and the *Daily Caller*, rendering it automatically illegitimate with most blue-state audiences.

Some people will say that is because the Uranium One/ Clinton Foundation matter simply isn't newsworthy. Maybe not. But if it isn't, are we sure we would know?

Right-wing audiences, almost irrespective of source, already discount most scoops about Republicans. That means even potentially devastating stories, like the troubling allegations of sexual misconduct which have been made in lawsuits against Trump, will be dismissed out of hand as just more politicized coverage.

The public hates us reporters in the best of times, when we're doing our jobs correctly, merely being conniving, prying little busybodies forever getting up into people's business.

But the summer of Trump could easily turn into an Alamo moment for the press. There are reporters who are quietly promising themselves they'll go back to being independent and above the fray in November, after we're past the threat of a Trump presidency.

But just ask the *National Review*: Once you jump in the politicians' side of the pool, it's not so easy to get out again. And what will they think of us then? Is there a word for "lower than scum"?

22

September 6, 2016: How Donald Trump Lost His Mojo

Flailing on race and immigration, his campaign in chaos, the candidate who made a brilliant farce of the election is now finding the joke is on him

A T FIRST, IT LOOKS LIKE THE SAME OLD ACT. WHAT COULD be more natural than a coiffed and bellicose Donald Trump, addressing a raucous crowd on a Friday afternoon in Manchester, New Hampshire, that great white-frustration campaign Mecca he blew through like a hurricane nine months ago during primary season?

"It is terrific to be back in New Hampshire!" he begins.

"TRUMP! TRUMP! TRUMP!" shouts the virtually all-white, mostly male crowd of fifty- and sixty- and seventy-somethings. Trump's speeches increasingly look like VFW raffle nights.

"It's really a very special place for me," Trump goes on. "This is where I won my first victory!"

The prepared remarks handed out by the campaign indicate that Trump's next line will begin with the antiseptic phrase "Over the next 74 days, we are all going to work very hard to win this state. . . ."

But this is Donald Trump, sworn enemy of the prepared remark.

He immediately jumps off-script to stay on his favorite subject: himself.

"If I didn't win here, who knows where I'd be," he says, mugging and humble-bragging for the crowd. "Maybe I'd be building buildings or something."

The audience roars. This is the Trump they fell in love with. It's the same über-confident, self-congratulating gasbag who bulldozed to the Republican nomination on the strength of long, unscripted rants that were glorious tributes to every teenager everywhere who has ever taken a test without studying. Now the scriptless wonder is back. Or is he?

"Hillary Clinton believes only in government of, by and for the powerful!" he booms, beginning a long rant on "Crooked Hillary." He speaks in harsh bursts of invective that sound at first like the same stream-of-consciousness turd clouds Trump spat out in great volumes during primary season.

But within a minute or two, he's muddling through a list of Clinton controversies in suspiciously grammatical language, and the air starts to leave the room.

He rails against the speaking fees paid to Bill Clinton by companies like the Swedish telecom giant Ericsson while it had business before Hillary's State Department, even using the phrase "the exemption of telecom giant Ericsson."

He denounces moves to give foundation donors suspicious reconstruction contracts in Haiti and a seat on an intelligence advisory board. Then, saying Clinton ran the State Department "like a personal hedge fund" (a phrase that makes no sense, even to people who hate hedge-fund managers), Trump mentions another controversy involving a Russian uranium company. Then, still another, involving the Swiss bank UBS.

It's a dead giveaway. The primary-season Donald Trump would never have been able to remember five things. Even more revealing is his rhetorical dismount: "But these examples," he shouts, "are only the tip of the Clinton-corruption iceberg!"

The real Donald Trump does not speak in metaphors, let alone un-mixed ones. The man who once famously pronounced "I know words, I have the best words" scorched through the primaries using the vocabulary of a signing gorilla ("China—money—bad!").

Last October, when Trump was an ascendant circus act whose every move mesmerized the global media, the *Boston Globe* did a linguistic analysis of the GOP field. The paper discovered that loserific hopefuls like Jim Gilmore and Mike Huckabee were speaking above the 10th-grade level. But Trump was crushing the competition using the language of a fourth-grader, below all of his competitors, including Ben Carson (sixth grade) and Ted Cruz (ninth grade).

It was a key to his success. In an era when the public above all hates professional politicians, Trump came off as unrehearsed and genuine. He was a lout and a monster, but at least he was ad-libbed.

All that's gone now. And it's not just the language that's different.

When he was in New Hampshire for the primaries, he acted like a drunken stockbroker who fell off the end of a bar into a presidential race. He made a mockery of the most overcovered and self-serious political pageant on Earth. There was no come-on, no calculation, no "ground game," nothing, just one unhinged rich person making it all up as he went along, crapping on the Jeb Bushes and "Little Marcos" for the sheer scatological joy of it. Forget about poll-tested speeches, it was a miracle he wore pants on the stump.

That this tasteless rampage lifted him to the Republican nomination was a perfect farce predictable to anyone who's ever seen *The Producers*. He acted like a man trying to lose, and won. But now . . .

Now he's trying to win, and he's in freefall. Polls show he will lose to one of the most unpopular Democratic nominees ever. And Trump, whose very name is supposed to be synonymous with hedonism and hoggish excess, looks in person like a picture of misery.

It's obvious that reading someone else's words depresses Trump to no end, which is why he's never really done it. His father's eulogy in 1999 is reportedly the one exception. "Those are the only prepared remarks he's ever delivered before now, to my knowledge," says his biographer Wayne Barrett. "He talks all the time about how he doesn't want to bore his audience. He's more worried about boring himself."

But he's boring himself a lot now, and it's hard not to wonder why. The man whose primary season slogan might as well have been "Trump '16: I Don't Give a Fuck" is not only carefully choosing his words now but appears panicked and indecisive, overwhelmed by his seemingly inevitable defeat.

Worse, he's sunk to the level of "strategy" to try to revive his flagging campaign, probably on the advice of some genius in the new rogues' gallery of crackpots and "alt-right" psychopaths (led by bullfroggish *Breitbart* chief Steve Bannon) he calls his inner circle.

And what strategy!

The Manchester crowd of sunburned white guys in jean shorts and Celtics gear looks on, mute and mystified, as Trump moves from the Clinton Foundation rant into his new "theme": Donald Trump as civil-rights champion!

The crowd whoops and hollers at first as Trump repeats the tried-and-true Republican trope that minorities are the victims of patronizing Democratic Party politics.

"Every policy Hillary Clinton supports is a policy that has failed and betrayed communities of color!" he begins, to cheers.

But the crowd grows more and more quiet as Trump lingers on the theme of black and Hispanic suffering.

"Nearly four in 10 African-American children live in poverty!" he says. "Fifty-eight percent of African-American youth are not working! More than 2,700 people have been shot in Chicago this year alone!"

And he just keeps going. There's no punchline about the failure of personal responsibility in inner-city homes, no lecture about the breakdown of two-parent families, no tirades against "free stuff." The crowd waits for a dog whistle that never blows. Instead, Trump just reads off one line after another about suffering in minority communities, almost like that's the point or something.

Trump's old stump speech was a blunt appeal to the frustrations of flyover America. It was a promise from a would-be strongman to clear out corrupt elites who, Trump said, had fattened themselves with donor cash as they shipped the regular workingman's job abroad, or handed them to minorities climbing the walls.

In places like Manchester, a moonscape of closed mills and industrial ruins, his furious "throw the bums out" speeches used to bull's-eye every audience.

But general-election Trump's new speech is like a bizarre Mad Libs exercise in which someone mass-inserted references to African-Americans where the old white-misery applause lines used to be.

In the crowd, there's slow clapping, and confusion. Finally, Trump wraps up by making a bold promise about the future under a Trump presidency.

"African-American citizens and Latino citizens," he promises, "will have the time of their life!"

What is this, the musical climax to *Dirty Dancing*? Has a stranger civil-rights speech ever been delivered?

Shortly afterward, a mumbling and bewildered crowd files out of the Radisson ballroom where the event had predictably been held (the Manchester Radisson will someday be preserved as a monument to presidential-campaign tedium). Nobody complains or anything, but a sense of letdown hangs over the whole building.

What the hell just happened? What was that speech about? Who was it for? And who kidnapped the old Donald Trump?

For most of the past year, it's been difficult to get a read on what "the Trump campaign" was thinking at any given moment, because "the Trump campaign" per se didn't exist.

The campaign was basically a few overheated ganglia some-where behind Trump's eyes.

His process was random enough that he himself often seemed surprised by the amazing things that came out of his mouth, sort of the way Eddie Van Halen used to raise an eyebrow when he thought he hit a particularly awesome note in a solo. Trump's head tilted one way, and a tirade against Macy's credit cards came out. It tilted the other way, and Trump compared El Chapo to a vacuum cleaner.

Nobody had "access" to the inner workings of that, not reporters, not his staff, and probably not even Trump him-self. And yet his poll numbers kept soaring. It was the cheap-est, most lightweight campaign organization ever. That he ended up securing the Republican nomination in this man-ner is an unsurpassable accomplishment in the history of winging it.

But eventually he reached a stage of the race where the whole enterprise simply got too big to manage entirely by whim, and that's when he got into trouble. Seat-of-pants Trump was an elusive, high-energy monstrosity, but doing-his-homework Trump was a disaster, to use one of his favor-ite words.

He made terrible decision after terrible decision. After spending all primary season savaging the Republican estab-lishment, he spent the months after he sewed up the nomi-nation alternately courting and denouncing the likes of Paul Ryan, John McCain and Kelly Ayotte.

Then, after bragging all year that he didn't need any-one's money, he suddenly started sucking up to party big-wigs and reportedly even fired his thuggish campaign manager, Corey Lewandowski, at the behest of donors as well as his own children.

He replaced Lewandowski with the similarly goonish political lifer Paul Manafort—Lewandowski and Manafort both look like the kind of people you'd find smoking Pall Malls in the trailer office of a repossessed-car lot. But Trump immediately began straining against Manafort's efforts to get him to stick to scripted speeches and stop bashing other Republicans, the parents of war dead, Mexican judges and other such unsuitable targets for general-election-season abuse.

Before long, the internal tensions leaked to the *New York Times*, which in an August 13th article detailed Manafort's fruitless efforts to get Trump to focus and stop shooting himself in the face. The article naturally infuriated the candidate, who then essentially ousted Manafort and replaced him with Bannon, chief of the far-right Breitbart media empire and perhaps the only person in America with a worse reputation than Trump for hotheadedness and choleric racism.

Trump would have been better off just conceding the loss from the outset and spending the general-election season going up in flames, showing up at debates guzzling martinis and wearing a lampshade on his head, directing daily tirades at cancer kids and nuns, playing the election like an Andy Kaufman prank.

Instead, he vacillated wildly, trying in one moment to look "presidential" before reversing course seconds later to purge his staff and go on politically destructive rampages.

These manic-depressive episodes caused him to plummet in the polls and ultimately left him on the maximally absurd strategic track: trying to right the ship and win back the political middle under the direction of Bannon, an infamous idiot, extremist and Internet conspiracy theorist whose ex-wife claimed in court filings that he "didn't want [his kids] to go to school with Jews." Trump as Eliza Doolittle and Bannon as Professor Higgins is surely the dumbest casting of *Pygmalion* ever tried.

By late August, the Trump-Bannon rebrand was well underway. The most obvious efforts were in the area of walking back Trump's reputation as a "racist," a word the campaign's internal polls showed too many people associated with the candidate.

Two days before the Manchester speech, for instance, Trump surprised everyone by telling his buddy Sean Hannity in a Fox-televised town hall that he was open to a "softening" on the immigration issue. "Everybody agrees we get the bad ones out," Trump said. "But when I meet thousands and thousands of people on this subject . . . they've said, 'Mr. Trump, I love you, but to take a person that has been here for 15 or 20 years and throw them and the family out, it's so tough, Mr. Trump.'"

TV audiences and journalists alike reacted in shock. Was this the same guy who plugged a return to Eisenhower's lurid "Operation Wetback" mass-deportation program last year?

The next morning, long-suffering Trump campaign spokeswoman Katrina Pierson was on TV, trying to explain. Pierson is a puzzling choice for a lead mouthpiece. She would lose at Boggle to Rob Gronkowski. She now had to reframe her candidate's apparent complete turnabout on his signature issue. To a CNN panel, Pierson said, "He hasn't changed his position on immigration. He has changed the words that he is saying."

The panel burst out laughing. Pierson tried to stay composed and brave her way through the rest of the segment, but it was like watching a kitten try to crawl out of a wood-chipper. Within moments, Pierson's tortured Orwellian construction was rocketing around the Internet, among other things inspiring thousands of Twitter jokes.

Famed swimsuit model Chrissy Teigen, for instance, acidly tweeted, "Not many of us could wake up and do what @KatrinaPierson does every day with a straight face. What an inspiration."

In a perfect mini set piece of the Trump campaign, Pierson retweeted this sarcastic tribute, thinking it a compliment. Even Trump's media expert is in a slump.

As for Trump's apparent flip-flop on immigration, it technically wasn't much of a change. As multiple observers have pointed out, Trump has all along occasionally thrown out tidbits such as "we'll keep the good ones." From the start, on this and on virtually every other issue, Trump has always tried to have it both ways.

Moreover, as Alex Nowrasteh of the Cato Institute points out, Trump's written platform doesn't draw a hard line on the issue. "Not that Trump is the kind of guy who cares what his position paper says," Nowrasteh says, "but there's nothing in it that insists that all undocumented immigrants have to go." Nowrasteh's theory is that the "softening" story was prompted by wishful thinking on the part of mainstream Republicans who are trying to make Trump more palatable. The idea of Trump changing positions is being pushed, he says, by "groups of Republicans who want to support him but are turned off by his rhetoric."

Indeed, just days before Trump's town hall with Hannity, the candidate held a Saturday meeting at Trump Tower in New York with his newly created "Hispanic Advisory Council" of Latino Trump supporters. Bannon and campaign manager Kellyanne Conway were also at the meeting. When it was over, members of the group leaked details of the discussion to the media, in particular to *BuzzFeed*, which in a headline said that Trump was indicating an "openness to legalization."

Trump campaign spokesman Steven Cheung coldly dismissed the report as "clickbait journalism." But then Trump himself delivered his bizarre "softening" riff at the Hannity event, seeming to confirm *BuzzFeed*'s report in every respect. What the hell was going on?

Nobody had a clue. Among the reporters following Trump around the country, there were only guesses. Trump's traveling press contingent is full of smart, hard-working folks but is tiny relative to campaigns past, between six and 12 reporters on a given day. This is a symbol of another missed opportunity by the Trump campaign, which not only sidelined journalists but banned some major outlets altogether.

Reporters traditionally traveled in huge numbers with the candidate and the candidate's staff, all on the same plane. Journalists drank with staffers at night and candidates periodically snuck into the press section to show a little leg. Whether it was John Kerry slinging footballs to hacks on the tarmac, George Bush giving nicknames to favored beat writers or Barack Obama posing for photos with press-section rookies, past presidential candidates made an effort to charm the media, no matter how much they secretly despised it.

If Trump were smart, he'd not only invite the press onto his plane, he'd regularly set up camp in the cheap seats with them, plying them with booze and Cuban cigars while stuffing C-notes into their shirt pockets, à la Rodney Dangerfield's Al Czervik character in *Caddyshack*. Trump is an expert schmoozer, and it's not like it costs a lot to influence the media. You can get most reporters to chill out with a beer and a box of cookies.

Charming the press was one of the few cards Trump had to play in a race that was always going to be an uphill climb. This is particularly true since the media covering Hillary Clinton have been similarly shut out.

Instead, the press not only flies in a separate plane from Trump, but flies with logistical staff only. You're well taken care of, but you see no aides, no spokespeople. There are virtually no "avails" with the candidate, and if you want a comment or a clarification, you can't just walk up the aisle. You've got to email a spokesperson halfway across the country, who may or may not answer, likely because he or she doesn't know the answer either.

Thus when the immigration flip-flop blew up, the Trump press corps had no way to know what was happening. They were told that a major address on immigration was coming in the next week or so, but no one told them when that would be. The situation was so absurd that when Trump gave a speech at one stop that happened to mention E-Verify and an exit-entry tracking system, some on the bus ride wondered if that was the big unveil.

"Hey," shouted one reporter, "was that the immigration speech?"

Shrugs all around. Who the hell knew?

Saturday afternoon, August 27th, the Iowa State Fairgrounds, outside Des Moines. Trump is scheduled to make an appearance here with a host of Iowa politicians, including the state's pop-culture heroine, and noted pig castrator, Sen. Joni Ernst.

The small traveling press corps following the candidate

glumly files out of a shuttle van into "Joni's Roast n' Ride," which turns out to be a mud-floored barn packed with yet another whooping-and-hollering all-white crowd dressed in biker regalia, mesh hats and flag-themed shirts.

It's a hardcore audience. Imagine the set of *Hee Haw* mixed with a Strom Thurmond rally, and you get the idea. If Colin Kaepernick walked in here by mistake, he would probably be skeletonized in seconds.

As the press files in, there is some bemused speculation as to whether or not Trump would have the stones to pull his "minority outreach" speech in this particular setting. "No way," whispers one reporter, looking around. "Not here."

When the candidate is finally introduced, he's late—he seems always to be late—and is alone. Trump rarely travels with his wife or children anymore. Stories that have surfaced about inconsistencies in Melania Trump's own immigration history have raised the specter of possible legal problems for the candidate's wife. Perhaps because of this, she's been less at his side lately.

Whatever the reason, the man who in primary season was often introduced as a beaming patriarch surrounded by adoring heir-spawn now seems sullen and diminished when he takes the stage.

In Iowa, he seems particularly off. Dressed in a blue blazer, a white button-down shirt with a high open collar, and a white "Make America Great Again" ball cap pulled down practically to his eyeballs, he looks stiff and lifeless from a distance, like a Pez-dispenser version of himself.

He also looks old. It's an impression enhanced by the terrible echoing acoustics in the barn, which make him sound like a man calling out Bingo numbers at a retirement home.

"Nothing means more to me-*me-me* . . . ," he begins, "than working to make our party the home of the African-American vote-*vote-vote* . . . once again-*again-again*. . . ."

He goes on to give the same bizarre speech about the troubles of African-Americans he's been giving for a week already, adding a line about the shooting death in Chicago of Nykea Aldridge, the 32-year-old cousin of NBA star Dwyane Wade.

In classic Trump-like fashion, he's already in the soup on this issue. Misspelling Wade's first name, Trump had earlier tweeted, "Dwayne Wade's cousin was just shot and killed walking her baby in Chicago. Just what I have been saying. African-Americans will VOTE TRUMP!"

Only Donald Trump can pivot from the murder of a beloved sports star's relative into a *Vote for me!* slogan in less than 24 hours. Not that it was a surprise: This is the same candidate who tweeted, "Appreciate the congrats for being right on Islamic terrorism," while the bodies of mass-murder victims in Orlando were still warm.

Back in the barn, Trump mentions "Dwyane Wade's cousin" again and then plunges into an even more protracted and detailed plea for the black vote. If Bernie Sanders had won the nomination and had made an attempt to change his anti-business image through a series of banker-friendly speeches delivered to undergrads at Oberlin and UC-Berkeley, it would feel something like this.

Here, Trump lays out two policy arguments for that theoretical poor inner-city African-American voter who would somehow be listening to this speech, delivered to a crowd of white bikers and farmers in an Iowa barn.

Argument one: If your life sucks already, and as a white billionaire I can only assume it does, why not try something new? "To those suffering, I say, vote for Donald Trump and I will fix it," he says. "What do you have to lose?"

Argument two is the stunner, a breathtaking attempt to pull all the irreconcilable rhetorical threads of his campaign together. "There is another civil-rights issue we need to talk about, and that's the issue of immigration enforcement," he says. "Every time an African-American citizen . . . loses their job to an illegal immigrant, the rights of that American citizen have been violated."

Yes, let's build a wall, but let's do it to help African-Americans! It's alt-right meets civil rights! The best crossover hit since "Walk This Way"!

There's muted applause, but also lots of glazed eyes staring up at the stage, not knowing how to respond. Still, after the speech, a local real estate developer named Don Whitham gives Trump's African-American outreach the thumb's-up. "The Republicans took them out of slavery. And we're trying to do it again," he says. "We're trying to take 'em out of enserfment."

He adds, voice breaking with emotion, "They're just being used by the damn politicians, that's all it amounts to!"

Apart perhaps from his most hardcore fans (and the occasional *Wall Street Journal* columnist), nobody seriously believes Trump has been trying to reach out to African-American voters. If he had, he might have spoken to some actual black people, and taken a position on an issue black audiences care about.

That he ended a week of "minority outreach" speeches pulling a crisp zero percent approval rating among black voters—zero percent!—speaks to the absurdity of taking his "outreach" campaign at face value.

Instead, the consensus is that Trump's whole effort was

geared toward reassuring moderate Republicans that he isn't a racist. "Bedrock level for a Republican is 45 percent—Trump is at 40 percent," says Simon Rosenberg, a longtime Democratic strategist and president of the New Democrat Network. "I can imagine Kellyanne Conway going through the numbers with him and just saying, 'Look, if you don't do something, you're looking at the biggest loss in party history.'" Basically, at this stage, Rosenberg concludes, "he's playing to avoid a blowout."

The only problem with this is, well, everything. If Trump was going to think strategically, the time to do it was from the very beginning, before he insulted menstruating women, the pope, Muslims, Mexicans, Whoopi Goldberg, Ronda Rousey, Carly Fiorina's face, Germany, and hundreds of other groups and individuals.

You do it before you do schlock impersonations of Chinese businesspeople ("We want deal!"), before you retweet a bogus meme claiming 81 percent of white homicide victims were killed by blacks (the real number is 15 percent), before you mimic people with neurological disorders, and before you suggest that gun enthusiasts might take a shot at your opponent.

And you definitely do it before you destroy the modern Republican Party by birthing into the mainstream an aggressive white-nationalist movement, whose entire identity is centered around walling itself off from America's future multicultural majority. In other words, you do it before you tear down a 162-year-old political organization to replace it with a smaller, more radicalized, more automatically losing coalition—not after.*

At the end of August, the campaign made a surprise an-

---

* In retrospect, Unhinged Trump was the perfect candidate for primary season, and Bannon's Pygmalion act was just enough to put a winning Republican coalition together. Maybe, on a darker level, Trump's "I love the African-Americans" act appealed to the "moderate" Republican who, like Trump, was more upset about being accused of being racist than he or she was concerned with the race issue in any other meaningful way. In either case, it was, on Bannon's part, brilliant strategy.

nouncement of a trip to Mexico, and following a year of unrestrained abuse of Mexicans, Trump shockingly ended up meeting with Mexican President Enrique Peña Nieto.

Trump spent that meeting meekly tiptoeing back a greatest-hits list of blustery primary-season remarks. Having spent all of last year promising that he would build a wall and make Mexico pay for it, he let Nieto tell him to his face that Mexico would not in fact pay for the wall. When asked about the wall, Trump said, "We discussed the wall, we didn't discuss payment." On NAFTA, which he promised to scrap in an effort to restore American jobs, Trump now promised only to keep jobs "in our hemisphere." Then the man who said Mexico was sending killers and rapists over the border on purpose called it a "great honor" to be invited to the presidential residence by Nieto, whom he described as a "friend."

Trump won the nomination by being the cruelest, most balls-out build-a-wall hard-liner. Now he was talking like Jeb Bush on immigration and Bill Clinton on NAFTA. What was the point of all that craziness and rancor and destruction? Who needs Donald Trump playing Jeb Bush, especially since the actual Jeb Bush might have had a chance of beating Hillary Clinton?

Then Trump zoomed up to Arizona and finally gave his "big immigration speech," doubling down on his most extreme rhetoric as if he hadn't just been south of the border, prostrating himself before the Mexican president. "Mexico will pay for the wall," he boomed. "A hundred percent. They don't know it yet, but they're going to pay for it."

He added a new plan to create "safe zones" in the Middle East (to be paid for by Persian Gulf countries, of course) for relocating Muslims turned back by "extreme vetting." The rollout was an immediate hit with former Klan leader David Duke, who called it "an excellent speech."

The Bannon-Trump plan appears to be to run simultaneously as a statesman and a nationalist lunatic. Either they're trying to drive their numbers down to zero as part of a kinky performance-art scheme, or the campaign is in complete chaos.

"The thing is, virtually every politician who runs for office for the first time loses," says Rosenberg. "These rich guys don't realize how nuanced a game it is. In their business, you get 10 percent margins, you're a huge success. In our business, you need 51 percent margins. It's tough. And they don't get it until it's too late."

The presidential campaign is the ultimate exploration of self. If you make it as far as the general election, you become one of the most analyzed personalities on Earth. Merciless reporters track down every relative, business partner, love interest and enemy you ever had, and pundits and armchair psychiatrists alike scrutinize every sentence you utter.

Making it to victory requires an unshakeable inner confidence beyond the capacity of most people. Most politicians get around this by being walking sales pitches instead of people, appearing as two-dimensional cardboard cutouts representing slates of party positions, their personalities merely serving as idiosyncratic background to the corporate presentation. In times of crisis, they can cling to the party line.

Trump is different. He ran as a party-smasher, a man among elitist mice, a traitor to the establishment who came down from corrupt Olympus to save the common people. "I know the game better than anyone," he told crowds. "I've been on the other side."

As a salacious high-velocity burn on a corrupted campaign process, he was initially a brilliant, if repulsive, success. He charged through the primary season like a pig on strychnine and won the nomination not because of who he was, but what he wasn't: a politician.

Therefore, uniquely perhaps in the history of presidential candidates, Trump's success hinged on his ability to stay true to himself. The promise of his campaign was Trump the man, all day, every day. If his voters wanted a politician, or even a non-politician who thought before he spoke, they'd have chosen one. Who could have foreseen we'd end up with the one thing more ridiculous than Donald Trump running for president: Donald Trump running for president and trying to be smart about it.

23

September 7, 2016: The Unconquerable Trump

Seemingly imploding on the trail, Trump gains in a national poll. WTF, America?

A STUNNING NEW CNN POLL CAME OUT THIS WEEK, showing Donald Trump in the lead against Hillary Clinton, 45–43 percent. Naturally, the release of this new survey coincided with my own *Rolling Stone* feature describing Trump in a "freefall," having "lost his mojo."

What can I say? Sometimes in journalism, you can't help looking like a buffoon.

Let's look at that poll, for if there's any truth to it (and there has been some other evidence of a "tightening" in the race), it would mean the ultimate worst-case scenario.

On the surface, Trump and new "campaign CEO" Steve

Bannon appear to be employing one of the dumbest campaign strategies presidential politics has ever seen.

The recent rebrand is a transparent effort to rehabilitate Trump's image as a racist loon. Bannon's play has been to wheel Trump out at campaign events shackled, Hannibal Lecter–style, to teleprompters. At each stop, the candidate tries to focus just long enough to read out a robotic script offering "minority outreach," while also signaling a "softening" and a "pivot" on his chief issue, immigration.

In person, watching Lecter-Trump labor to push this "minority outreach" script up a hill for 45 minutes or so is embarrassing to the point of being physically uncomfortable.

His "What do you have to lose?" appeals to African-American voters recall the cringe-inducing "My heart is as black as yours" routine of infamous New York Democrat Mario Procaccino, whose 1969 mayoral run has been described as the most incompetent campaign in American history.

It seems impossible that Trump's Dr. King act would convince an educated person of anything. Just try to picture the mind that would be persuaded by these speeches. It's not an easy image to conjure.

But in perhaps the ultimate demonstration of Murphy's Law, it seems to have worked. The Bannon-Trump strategy at least looks this week like a success, even if it was just in the area of scoring one headline in one perhaps-flawed poll.

It's developments like this that explain why the most successful third-party candidate in polls this season—and the only one who attracts wide support among liberals, conservatives and independents—is a giant meteor hitting the earth. (The "Sweet Meteor O'Death" scored 13 percent support, including an impressive 27 percent of independents, in a July poll.)

After all, if Trump-Bannon's nitwit strategy can succeed, that's a powerful argument in favor of the species needing a reboot.

Or maybe the problem is confined to those of us here in America.

Just look at the math. The total popular vote in 2012 was 129,237,642 people. Assuming a similar turnout, in a theoretical world where Donald Trump scores 45 percent of the vote, that would mean a hair over 58 million human beings casting a vote for a man who thinks vaccines need to be administered one at a time, because "tiny children are not horses."

Unlike George W. Bush, a pliable ignoramus surrounded by cunning government lifers who were the real candidates for the job, Trump is surrounded by determined conspiracy theorists incapable of speaking English or completing a coherent thought.

His spokesperson Katrina Pierson said Barack Obama's policies "probably" caused the death of a soldier killed in Iraq—in 2004! When confronted about her mistake, she said, "That's why I used 'probably.'"

These are the sort of people whose first move upon entering the Oval Office would probably be to order the file on Area 51, or to check the back of the Declaration of Independence for treasure maps. And yet, somewhere north of 55 million voters, and huge majorities of white people, seem prepared to cast votes for this crew.

Trump would probably require miraculous reversals in demographic trends to win. Most likely, he'd need either absurdly low turnout among minorities and college-educated voters, or an unheard-of increase in turnout among non-college-educated white voters.

But such eventualities can't be counted out. Trump has enjoyed an extraordinary run of sinister luck since the beginning of this race. The seas have parted for him over and over again in a pattern so improbable, it makes one guess at the existence of a Supreme Being with a serious grudge against the United States.

I bet on Trump to win the Republican nomination last summer, but it didn't seem like easy money then. Trump's path to victory in the nomination seemed to depend upon the unfolding of something like a conspiracy of incompetence by his primary opponents.

The likely victory scenario required some combination of John Kasich, Ben Carson, Jeb Bush, Chris Christie, Marco Rubio and Ted Cruz staying in the race too long, preventing Trump from having to win a one-on-one race.

That did happen, thanks in part to a series of unhappy accidents. Marco Rubio's New Hampshire implosion, for instance, may have opened the door for already-conceding John Kasich's surprise second-place showing in the same state. This kept both candidates in through Super Tuesday, allowing Trump to waltz to victory needing only a plurality of voters.

Trump's Republican opponents proved perfect foils for his suicide-bomber political style. One by one, they each walked into the trap of engaging him in exchanges of schoolyard insults, causing senators and governors to quickly lose their respectable titles in favor of new monikers like "low-energy Jeb" and "Little Marco" and "Lyin' Ted."

Trump's opponents all looked offended and thrown off-script by his attacks, while Trump came across as the same bleating, thin-skinned nut whether anyone engaged him or not. His opponents never figured out that Trump is incapable of losing such contests of insults, since he lacks the self-awareness to feel it when verbal punches land.

The physical proximity afforded by the endless debates was another factor. When you have to share a stage with a candidate determined to turn every event into a circus, it's pretty hard to play the "I'm above the fray" card. He devoured camera time even in moderated debates, enhancing the impression that he was the dominant personality.

But all of these advantages were supposed to evaporate in general-election season. Instead of needing a plurality of Republicans, he now needed a plurality (and perhaps a majority) of all voters. Moreover his opposition was no longer a field of 16 nincompoops, but a single historically skilled political infighter who happened also to be one of the most famous and admired women on earth.

Unlike Ted Cruz or Marco Rubio, Hillary Clinton was not going to get into a "mine's bigger than yours" bro-brawl with Trump on live TV. She was sure to do the smart thing: let Trump hang himself with his own stupidity for as long as possible, and then ultimately turn the election into a referendum on dull competence versus cattle cars, race war and global isolation—an easy choice, the political version of Eddie Izzard's "cake or death" joke.

This is exactly how it seemed to play out. After the conventions, Trump plunged into new scandals and controversies on a nearly minute-to-minute basis, from a loony battle with the family of a dead war vet to a claim that Obama "founded ISIS" to a bizarre remark about what daughter Ivanka should do if sexually harassed in the workplace by a Roger Ailes type ("find a new career").

Then, in the face of plummeting poll numbers and mocking headlines, he panicked and emerged from a campaign reorganization tethered to an insane plan to walk all of this damage back by singing homilies to African-American despair in front of all-white crowds.

It should have been fatal. It wasn't. Whether the CNN poll taken at the end of this incredible sequence of events that shows him in the lead is accurate or not, is irrelevant. The fact that it's even close is an awesome indictment of us all.

It's also a testament to Trump's uncanny inability to fail even when he seems to be trying his hardest to do so. Not even the most exaggerated view of Hillary Clinton's deficiencies as a candidate explains it. It feels a lot more like *Idiocracy* coming powerfully to life at exactly the wrong moment.

I still don't think Trump really has a chance, but we're sure headed toward a scary ending.

24

October 16, 2016: The Failure and Fury of Donald Trump

Win, lose or drop out, the Republican nominee
has laid waste to the American political system.
On the trail for the last gasp of the ugliest
campaign in our nation's history

SATURDAY, EARLY OCTOBER, AT A FAIRGROUND 40 MINUTES southwest of Milwaukee. The very name of this place, Elkhorn, conjures images of past massacres on now-silent fields across our blood-soaked history. Nobody will die here; this is not Wounded Knee, but it is the end of an era. The modern Republican Party will perish on this stretch of grass.

Trump had been scheduled to come here today, to kiss defenseless babies and pose next to pumpkins and haystacks at Wisconsin congressman and House Speaker Paul Ryan's annual "GOP Fall Fest."

Instead, the two men declared war on each other. The last straw was the release of a tape capturing Donald Trump uttering five words—"Grab them by the pussy"—during an off-camera discussion with former *Access Hollywood* host Billy Bush about what you can do to women when you're a star.

Keeping up with Trump revelations is exhausting. By late October, he'll be caught whacking it outside a nunnery. There are not many places left for this thing to go that don't involve kids or cannibalism. We wait, miserably, for the dong shot.

Ryan, recoiling from Trump's remarks, issued a denunciation ("Women are to be championed and revered, not objectified"), disinviting Trump from his Elkhorn celebration, which was to be the first joint campaign appearance by the country's two highest-ranking Republicans.

As a result, the hundreds of Republican faithful who came spoiling for Trumpian invective, dressed in T-shirts reading things like DEPLORABLE LIVES MATTER and BOMB THE SHIT OUT OF ISIS, and even FUCK OFF, WE'RE FULL (a message for immigrants), ended up herded out here, as if by ruse, to get a big dose of the very thing they'd rebelled against.

They sat through a succession of freedom-and-God speeches by Wisconsin Republicans like Rep. Jim Sensenbrenner, Sen. Ron Johnson, Gov. Scott Walker and Ryan, who collectively represented the party establishment closing ranks and joining the rest of the country in denouncing the free-falling Trump. Once an unstoppable phenomenon who had the media eating out of his controversial-size hands, Trump, in the space of a few hours, had become the mother of all pop-culture villains, a globally despised cross of Dominique Strauss-Kahn, Charlie Sheen and Satan.

To the self-proclaimed "Deplorables" who came out to see Trump anyway, Ryan's decision was treason, the latest evidence that no matter what their party affiliation, Washington politicians have more in common with one another than with regular people.

"Small-ball Ryan," groused Trump supporter Mike Goril, shaking his head, adding to this election cycle's unsurpassable all-time record for testicular innuendo.

Speaker after speaker ascended the stage to urge Republican voters to vote. But with the exception of Attorney General Brad Schimel, who got a round of applause when he grudgingly asked the audience to back Trump for the sake of the Supreme Court, every last one of them tiptoed past the party nominee's name. One by one, they talked around Trump, like an unmentionable uncle carted off on a kiddie-porn rap just before Thanksgiving dinner.

Metaphorically anyway, Trump supporters like Goril were right. Not one of these career politicians had the gumption to be frank with this crowd about what had happened to their party. Instead, the strategy seemed to be to pretend none of it had happened, and to hide behind piles of the same worn clichés that had driven these voters to rebel in the first place.

The party schism burst open in the middle of a speech by Wisconsin's speaker of the State Assembly, Robin Vos. Vos is the Billy Mays of state budget hawks. He's a mean-spirited little ball of energy who leaped onto the stage reminding the crowd that he wanted to eliminate the office of the treasurer to SAVE YOU MONEY!

Vos went on to brag about having wiped out tenure for University of Wisconsin professors, before dismounting with yet another superawkward Trumpless call for Republicans to turn out to vote.

"I have no doubt that with all of you standing behind us," he shouted, "and with the fantastic record of achievement that we have, we're going to go on to an even bigger and better victory than before!"

There was scattered applause, then someone from the crowd called out:

"You uninvited Donald Trump!"

Boos and catcalls, both for and against Vos and the Republicans. Most in the crowd were Trump supporters, but others were angry with Trump for perhaps saddling them with four years of Hillary Clinton. These camps now battled it out across the field. A competing chant of "U-S-A! U-S-A!" started on the opposite end of the stands, only to be met by chants from the pro-Trumpers.

"We want Trump! We want Trump!" "U-S-A! U-S-A!"

Ryan, the last speaker, tried to cut the tension with a leaden joke about the "elephant in the room." But he still refused to speak Trump's name, or do more than refer the crowd to a written statement. He just smiled like it was all OK, and talked about what a beautiful day it was.

Ryan's cowardly play was reflective of the party as a whole, which has yet to own its role in the Trump story. Republican ineptitude and corruption represented the first crack in the facade of a crumbling political system that made Trump's rise possible. As toxic as Trump was, many outside observers were slow to pick up on the threat because they were so focused on how much Republicans like Ryan deserved him.

Trump's early rampage through the Republican field made literary sense. It was classic farce. He was the lewd, unwelcome guest who horrified priggish, decent society, a theme that has mesmerized audiences for centuries, from *Vanity Fair* to *The Government Inspector* to (closer to home) *Fear and Loathing in Las Vegas*. When you let a hands-y, drunken slob loose at an aristocrats' ball, the satirical power of the story comes from the aristocrats deserving what comes next. And nothing has ever deserved a comeuppance quite like the American presidential electoral process, which had become as exclusive and cut off from the people as a tsarist shooting party.

The first symptom of a degraded aristocracy is a lack of capable candidates for the throne. After years of indulgence, ruling families become frail, inbred and isolated, with no one but mystics, impotents and children to put forward as kings. Think of Nikolai Romanov reading fortunes as his troops starved at the front. Weak princes lead to popular uprisings. Which brings us to this year's Republican field.

There wasn't one capable or inspiring person in the infamous "Clown Car" lineup. All 16 of the non-Trump entrants were dunces, religious zealots, wimps or tyrants, all equally out of touch with voters. Scott Walker was a lipless sadist who in centuries past would have worn a leather jerkin and thrown dogs off the castle walls for recreation. Marco Rubio was the young rake with debts. Jeb Bush was the last offering in a fast-diminishing hereditary line. Ted Cruz was the Zodiac Killer. And so on.

The party spent 50 years preaching rich people bromides like "trickle-down economics" and "picking yourself up by your bootstraps" as solutions to the growing alienation and financial privation of the ordinary voter. In place of jobs, exported overseas by the millions by their financial backers, Republicans glibly offered the flag, Jesus and Willie Horton.

In recent years it all went stale. They started to run out of lines to sell the public. Things got so desperate that during the Tea Party phase, some GOP candidates began dabbling in the truth. They told voters that all Washington politicians, including their own leaders, had abandoned them and become whores for special interests. It was a slapstick routine: Throw us bums out!

Republican voters ate it up and spent the whole of last primary season howling for blood as Trump shredded one party-approved hack after another. By the time the other 16 candidates finished their mass-suicide-squad routine, a tail-chasing, sewer-mouthed septuagenarian New Yorker was accepting the nomination of the Family Values Party.

Now, months later, as Trump was imploding, Ryan was retreating to ancient supply-side clichés about how cutting taxes will bring the jobs back. "We've got to scrap this tax code and start over," he said.

As Ryan droned on, well back behind the stands, two heavyset middle-aged women in Trump/Pence T-shirts shook their heads in boredom. One elbowed the other.

"Wanna grab my crotch?"

This is Wisconsin, after all. You can tell immigrants to fuck off, but you can't say the p-word the day before church, or a Packers game.

The other woman chuckled, then reached down to her own, as if to say, "Grab this!"

Both women busted out laughing. When the event was done, as the crowd of other seething Deplorables filed past them, they and a few others remained in their chairs, staring fatalistically at the empty stage.

The scene couldn't have been more poignant. Duped for a generation by a party that kowtowed to the wealthy while offering scraps to voters, then egged on to a doomed rebellion by a third-rate con man who wilted under pressure and was finally incinerated in a fireball of his own stupidity, people like this found themselves, in the end, represented by literally no one.

Not many people are shedding tears for the Republican voter these days, perhaps rightly so. But the sudden crash-ending of the Trump campaign only made official what these voters have suspected for years: They've been represented by an empty stage all along. Why not sit there and stare at it for a little longer?

Wilkes-Barre, Pennsylvania, the Mohegan Sun Arena, two days later. As he has done multiple times in the past year, Trump has seemingly rebounded from certain disaster. A second debate with Hillary Clinton did not go quite so disastrously as the first, despite horrible optics (he appeared obese from stress and stalked Clinton onstage, as if wanting to bite her back à la Marv Albert) and even worse behavior (he threatened to jail his opponent, a straight-up dictator move you'd expect from a Mobutu, Pinochet or Putin).

Whether or not he "won" the debate was immaterial. He at least impressed pious Mike Pence, Trump's sad-sack running mate, who reportedly had been considering withdrawing from the ticket over the whole pussy thing. "Big debate win!" Pence tweeted, ending rumors of an internal mutiny. "Proud to stand with you as we #MAGA!"

That's hashtag Make America Great Again, in case you didn't believe Mike Pence is hip. (The new white-power movement, like a lot of fraternities, is short on brains, but long on secret passwords and handshakes.) The man who once opposed clean needles on moral grounds was now ready to march through history with a serial groper and tit-gazer.

In Wilkes-Barre, home to a recent Klan leafleting, and a key electoral-map battleground, the turnout for Trump's rally was a vast sea of white faces and profane signage. SHE'S A CUNT—VOTE TRUMP read the T-shirt of one attendee. BILL! MONICA GAVE YOU WHAT? read the caption over a photo of a grinning Hillary, plastered on the side of one of a scary triad of 18-wheelers decked out in anti-Clinton invective. On line going into the event, some more mild-mannered visitors explained why there was nothing that could dissuade them from voting Trump. "Even if it's small, there's a chance that he's going to do something completely different, and that's why I like him," said Trent Gower, a soft-spoken young man. "And when he talks, I actually understand what he's saying. But, like, when fricking Hillary Clinton talks, it just sounds like a bunch of bullshit." Inside the arena, passions were running high. Kids zoomed back and forth in Trump/Pence shirts. Some future visitors to probate court even brought their little boy to the event dressed in Trump garb, with a blazer and a power tie. Trump called the lad up onstage.

"Would you like to go back to your parents, or stay with Trump?" Trump asked. No one since Rickey "Rickey can't find Rickey's limo" Henderson has referred to himself in the third person with the same zeal as Trump.

The boy paused.

"Trump!" he said finally, to monstrous applause.

That was the highlight of the evening, unless you want to count Rudy Giuliani's time onstage, with his eyes spinning and arms flailing like a man who'd come to a hospital lost-and-found in search of his medulla oblongata. In recent weeks, Giuliani has looked as though he's been experimenting with recreational Botox. His new thing is to say something insane and then let his face freeze for a second, as if for the last time. In Wilkes-Barre, he started saying something rude about the Clinton Foundation: "Boy, that is phony as . . . I can't say the word because I have to be . . . nice."

Open mouth: freeze.

He stared helplessly at the crowd for a moment, then pointed upward, like he remembered something. "I might say it in the locker room!" he said, to cheers.

How Giuliani isn't Trump's running mate, no one will ever understand. Theirs is the most passionate television love story since Beavis and Butt-head. Every time Trump says something nuts, Giuliani either co-signs it or outdoes him. They will probably spend the years after the election doing prostate-medicine commercials together.

In the far-right world, every successive villain has always been worse than the last. It's quaint now to think about how Al Gore was once regarded as the second coming of Lenin, or that John Kerry was a secret communist agent. Then the race element took Obama-hatred to new and horrifying places. But Trumpian license has pushed hatred of Hillary Clinton beyond all reason. If you don't connect with it emotionally, you won't get it. For grown men and women to throw around words like "bitch" and "cunt" in front of their kids, it means things have moved way beyond the analytical.

Where is it all coming from? The most generous conceivable explanation is that the anger stems from a sense of abandonment and betrayal by the political class. This doesn't explain the likes of Giuliani and Trump, but if you squint really hard, it maybe explains some of what's going on with his supporters.

Although a lot of Clinton backers believe she's being unfairly weighed down by negative reports about the Clinton Foundation and her emails, her most serious obstacles this year were less her faults than her virtues. The best argument for a Clinton presidency is that she's virtually guaranteed to be a capable steward of the status quo, at a time of relative stability and safety. There are criticisms to make of Hillary Clinton, but the grid isn't going to collapse while she's in office, something no one can say with even mild confidence about Donald Trump.

But nearly two-thirds of the population was unhappy with the direction of the country entering the general-election season, and nothing has been more associated with the political inside than the Clinton name.

The suspicions heightened on the same day that Trump's infamous "pussy" tape leaked, when WikiLeaks released papers purporting to be excerpts of Clinton's speeches to corporate and financial titans like Goldman Sachs, Deutsche Bank and GE. Her campaign had stalwartly refused to release these during the primary against Bernie Sanders. After the Wiki release, however, one had to wonder why the Clinton camp had bothered to keep the papers secret.

The "secret" speeches in some ways showed Hillary Clinton in a more sympathetic light than her public persona usually allows. Speaking to bankers and masters of the corporate universe, she came off as relaxed, self-doubting, re-flective, honest, philosophical rather than political, and unafraid to admit she lacked all the answers.

The transcripts read like freewheeling discussions with friends about how to navigate an uncertain future. In one speech, she conceded a sense of disconnect between the wealthy and the middle class to which she used to belong. This, she said, was a feeling she never had growing up, when the country seemed to be more united.

"And now, obviously," she told executives from Gold-man, "I'm kind of far removed because of the life I've lived and the economic . . . fortunes that my husband and I now enjoy."

This frank, almost regretful admission rendered her more real in a few sentences than those cliché-ridden speeches about her hardscrabble background as the grand-daughter of a Scranton lace-factory worker.

In a speech before the Brazilian Banco Itaú, Clinton talked about her vision for the future. "My dream is a hemi-spheric common market, with open trade and open bor-ders," she reportedly said. She wanted this economy "as green and sustainable as we can get it, powering growth and opportunity for every person in the hemisphere."

In classic Clintonian fashion, her camp refused to con-firm the authenticity of the emails, while also not denying them either. But why not just own the emails? Why all the cagey non-denial denials?

The themes Clinton discussed with the banks were awesome, sweeping and of paramount importance, espe-cially coming from someone in such a unique position to shape the world's future. They collectively represented ex-actly the honest discussion about what is ahead for all of us that no one in power has ever really had with the rest of the country.

The "scandal" of the Wiki papers, if you can call it that, is that it captured how at ease Clinton was talking to bankers and industrialists about the options for the organization of a global society. Even in transcript form, it's hard not to realize that the people in these rooms are all stakeholders in this vast historical transformation.

Left out of the discussion over the years have been people like Trump's voters, who coincidentally took the first hit along the way in the form of lowered middle-class wages and benefits. They were also never told that things they cared about, like their national identity as Americans, were to have diluted meaning in the more borderless future.

This is why the "basket of deplorables" comment rankled so badly. It's not like it was anywhere near as demeaning or vicious as any of 10,000 Trump insults. But it spoke to a factual disconnnect.

It isn't just that the likely next president feels alienated from people in places like Wilkes-Barre, so close to her ancestral home. It's that, plus the fact that she feels comfortable admitting this to the likes of Goldman's Lloyd Blankfein, to whom she complained about the "bias against people who have led successful and/or complicated lives."

All of which is interesting, and maybe a problem we Americans can have a sober discussion about once we finish bayoneting each other over "pussy" or Miss Universe's weight or the Central Park Five (only Trump could go back in time and revictimize the survivors of one of the most infamous law-enforcement mistakes of all time), or whatever other lunacies we'll be culture-warring over in the last weeks of this mercifully soon-to-end campaign.

It is true that if you talk to enough Trump supporters, you will eventually find an ex-Democrat or two who'll cop to being disillusioned by the party's turn away from the middle class. "My parents were FDR Democrats," says Tim Kallas of Oak Creek, Wisconsin. "I was born and raised to believe that Democrats were for the workingman." A self-described "child of the MTV generation" who has plenty of liberal friends and rocks a long silver ponytail, Kallas says he became disenchanted with the Democrats sometime during Bill Clinton's second term. He was troubled by the Wiki speeches, and says he never signed up for the globalist program. "If you look at what's going on in Europe with the Brexit vote, it's the same conclusion that voters in England came to," he says. "Why are the problems in Greece, or whatever, my problem?"

This sounds sensible enough, but it stops computing when you get to the part where the solution to the vast and complex dilemmas facing humanity is Donald Trump, a man who stays up at night tweeting about whether or not Robert Pattinson should take back Kristen Stewart. (He shouldn't, says Trump: "She cheated on him like a dog and will do it again—just watch. He can do much better!") This is a man who can't remember what he did 10 seconds ago, much less decide the fate of the nation-state.

Whatever the original source of disaffection among these Republican voters, the battle has morphed into something else, as Trump himself proved the morning after Wilkes-Barre. He went on one of his trademark Twitter rampages, this time directed at Ryan.

The House speaker had held a conference call with elected Republicans, telling them they were free to yank support from Trump if they thought it would help them win in November. This sounds like a good decision, until you consider that it's one he should have made the moment Trump sealed the nomination. As always, the Republicans acted far too late in disavowing vicious and disgusting behavior in their ranks. Then again, it's hard to keep the loons out when you're scraping to find people willing to sell rich-friendly policies to a broke population. The reaction among hard-line legislators was predictable: You're telling us *now* we can't be pigs?

Arizona Rep. Trent Franks told Ryan that Clinton reaching the White House would result in fetuses being torn "limb to limb," while Southern California's cretinous boob Dana Rohrabacher called Ryan "cowardly," and said Trump's "pussy" comment was just a "60-[year-old] expressing sexual attitude to a younger man."

Trump, meanwhile, unleashed an inevitable string of self-destructive tweets.

9:05 a.m.: "Our very weak and ineffective leader, Paul Ryan, had a bad conference call where his members went wild at his disloyalty."

10 a.m.: "It is so nice that the shackles have been taken off me and I can now fight for America the way I want to."

Shackled! Only in America can a man martyr himself on a cross of pussy.

There's an old Slavic saying about corruption: One thief sits atop another thief, using a third thief for a whip. The campaign trail is similarly a stack of deceptions, with each implicit lie of the horse race driving the next.

Lie No. 1 is that there are only two political ideas in the world, Republican and Democrat. Lie No. 2 is that the parties are violent ideological opposites, and that during campaign season we can only speak about the areas where they differ (abortion, guns, etc.) and never the areas where there's typically consensus (defense spending, surveillance, torture, trade, and so on). Lie No. 3, a corollary to No. 2, is that all problems are the fault of one party or the other, and never both. Assuming you watch the right channels, everything is always someone else's fault. Lie No. 4, the reason America in campaign seasons looks like a place where everyone has great teeth and $1,000 haircuts, is that elections are about political personalities, not voters.

These are the rules of the Campaign Reality Show as it has evolved over the years. The program is designed to reduce political thought to a simple binary choice and force more than 100 million adults to commit to one or the other. Like every TV contest, it discourages subtlety, reflection and reconciliation, and encourages belligerence, action and conflict.

Trump was the ultimate contestant in this show. It's no accident that his first debate with Hillary Clinton turned into the Ali-Frazier of political events, with a breathtaking 84 million people tuning in, making it the most watched political program in American history.

Anyone who takes a close-enough look at how we run elections in this country will conclude that the process is designed to be regressive. It distracts us with trivialities and drives us apart during two years of furious arguments. It's a divide-and-conquer mechanism that keeps us from communicating with one another, and prevents us from examining the broader, systemic problems we all face together.

In the good old days, when elections were merely stupid and not also violent and terrifying, we argued over which candidate we'd rather have a beer with, instead of wondering why both parties were getting hundreds of millions of dollars from the same people.

Trump, ironically, was originally a rebel against this process, the first-ever party-crasher to bulldoze his way past the oligarchical triad of donors, party leaders and gate-keeping media. But once he got in, he became the ultimate servant of the horse race, simultaneously creating the most-watched and most regressive election ever.

He was unable to stop being a reality star. Trump from the start had been playing a part, but his acting got worse and worse as time went on, until finally he couldn't keep track: Was he supposed to be a genuine traitor to his class and the savior of the common man, or just be himself, i.e., a bellicose pervert with too much time on his hands? Or were the two things the same thing? He was too dumb to figure it out, and that paralysis played itself out on the Super Bowl of political stages. It was great television. It was also the worst thing that ever happened to our electoral system.

Trump's shocking rise and spectacular fall have been a singular disaster for U.S. politics. Built up in the press as the American Hitler, he was unmasked in the end as a pathetic little prankster who ruined himself, his family and half of America's two-party political system for what was probably a half-assed ego trip all along, adventure tourism for the idiot rich.

That such a small man would have such an awesome impact on our nation's history is terrible, but it makes sense if you believe in the essential ridiculousness of the human experience. Trump picked exactly the wrong time to launch his mirror-gazing rampage to nowhere. He ran at a time when Americans on both sides of the aisle were experiencing a deep sense of betrayal by the political class, anger that was finally ready to express itself at the ballot box.

The only thing that could get in the way of real change—if not now, then surely very soon—was a rebellion so maladroit, ill-conceived and irresponsible that even the severest critics of the system would become zealots for the status quo.

In the absolute best-case scenario, the one in which he loses, this is what Trump's run accomplished. He ran as an outsider antidote to a corrupt two-party system, and instead will leave that system more entrenched than ever. If he goes on to lose, he will be our Bonaparte, the monster who will continue to terrify us even in exile, reinforcing the authority of kings.

If you thought lesser-evilism was bad before, wait until the answer to every question you might have about your political leaders becomes, "Would you rather have Trump in office?"

Trump can't win. Our national experiment can't end because one aging narcissist got bored of sex and food. Not even America deserves that. But that doesn't mean we come out ahead. We're more divided than ever, sicker than ever, dumber than ever. And there's no reason to think it won't be worse the next time.

25

November 10, 2016: President Trump: How America Got It So Wrong

Journalists and politicians blew off the warning signs of a Trump presidency—now, we all must pay the price

Tuesday, November 8th, early afternoon. Outside the Trump Tower in Manhattan, a man in the telltale red Make America Great Again hat taps me on the shoulder.

"You press?" he says, looking at a set of lanyards around my neck.

I nod.

"Fuck yourself," he says, thrusting a middle finger in my face. He then turns around and walks a boy of about five away from me down Fifth Avenue, a hand gently tousling his son's hair.

This was before Donald Trump's historic victory. The message afterward no doubt would have been the same. There's no way to overstate the horror of what just went down. Sure, we've had some unstable characters enter the White House. JFK had health problems that led him to take amphetamine shots during the Cuban Missile Crisis. Reagan's attention span was so short, the CIA had to make mini-movies to brief him on foreign leaders. George W. Bush not only didn't read the news, he wasn't interested in it ("What's in the newspapers worth worrying about?" he once asked, without irony).

But all of these men were just fronts for one or the other half of the familiar alternating power structure, surrounded by predictable, relatively sober confederates who managed the day-to-day. Trump enters the White House as a lone wrecking ball of conspiratorial ideas, a one-man movement unto himself who owes almost nothing to traditional Republicans and can be expected to be anything but a figurehead. He takes office at a time when the chief executive is vastly more powerful than ever before, with nearly unlimited authority to investigate, surveil, torture and assassinate foreigners and even U.S. citizens—powers that didn't seem to trouble people much when they were granted to Barack Obama.

Shunned during election season by many in his own party, President-elect Trump's closest advisers are a collection of crackpots and dilettantes who will make Bush's cabinet look like the Nobel committee. The head of his EPA transition team, Myron Ebell, is a noted climate-change denier. Pyramid enthusiast and stabbing expert Ben Carson is already being mentioned as a possible Health and Human

Services chief.* Rudy Giuliani, probably too unhinged by now for even a *People's Court* reboot, might be attorney general. God only knows who might end up being Supreme Court nominees; we can only hope they turn out to be lawyers, or at least people who played lawyers onscreen. And sitting behind this fun-house nightmare of executive-branch worthies (which *Politico* speculates will be one of the more "eclectic" cabinets ever) will be a rubber-stamping all-Republican legislature that will attract the loving admiration of tinhorn despots from Minsk to Beijing.

Trump made idiots of us all. From the end of primary season onward, I felt sure Trump was en route to ruining, perhaps forever, the Republican Party as a force in modern American life. Now the Republicans are more dominant than ever, and it is the Democratic Party that is shattered and faces an uncertain future.

And they deserve it. The Democratic Party's failure to keep Donald Trump out of the White House in 2016 will go down as one of the all-time examples of insular arrogance. The party not only spent most of the past two years ignoring the warning signs of the Trump rebellion, but vilifying anyone who tried to point them out. It denounced all rumors of its creeping unpopularity as vulgar lies and bullied anyone who dared question its campaign strategy by calling them racists, sexists and agents of Vladimir Putin's Russia.

But the party's willful blindness symbolized a similar arrogance across the American intellectual elite. Trump's election was a true rebellion, directed at anyone perceived

* Ben Carson was named secretary of housing and urban development on December 5, 2016.

to be part of "the establishment." The target group included political leaders, bankers, industrialists, academics, Hollywood actors, and, of course, the media. And we all closed our eyes to what we didn't want to see.

The almost universal failure among political pros to predict Trump's victory—the few exceptions, conspicuously, were people who hailed from rust-belt states, like Michael Moore—spoke to an astonishing cultural blindness. Those of us whose job it is to cover campaigns long ago grew accustomed to treating The People as a kind of dumb animal, whose behavior could sometimes be unpredictable but, in the end, almost always did what it was told.

Whenever we sought insight into the motives and tendencies of this elusive creature, our first calls were always to other eggheads like ourselves. We talked to pollsters, think-tankers, academics, former campaign strategists, party spokes-hacks, even other journalists. Day after day, our political talk shows consisted of one geek in a suit interviewing another geek in a suit about the behaviors of pipe fitters and store clerks and cops in Florida, Wisconsin, Ohio and West Virginia. We'd stand over glitzy video maps and discuss demographic data points like we were trying to determine the location of a downed jetliner.

And the whole time, The People, whose intentions we were wondering so hard about, were all around us, listening to themselves being talked about like some wild, illiterate beast.

When *60 Minutes* did its election-eve story about the mood of the electorate, they had to call up a familiar Beltway figure, pollster Frank Luntz, to put together a focus group. Luntz's purpose was to take the white-hot rage and disgust hurled at him by voters on both sides of the aisle during the "focus group" portion, and translate it all into a media-speak during the sit-down. Luntz did his job and gave Steve Kroft his sound-bite diagnosis of The People's temperature. "That's not blowing off steam," he said. "That is a deep-seated resentment."

Deep-seated resentment. There was a catchy, succinct line, over which we could all collectively stroke our chins in quiet contemplation. That's as opposed to what the voters intended, which was to sock us all so hard for our snobbism and intellectual myopia that those very chins of ours would get driven straight through the backs of our skulls.

There was a great deal of talk in this campaign about the inability of the "low-information" voter to understand the rhetoric of candidates who spoke above a sixth-grade language level. We were told by academics and analysts that Trump's public addresses rated among the most simplistic political rhetoric ever recorded.

But that story cut in both directions, in a way few of us silver-tongued media types ever thought about. The People didn't speak our language, true. But that also meant we didn't speak theirs.

Beavis and Butt-head creator Mike Judge's *Idiocracy*, ostensibly a comedy but destined now to be remembered as a horror movie, was often cited this past year as prophecy. The film described a future dystopia of idiot Americans physically unable to understand the tepid grammatical speech of a half-smart time traveler from the past. Many reporters, myself included, found themselves thinking about this film when we heard voters saying they were literally incapable of understanding the words coming out of Hillary Clinton's mouth.

"When [Trump] talks, I actually understand what he's

saying," a young Pennsylvanian named Trent Gower told me at a Trump event a month ago. "But, like, when fricking Hillary Clinton talks, it just sounds like a bunch of bullshit."

So these Trump voters had a comprehension problem. But we were just as bad. We couldn't understand what they were saying to us. We refused to accept every signal about whom they hated, and how much. Why? Because Trump's voters were speaking a language that has been taboo in America for decades, if not forever.

Nobody in this country knows how to talk about class. America is like a giant manor estate where the aristocrats don't know they're aristocrats and the peasants imagine themselves undiscovered millionaires. And America's cultural elite, trained for so long to think in terms of artificial distinctions like Republicans and Democrats instead of more natural divisions like haves and have-nots, refused until it was too late to grasp the meaning of the rage-storm headed over the wall.

Just like the leaders of the Republican Party, who simply never believed its electorate wouldn't drop and roll over on command when the time came, we media types never believed all that anger out there was real, or at least gathered in enough force to matter.

Most of us smarty-pants analysts never thought Trump could win because we saw his run as a half-baked white-supremacist movement fueled by last-gasp, racist frustrations of America's shrinking silent majority. Sure, Trump had enough jackbooted nut jobs and conspiracist stragglers under his wing to ruin the Republican Party. But surely there was no way he could topple America's reigning multicultural consensus. How could he? After all, the country had already twice voted in an African-American Democrat to the White House.

Yes, Trump's win was a triumph of the hideous racism, sexism and xenophobia that has always run through American society. But his coalition also took aim at the neoliberal gentry's pathetic reliance on proxies to communicate with flyover America. They fed on the widespread visceral disdain red-staters felt toward the very people Hillary Clinton's campaign enlisted all year to speak on its behalf: Hollywood actors, big-ticket musicians, Beltway activists, academics, and especially media figures.

Trump's rebellion was born at the intersection of two toxic American myths, the post-racial society and the classless society.

Candidate Trump told a story about a conspiracy of cultural and financial elites bent on finishing off a vanishing white middle-class nirvana, first by shipping jobs overseas and then by waving hordes of crime-prone, bomb-tossing immigrants over the border.

These elites lived in both parties, Trump warned. The Republicans were tools of job-exporting fat cats who only pretended to be tough on immigration and trade in order to win votes, when all they really cared about were profits. The Democrats were tools of the same interests, who subsisted politically on the captured votes of hoodwinked minorities, preaching multiculturalism while practicing globalism. Both groups, Trump insisted, were out of touch with the real American voter. Neither party saw the awesome potential of this story to upend our political system.

Republicans had flirted with racist (and sexist) rhetoric for decades, refusing to the last to understand how dangerous this behavior was. They never imagined their voters would one day demand that they act on all this race-baiting talk. They believed their own pablum about racism being a thing of the past and reverse discrimination being the true threat to the American polity.

Meanwhile, the Democratic leadership, even as it was increasingly indebted to banks and corporations, never imagined that it could be the target of a class uprising. How could we be seen as aristocrats? We get union endorsements! We're the party of FDR! We're pro–civil rights! And so on.

Trump drove his tens of millions of followers right through each of these major-party blind spots. He called the Republicans' bluff on race almost from the start with his crazy Mexican wall idea, which instantly positioned the rest of the party field as nationalist pretenders. As for the Democrats, he lucked into a race against a politician he would portray as a 30-year symbol of a Beltway-insider consensus, one he said had left Middle America behind through trade deals like NAFTA.

Way back in February, after following Trump in New Hampshire, I guessed at the probable nominee's general-election strategy: "Trump will surely argue that the Clintons are the other half of the dissolute-conspiracy story he's been selling, representing a workers' party that abandoned workers and turned the presidency into a vast cash-for-access enterprise, avoiding scrutiny by making Washington into Hollywood East and turning labor leaders and journalists alike into starstruck courtiers."

Back then, I thought Trump had a real chance at the presidency. But later I made the same mistake most every other reporter did. I listened to polls and media outlets, instead of people. I thought Trump's maladroit and ridiculous

general-election campaign, in which he went back on virtually every major primary-season promise while being revealed through seemingly hourly scandals as one of the
world's most corrupt and personally repulsive individuals,
would do him in. He would lose and lose huge, ending up a
footnote to history, having served no purpose beyond the
destruction of the Republican Party. Conventional wisdom
said so, and wasn't conventional wisdom always right?

Not quite. We journalists made the same mistake the
Republicans made, the same mistake the Democrats made.
We were too sure of our own influence, too lazy to bother
hearing things firsthand, and too in love with ourselves to
imagine that so many people could hate and distrust us as
much as they apparently do.

It's too late for any of us to fix this colossal misread and
lapse in professional caution. Now all we can do is wait to
see how much this failure of vision will cost the public we
supposedly serve. Just like the politicians, our job was to
listen, and we talked instead. Now America will do its own
talking for a while. The world may never forgive us for not
seeing this coming.

26

November 18, 2016: President Obama's Last Stand

Even Obama's critics will soon have plenty of
reasons to appreciate him

Bᴀʀᴀᴄᴋ Oʙᴀᴍᴀ ʀᴀɪsᴇᴅ ᴀɴ ᴇʏᴇʙʀᴏᴡ ᴏʀ ᴛᴡᴏ ᴛʜɪs ᴡᴇᴇᴋ, when he had this to say about why the Democrats just lost the White House:

"You know, I won Iowa not because the demographics dictated that I would win Iowa. It was because I spent 87 days going to every small town and fair and fish fry and VFW hall, and there were some counties where I might have lost, but maybe I lost by 20 points instead of 50 points. . . . There are some counties maybe I won that people didn't expect because people had a chance to see you and listen to you."

Ouch. There's no way to read that except as a stinging

indictment of the Clinton campaign's failure to compete in "lost" territory.

In the past week, Obama has ventured some explanations for Donald Trump's rise. He pointed out that Trump had made a "connection" with his voters that was "powerful stuff."

This felt like a double-edged dig, thrown at both the rabid lunacy of Trump's crowds and Hillary Clinton's infamous (and oft-disputed) struggles on the personal-connection front.

Obama said Trump reached people who are "feeling deeply disaffected," and added during remarks in Greece that "we have to deal with issues like inequality . . . and economic dislocation." He noted, in the context of both the Brexit vote and Trump's win, that these issues perhaps "[cut] across countries."

Obama's remarks have been coolly received, to say the least, among blue-staters and in traditionally Democratic-friendly media outlets. Dana Milbank of the *Washington Post* blasted the outgoing president for his "above the fray approach." Others have wondered why Obama has not taken on a "more antagonistic posture."

There are a lot of people these days wondering if the election of the race-baiting Donald Trump will end up staining or outright repudiating the legacy of Barack Obama. I think it will be the other way around. Trump's presidency is almost sure to throw the best qualities of this unique and powerful historical figure into relief.

Trump was carried into the White House by an electorate that outlets like the *Harvard Business Review* tell us was obsessed with the concept of "manly dignity," but it's Obama

who has been the great model for young men of his generation. And ten years from now, when the millions of young
people who grew up during his presidency start to enter the
workforce and become leaders and parents, we'll see more
clearly what he meant to this country.

As a politician, Obama wasn't exactly without disappointments. Reporters who covered his first presidential
campaign in 2007–2008 will laugh if they go back to their
notes and read the promises he made back then.

In Philadelphia in April of 2008 Obama told the AFL-
CIO in no uncertain terms they could trust him not to sign
bad deals like the South Korea Free Trade agreement. "You
can trust me when I say that whatever trade deals we negotiate when I'm president will be good for American workers," he proclaimed. Four years later he was aggressively
lobbying that same deal and promising that it would create
70,000 jobs, and supported the even worse Trans-Pacific
Partnership to the end.

He told us repeatedly he would never have a registered
lobbyist in the White House, and practically minutes into
his presidency he was making Mark Patterson, a Goldman
lobbyist, the number two man at Treasury. He promised to
support drug reimportation from Canada and gave up on
that after a few discussions with Pharma bigwigs.

He pledged to push for "a world without nuclear weapons" at the beginning of his presidency, and was pushing for
a brand-new trillion-dollar program by the end of it. He
pledged to clean up Wall Street and then presided over a
historic stretch of regulatory and prosecutorial inaction.
The betrayals on security-state issues like drone assassination, secrecy and surveillance have been breathtaking.

On all these questions Obama seemed either to be unable to assert himself in the center of a hurricane of interests, or else he was really just a run-of-the-mill corporate Democrat regressing to an insincere mean one once Election Day was safely in the rearview mirror.

Still, if it was the latter, the usual policy disappointments somehow felt less awful in his hands. Obama seemed also to be fighting a two-front war as president and it was the other narrative, the historical battle, where his considerable intelligence seemed more focused.

He faced an extraordinary challenge, entering the White House as the first African-American president at a time when the economy was in ruins and the culture war was spiraling out of control. His political path forward was a tightrope. A presidency weighed down by corruption, indecisiveness or personal weaknesses would have been a disaster.

Imagine the reaction if Barack Obama had been caught in Kennedy- or Clinton-style bedroom scandals, or even if he'd spoken publicly in the style of Carter's "malaise" speech, or suffered a bad come-from-ahead second-term loss à la George H. W. Bush.

Any of the above would have led to the door closing on African-American politicians at the national level for a long time, a generation maybe. This burden was every bit as unfair as the one Hillary Clinton just had to shoulder as the first woman to win a major-party presidential nomination. It was crucial not only that he win, but win twice, and convincingly, and on the power of his own charisma and resolve.

He also had to manage this while somehow not allowing himself to be rattled by the torrent of abuse he received. Think of the discipline and equanimity it must have taken to not show anger and maintain an air of positivity given the vicious absurdities he had to work through, including the ones emanating from none other than Donald Trump about his birth origin.

The birther controversy was racism and profiling elevated to a Wagnerian level: Here was a black man who'd made it all the way to the Oval Office, and a giant portion of the population still considered him to be literally trespassing.

That such an idiotic campaign may have launched Trump into the White House to succeed Obama is an incredibly bitter pill, but this story isn't exactly over yet. When Trump takes over he will immediately have to reckon with Obama's example, and this is a historical popularity contest His Orangeness seems doomed to lose.

From a personality standpoint, Obama is everything Trump isn't. He's in control of his emotions, thick-skinned, self-aware, ingratiating, strategic and temperamentally (if not politically) consistent. A striking quality of Obama as president is that he did his job without seeming to need to take credit for things all of the time, which kept the political price down on many of his decisions.

People rarely make it to the presidency without first acquiring a weakness for embarrassing self-glorifying spectacles like George W. Bush's asinine "Mission Accomplished" flight. When presidents throw parades for themselves after every tiny political win, it only makes the fall from grace hurt that much more when circumstances inevitably cycle back downward. Most of them never learn because most politicians are pathological: 99 percent of them are ruled by drives rather than thoughts.

Obama wasn't that way. To use a hokey sports metaphor, he did his job in the manner of an offensive lineman: The less you heard about him, the better he was probably doing. (Obama would appreciate the comparison. He will go down with Dick Nixon and George W. Bush as one of the most unhealthily genuine sports fans to occupy the Oval Office.)

His performance this week testified greatly to this quality. He didn't have a lot to say about the election results, but what few lines he did speak conveyed a lot. This is a characteristic of strong people. Contrast this to Donald Trump, who vomits out great quantities of verbiage, taking so many positions at once that no one of them has much meaning after a while.

President-elect Trump will surely talk himself into a jackpot a dozen times before inauguration. Obama hasn't done it, really, since his infamous "guns and religion" speech. Eight years is an awfully long time to go without blinking.

Obama's parting message, about how he won Iowa, was a calm admonition to his own party to not give up on those sections of the country where the "demographics" don't suggest success.

This was an extraordinary statement to make in the wake of such a massive affirmation of racist and xenophobic attitudes. At one of our lowest moments, the person at the very center of this horrible maelstrom of hate was the one urging us not to give up. Obama's detractors may not hear this message now. But history will.

Donald Trump may have won the White House, but he will never be a man like his predecessor, whose personal example will now only shine more brightly with the passage of time. At a time when a lot of Americans feel like they have little to be proud of, we should think about our outgoing president, whose humanity and greatness are probably only just now coming into true focus.

Epilogue

Just after dawn, November 9, 2016. I'm in shock. Right up until the end, I didn't believe America would actually do it.

What just happened? What I saw all year was a bumbling train wreck of a candidate who belched and preened his way past a historically weak field of Republicans, then seemed to spend all summer staggering toward the nearest exit.

Trump was an accidental candidate, a goof playing out a whim, like the guy who walked across America backward. Assuming great effort on his part, you could see him making it to the finish line alive. But winning? What did we all miss?

Only upon reflection does it make an awful kind of sense.

Trump's election marks the end of an era. In particular, the one that began back on August 28, 1963, with Martin Luther King's "I Have a Dream" speech, establishing—no matter how incomplete, how unfulfilled—the template for 50 years of race relations.

Of course we don't remember today that white residents in 1963 fled the capital before the March on Washington, suffering from what *Life* magazine called "the worst case of invasion jitters since the First Battle of Bull Run."

Nor do we remember that John F. Kennedy's head of domestic intelligence at the time, William Sullivan, reacted to the speech by declaring that King was "the most dangerous Negro of the future in this Nation from the standpoint of communism, the Negro and national security."

King turned out to be anything but a dangerous man. His rise didn't precipitate a communist takeover. His legacy instead was nonviolence, reconciliation and a generation of young people of all races who grew up after his death believing that acceptance of others is a primary duty of citizenship.

King told us we were people before we were anything else: white or black, young or old, male or female, rich or poor, born here or born elsewhere. Even if we never came close to realizing it, the notion that we all had to find a way to live together was the organizing principle of our society for 50 years. Many of the people voting in this election never knew anything else.

Then Trump came along.

Presidential elections, no matter what else they're about, are ultimately all referenda on race. Conventional wisdom heading into this election said the Republican Party needed to adjust even more in the direction of racial universalism.

Republican big-dollar donors and party chiefs after 2012 went through the same exercise in willful blindness that Democrats will undoubtedly go through for the next four years, searching out every explanation for a crushing loss except for the ones that inculpated them.

Republicans didn't blame their plan to reduce Medicare benefits for people under 55, or their anemic job proposals, or their proud dedication to free trade policies.

No, it couldn't have been any of those things. As former speechwriter to George W. Bush David Frum explained in

the *Atlantic* in January 2016, the Republican donor class believed the path to victory for Republicans involved voters
accepting a softening on the immigration issue. So they set
about raising money for "crossover" Republicans pushing
path-to-citizenship ideas, like Jeb Bush.

As Frum pointed out, the impact of immigration for
this brand of Republican donor was limited enough ("more
interesting food!") that they were really agnostic on the
issue. They expected their voters out there to feel the same.

They didn't. Instead, they flocked to Trump, who specifically ran against those "establishment" Republicans and
their uninspiring aristocrat candidate, Bush. Trump's run
promised voters something the Republican leadership never
even considered as a strategy—i.e., a radical overthrow of
that 50-year consensus on race, during which time even
most Republicans paid lip service to King's vision.

As Trump's run progressed, the ideology behind it came
into focus. In the summer he named a new campaign
"CEO," Steve Bannon. Bannon was best known as the head
of the noxious *Breitbart* site but for some time had also been
perhaps the leading figure in a revolutionary anti-universalist
movement that explicitly rejected the King doctrine.

The so-called alt-right movement, like all movements
dreamed up by intellectual revolutionaries, is obsessively
concerned with defining itself. As such it has left behind a
voluble literature detailing its history and priorities.

Earlier in 2016, Bannon's *Breitbart* site even published
an exultant "Establishment Conservative's Guide to the
Alt-Right," written by Allum Bokhari and barnstorming
campus villain Milo Yiannopoulos, for the benefit of the
soon-to-be-vanquished class of David Brooks/George Will
Republicans.

This tract outlined the main principles of the new movement, the first apparently being that the thing distinguishing them from skinheads is that they all went to college:

> Skinheads, by and large, are low-information, low-IQ thugs driven by the thrill of violence and tribal hatred. The alternative right are a much smarter group of people—which perhaps suggests why the Left hates them so much. They're dangerously bright.

The *Breitbart* manifesto was unpleasantly familiar stylistically, and would be to anyone who's had the misfortune (as I have, having studied in the Soviet Union) to read a lot of Marxist/Leninist writing.

These alt-righters are clearly influenced by Lenin, not in his leveling instincts, of course, but in his tactics. Just like the Bolsheviks, the alt-righters see themselves as the elite vanguard of a much larger population of proles, whom they deign to call "low-information" voters.

"Although the alt-right consists mostly of college-educated men," the piece declares, "it sympathises with the white working classes and, based on our interviews, feels a sense of *noblesse oblige*."

Or, as Trump would put it: "I love the poorly educated!"

Unlike the Bolsheviks, who were internationalists and globalists, the alt-righters are proudly provincial. Their goals are "a new identity politics that prioritises the interests of their own demographic," is how Allum/Milo verbalized the idea.

Culture over economics is another theme. They dislike modern "establishment" conservatives because, like Clinton

Democrats, they embrace a globalist politics that de-emphasizes national identity. They talk a lot about the "preservation of their own tribe."

They believe that if ethnic groups spill over the border in big enough numbers, they will eventually "come to blows" with other groups, like for instance white Americans. This is one of the cardinal beliefs of the alt-right, and it's an outgrowth of early twentieth-century white supremacist Ben Klassen's "Racial Holy War" concept.

You can go on any alt-right message board, for instance 4chan or Stormfront, and see people speculating about when "RaHoWa" is coming. This is the new right's version of "pure communism," or the Rapture—the beautiful paradisical thing to be dreamed of in the future. It's not terribly indistinguishable from Charlie Manson's homicidal "Helter Skelter" theology.

As *Breitbart* puts it, integration "won't be successful in the 'kumbaya' sense." This is a profoundly pessimistic movement, angry, disappointed, born of frustration and insecurity and failure.

Early in the race, Trump seemed more like a consumer of alt-right ideas than a progenitor of them. He came off like a guy who read some stuff on the Internet that got him so worked up, he ran for president. This helped him connect with ordinary voters, because they read the same material. Trump was just like them!

The question of whether or not Trump was a conscious purveyor of these revolutionary concepts is hard to decipher, since Trump is a man who embraces and discards ideas at light speed. On the stump he seems unstable, easily distracted, and as likely driven by gas as ideology. His dominant idea is usually the one that most recently entered his head.

Still, Trump was the perfect vehicle for the movement. A lot of Trump's policy ideas spoke directly to its cherished themes. Alt-righters love walls. They believe other "tribes," like Muslims for instance, inherently look out for their own, and therefore limiting their entry into the country "until we figure out what's going on" is not racist but merely self-preserving.

Moreover Trump's constant mocking violations of modern cultural taboos, his jokes about Megyn Kelly's "wherever" and impersonations of disabled Serge Kovaleski and his rants about Carly Fiorina's face and Hillary Clinton's "massive" hair, all line up with the ethos of the alt-righters.

These "dangerously bright" people think their Internet trolling is hilarious and ideologically justified. They actually think about this, consciously, as a strategy, which is another reason to think they just got incredibly lucky when the Republican nominee turned out to be Trump, a man whose trolling is reflexive and pathological, anything but thought out.

The alt-righters see themselves as the twenty-first-century version of the New Left of the 1960s and 1970s who were forever "swearing on TV, mocking Christianity, and preaching the virtues of drugs and free love." Only their thing is idiotic caricatures of Jews, Muslims, women, etc.

The alt-right positions Dr. King's "dream" as false medicine forced upon us by our parents, a thing to be lampooned as cruelly as possible, the way we picked on *Reefer Madness* or Jerry Falwell's "first time."

I didn't see or understand the power of the alt-right message until late in the campaign. Trump himself doesn't seem like the kind of guy you'd imagine hanging out with an effete wimp like Milo Yiannopoulos. It's easier to picture him with Mike Tyson and Kid Rock. Moreover, when I went out on the trail and talked to Trump voters, these snide campus-troll types were nowhere to be found.

My idea of a Trump voter, almost until the end, was one endless crowd of mostly older white people in mesh hats, carrying little American flags, standing with their hands clasped in a barn (in Iowa) or an agricultural fairgrounds (Wisconsin), begging for a return to a lost America that never existed.

Not one of these people had the education to be offended, as alt-righters were, that there had been calls to tear down statues of Cecil Rhodes or Queen Victoria in England. A lot of them were veterans and longtime blue-collar workers who had been shuttled from bad idea to bad idea over the years, as Republican snake-oil salesmen had descended into the heartland pointing fingers at cultural villains to the east and west. Trump seemed like just the latest.

But with Bannon's help, Trump's rhetoric unleashed a monstrous energy in these crowds. It turned out it took just a little push to move the traditional doddering Republican voter from tepid free-market internationalism to furious "tribal preservation." In retrospect no one should have been surprised that voters were so unimpressed by the Republican Party establishment's repeated cries that Trump was "not a conservative."

Not a conservative? So what? Neither were most of these people. True, they didn't love government regulations and taxes, but that wasn't as central to their identity as, well, their identity.

The old Bush/Reagan Republicans used identity as a mere palate cleanser for their real political mission, energetic programs of laissez-faire capitalism.

Trump made identity the main course. He unleashed something dark and violent in the American psyche. He gave voters permission to disbelieve in a common future with the rest of America and offered the option of confrontation instead.

Pull a lever for me, he promised, and you'll horrify them all. And they did it. Sixty million of them chose it. They wanted us to feel the way we feel this morning. They wanted to watch our faces as the dream went up in smoke.

In retrospect, the campaign really turned when Bannon came aboard. In classic Leninist fashion, he won the political battle with a strategic surrender, by having Trump publicly denounce almost all of the alt-right's principles.

Trump crisscrossed the country on an "African-American outreach" tour. He went to Mexico and supplicated before President Enrique Peña Nieto, who got to tell Trump to his face he wouldn't be paying for any wall. And the Trump campaign signaled over and over again that it was open to a "softening" on immigration, a seemingly heretical concept and a betrayal of everything he said during primary season.

Asked about Trump's change of heart, campaign spokesclown Katrina Pierson quipped, "He hasn't changed his position on immigration. He has changed the words that he is saying."

I was with Trump's press corps on a bus in New York, waiting to be shepherded to a flight to New Hampshire, when that comment came out. All of the reporters, myself included, burst out laughing. The general consensus was that Pierson was a dolt and that whatever they were doing with the immigration issue, it was suicide.

It wasn't. It was brilliant. They were sticking the alt-right revolution back in the Trojan Horse in order to move it forward. Someone had finally wedded Trump's crazy energy to a strategy. The beauty of the plan is that it didn't require that Trump himself have a conversion. He squirmed and pouted through the whole "outreach" exercise, like Huck Finn fighting a bath. His core voters never stopped believing he was the uncouth madman with whom they'd fallen in love. Millions of other Republicans thought he'd tiptoed back to respectability. Bannon was doing the exact thing the choleric Trump by himself could not. He was building a coalition.

A few days after the election, postmortems began to trickle out of Washington. Right on cue, the Democrats began pointing fingers at everyone but themselves.

A *Politico* report describes the good-bye address between top Clinton aides and campaign staff:

> Sexism. The media. James Comey.
> On a call with surrogates Thursday afternoon, top advisers John Podesta and Jennifer Palmieri pinned blame for Hillary Clinton's loss on a host of uncontrollable headwinds that ultimately felled a well-run campaign. . . .
> They offered no apology for the unexpected loss.

The piece quoted surrogates who seethed as they listened to the Clinton brain trust deflect responsibility: "She got this gift of this complete idiot who says bizarre things and hates women and she still lost," a Clinton fund-raiser told *Politico*. "They lost in a race they obviously should have won. They need to take some blame."

Like Steve Bannon, Bill and Hillary Clinton were revolutionaries. The original Clinton revolution was also an intellectual revolt, born not of popular frustration but the intramural angst of Washington politicos frustrated by repeated Republican electoral successes.

Stung by Walter Mondale's landslide loss in 1984, the new Democratic Leadership Council pushed a "third way" strategy. Founding documents like the DLC's 1990 New Orleans Declaration—written when Bill Clinton was DLC chair—described a simple pragmatic trade: less bleeding-heart politics, more Democratic presidents.

The only "ideas" at the core of the DLC strategy were that Democrats were better than Republicans, and that winning was better than losing. To make Democrats more competitive, they made two important changes. One was the embrace of "market-based" solutions, which opened the door for the party to compete with Republicans for donations from Wall Street and heavy industry.

The other big trade-off was on race. The Clinton revolution was designed as a response to Dick Nixon's Southern Strategy, which was based on dominating among whites from the South who nurtured resentments about the post–civil rights consensus.

To win those white voters back, the Clintons "triangulated" against liberal orthodoxies, pledging to end "welfare as we know it" and to punish criminals instead of "explaining away their behavior." Liberal dog-whistling, if you will. Candidate Bill Clinton even went out of his way to attend the execution of a mentally deficient black man named Ricky Ray Rector during the 1992 campaign to signal his seriousness.

The original DLC positions on policing sound almost identical to current Trumpian rhetoric. "The U.S. has unwittingly allowed itself to unilaterally disarm in the domestic war against violent crime," the group wrote, as part of its argument for a bigger federal role in law enforcement and the expanded use of "community policing."

These moves worked in large part because of the personal magnetism of the Clintons. Bill and Hillary both seemed energetic and optimistic. Much of the world was enthralled by them, this power couple of intellectual equals. They were something modern, with their can-do positive attitude, which was marketed almost like a political version of Nike's "Just Do It" campaign.

Moreover, Bill Clinton was nobody's idea of a plutocrat back then. He was a self-made success story from a hardscrabble background, raised by a single mom in a rural Arkansas town literally called Hope. He was thought of both as an overgrown hillbilly *and* "the first black president."

Clinton looked like a man of the people. He had to be torn away from campaign stops and chatted up everyone from truckers to waitresses to toll operators. He even had a bad junk-food habit, a quality then-Bill shares with today's Donald Trump.

It helped that Bill Clinton's first presidential opponent, George H. W. Bush, was a calcified Connecticut aristocrat who had been pampered in power for so long, he didn't know how checkout lanes worked when he visited a supermarket.

They won, and kept winning, their success papering over fault lines building in the party.

In the sixteen years after Bill left office, a lot changed. For one thing, the Clintons personally emerged from the experience of the presidency deeply embittered by press criticism. They became fatalistic rather than optimistic about the burdens of power.

In that *Politico* piece after the election, an unnamed "longtime confidant" explained that Hillary and Bill decided to embark on a moneymaking campaign after Bill left office because they figured they would get criticized either way.

"Her outlook is, 'I get whacked no matter what, so screw it,'" the person explained. "I've been out here killing myself for years and years and if I want to give the same speech everyone else does, I will."

So the Clintons went from being plausibly accessible to ordinary people to living in a world where it was nobody's business if they wanted to make $153 million in speaking fees.

Soon they were the politicians who'd been on Olympus so long, they couldn't navigate the metaphorical supermarket line. Shortly before she announced her 2016 run, Hillary gave a speech to Goldman Sachs executives admitting that she was "kind of far removed because [of] the economic, you know, fortunes that my husband and I now enjoy."

There was another change.

The original Clinton strategy of the Nineties had stressed a rejection of liberal mantras about identity politics, and even the 2008 Hillary Clinton campaign had aggressively run against the "fairy tale" of Barack Obama.

That Hillary Clinton generated quite a lot of heat among white voters on the campaign trail. The emotional high point of her campaign came during the Pennsylvania primary, after Barack Obama had made his infamous "they cling to guns and religion" speech.

Hillary Clinton wasted no time in calling Obama "elitist and out of touch," hammering him for his "demeaning remarks . . . about people in small-town America."

I was at some of her Pennsylvania rallies that year, when she railed against her eggheaded opponent and riffed on her background as the "granddaughter of a factory worker" who was raised "outside" of a big city. Her mostly white and middle-class audiences whooped and hollered.

Hillary may have been very wealthy already by then. But the former "Goldwater Girl" clearly enjoyed playing the role of the champion of the silent majority. Her stump speech in that race was an almost exact replica of Nixon's "forgotten Americans" theme from 1968: Hillary's version was a call to the "invisible Americans" of the betrayed middle class.

But she lost that race, and the size and breadth of the Obama victory against McCain inspired the change to what her aides described to reporters as the "far narrower" Obama mobilize-the-base strategy in 2016.

But decades of those triangulating politics made her an unconvincing vehicle for that plan, and unforeseen developments like the Bernie Sanders campaign forced her to spend an enormous amount of time trying to hold the Democratic coalition together.

Meanwhile, on the other side, she was now pushing a strategy that couldn't possibly have been less appealing to the so-called white working-class voter. Always an economic globalist, Hillary Clinton was now an enthusiastic convert to multiculturalism as well, the worst conceivable combination.

In the end, the Clinton revolution went the way of a lot of revolutions. The longer any group of intellectuals sits at or near power, the more they tend to drift away from their founding ideas and resort more and more to appeals to authority.

Trump's rise massively accelerated this process. By late summer 2016, the Clinton campaign spent virtually all its time either raising explorations of Trump's evil up the media flagpole or denouncing anyone who didn't salute fast enough.

The Clinton campaign dismissed flyover Republicans as a "basket of deplorables" and then developed their own Leninist mania for describing factional enemies and skeptics within their own tent. In place of parasites, cosmopolitanites and wreckers, the campaign railed against "Bernie Bros," "neo-Naderites," "purity-testers" and a long list of other deviants.

In 2014, before the start of his wife's presidential run, Bill Clinton was saying things like, "The biggest threat to the future of our children and grandchildren is the poison of identity politics that preaches that our differences are far more important than our common humanity."

But by the last months of the general election race, the Clinton camp had done a complete 180 on identity politics, deploying it as a whip in an increasingly desperate effort to keep their coalition in place. They used language against other Democrats they would previously never have used against Republicans. Even ex-hippies and New Dealers were denounced as bigots whose discomfort with Clinton was an expression of privilege and an attack against women, people of color and the LGBT community.

Meanwhile members of the press who wrote anything negative about Clinton, made jokes, or even structured their ledes in the wrong way could be guilty of anything from "both-sidesism" (Lenin would have loved this tongue-mangling term) to "false equivalency" to the use of "weap-onized" information, to say nothing of actual treason.

"You are a criminal agent of Putin conspiracy. And a profound enemy of progressive politics," raged Democratic strategist Bob Shrum to journalist Glenn Greenwald, after the latter made a sarcastic comment about the campaign's outrage toward previously lauded FBI director James Comey.

There are a lot of people who will probably say that all of these tirades against Clinton's critics were on the mark. But it's surely also true that once you reach the stage of being angry with people for wanting a reason to vote for you, you've been in this game too long.

The Clintons probably should have left politics the moment they decided they didn't care what the public thought about how they made their money. Their original genius was in feeling where the votes were on the map and knowing how to get them. But that homing mechanism starts to falter once you make a conscious decision to tune out public criticism as irrational and inevitable.

It was a huge gamble to push forward toward the White House after they crossed this mental line. Moreover to run for president at a time when you're admitting in private that you're out of touch with regular people is wildly irresponsible, a violation of every idea even they once had about how to win elections.

All of these things played a role in the still-stunning loss to Trump. They spent virtually all their time attending corporate fund-raisers—more than 400 of them, according to one source I spoke to in Washington the day after the election—and relatively little on traditional canvassing. And they relied upon a preposterous computerized fortune-telling machine called "Ada" to gauge the feelings of voters, instead of sounding them out in person.

After the loss to Trump, the inclusive, upbeat Fleetwood Mac vibe of the original Clinton revolution vanished forever, replaced by anger, recrimination and willful myopia. A movement begun by future-embracing intellectuals ended on notes like, "I don't want to hear it," which became a ubiquitous phrase in Democratic circles.

"Samantha Bee Doesn't 'Want to Hear a Goddamn Word' About Black Turnout" was *HuffPo*'s headline, after the comic's postelection tirade against any explanations for Trump's rise other than "white people."

"I don't want to hear it" became an expression of solidarity. It felt like a real-world extension of a social media response, where publicly blocking people during this season became a virtue even among upper-class white guys (*Vox*'s Matt Yglesias boasting in the summer of 2016 about having blocked 941 people on Twitter is one bizarre example).

The "hear no evil" campaign was surely in part messaging from the Clinton campaign, which went from poohpoohing any poll numbers that showed a tight race (the media was often blamed for pushing poll numbers "without context" in search of a better horse race) to describing Trump's victory as the inevitable triumph of an irrepressible white nationalist movement.

We somehow went from "suggesting it's close is a vicious lie" to "we never had a chance" overnight.

The Clintons throughout their history had been survivors. They made it through controversy after controversy by unfailingly finding the lee shore in a storm. Their talent at spinning was legendary.

Any journalist who ever tried to call a Clinton aide for a

comment on a negative story was inevitably treated to a master class in double-talk. The bad thing didn't happen, or they didn't do the bad thing if it was done, or even if they did do it you shouldn't report it, because it helped worse people, and so on. They were like junkies: They always had a story. Their confidence was unshakeable and exhausting, their will to persevere a thing to behold.

But in the end, they ran out of stories, except one last one: They lost because there was no hope. They went from optimism, to fatalism, to absolute pessimism, all in the space of 25 years.

The pessimism of the Democratic leadership is like that of a person in a catatonic crisis. Once they were heroes for finding a way to win by selling out just enough on race and economics. But now that that strategy has been closed, they seem stunned to the point of paralysis by the seemingly incurable divisions of our society, as if they're seeing them for the first time.

Meanwhile the pessimism of Trump's revolution is intentional, impassioned, ascendant. They placed a huge bet on America's worst instincts, and won. And the first order of business will be to wipe out a national idea in which they never believed.

Welcome to the end of the dream.

Acknowledgments

THIS WOULD NOT EVEN HAVE BEEN A BOOK WITHOUT THE help of my longtime editor, Chris Jackson, who worked very hard in a short period of time to put all of this together, along with his assistant editor Nicole Counts and his Random House and Spiegel & Grau colleagues. Lydia Wills, my agent, also helped push this compilation into print.

This has been a difficult time for *Rolling Stone*, for obvious reasons. During the time period covered in this book it was dealing with the fallout of the UVA scandal, which affected a great many people, some outside the magazine, some within it. I empathize with the former, but I know more about the latter, as many friends and colleagues left the magazine in the last years. Will Dana, who was the first editor to send me on the campaign trail, is missed, as is longtime copy chief Coco McPherson. I owe a debt to editors Jason Fine and Sean Woods for continuing with the magazine's campaign tradition this year. It was a special pleasure to work with illustrator Victor Juhasz (I'm beginning to think we're going to be buried together). About Jann Wenner I should say that not many publishers and/or editors would permit a dissenting column after an official endorsement, which is what happened this time around. Jann's original vision of covering campaigns in a rock magazine using the personalized diary style that Hunter Thompson employed was an innovation that will live on for a long time, and it really has been an honor to continue the tradition, especially in this unforgettable, if horrible, year.

Lastly, I must thank my loving wife, Jeanne, and my children, Max and Nate, to whom I was always so happy to return after a campaign trip.

About the Author

MATT TAIBBI, author of the *New York Times* best-sellers *The Divide*, *Griftopia*, and *The Great Derangement*, is a contributing editor for *Rolling Stone* and winner of the 2008 National Magazine Award for columns and commentary.

@mtaibbi